Northwestern University Publications
in Analytical Philosophy

THE

Epistemology

OF

G. E. Moore

E. D. Klemke

Northwestern University Press

EVANSTON·1969

*E. D. Klemke is Professor of Philosophy at
Roosevelt University, Chicago, Illinois.*

Permission has been granted to quote from the following books: G. E. Moore, *Some Main Problems of Philosophy*, Allen & Unwin, London, 1953. G. E. Moore, *Philosophical Papers*, Allen & Unwin, London, 1959. *The Philosophy of G. E. Moore*, ed. P. A. Schilpp, 2d ed., copyright © 1952 Open Court Publishing Company, LaSalle, Illinois.

TO
May Brodbeck
AND
Herbert Hochberg

Contents

Preface

IT IS NO EXAGGERATION to say that G. E. Moore is among the foremost of twentieth-century philosophers. Certainly, in the Anglo-American tradition, he, along with Bertrand Russell, may be ranked among the top figures. It is appropriate that current histories and surveys of contemporary philosophical analysis devote chapters to Moore. Moore's negative or destructive influence may be seen in the fact that he and Russell dealt severe blows to the philosophical tendency which had dominated Britain for many years—namely, Idealism. Even if none of his doctrines attains permanence, Moore will doubtless be remembered for this achievement alone. But Moore's constructive influence must not be minimized either. Several philosophers and movements—Russell, logical positivism, "Oxford Analysis"—are indebted to him. (In the case of Russell, at least, the indebtedness was mutual.) This is to say not that any of these totally accepted Moore's views, but only that, in some sense or other, Moore had a significant influence upon many of his contemporaries.

Hence, analysis and evaluation of Moore's philosophical works are surely in order.

I have limited my examination to those works of Moore which are primarily epistemological in nature. Moore's ethical views are specifically omitted from consideration here, except insofar as they illustrate some epistemological point. I have relied primarily upon the original writings themselves, having found most secondary sources to be either of little help or somewhat misleading. (I have commented upon some of the latter cases.) The topics which I have considered are arranged under three main headings. In Part One, I have discussed problems—some of which Moore wrote about at great length—which are methodological in nature: Moore's notion of philosophy, his appeal to common sense, the place of ordinary language, the meanings of 'meaning', and various kinds of analysis. In Part Two, I have taken up such topics as the kinds of knowledge which Moore finds possible, theories of truth, and the relation of consciousness to knowledge. In Part Three, I have dealt with a specific epistemological problem, perception, about which Moore wrote many papers. As far as I can determine, these exhaust the topics which are primarily epistemological. I am aware, however, of the fact that a rigid distinction between metaphysics and epistemology is untenable.

I have taken into consideration all of Moore's works, but I have not stressed the two posthumously published works, edited by C. Lewy. One is not sure as to whether Moore would approve of many of the passages which occur in the *Commonplace Book,* and *Lectures on Philosophy* appeared after this work had been completed.

Although this book is primarily the result of my own study of and thought about Moore's philosophy, I should like here to express my appreciation to those among my former teachers who have either directly or indirectly influenced my own philosophical development or provided the challenge of alternatives. Among these are Professors Gustav Bergmann, May Brodbeck, Robert Browning, William A. Earle, Herbert Hochberg, Paul L. Holmer, Asher Moore, and Wilfrid Sellars. I should also like to express my appreciation to the friends and colleagues who have helped in many ways with regard to the completion and publication of this work or who have provided encouragement. I am especially grateful to Professors Moltke S. Gram, F. Arthur Jacobson, and Henry Veatch; Dr. Ruth Burrows; Messrs. Truman Metzel and G. Moor; and Dean Otto Wirth and President Rolf A. Weil of Roosevelt University, who granted me a reduced teaching load so that I could complete this work. Among those to whom I owe the most, two of my friends and former teachers stand out, and it is to them that this book is dedicated.

E. D. KLEMKE

Evanston, Illinois
August 1968

Note

The following abbreviations have been used in the footnotes and the Bibliography:

WORKS OF G. E. MOORE

"Def."   "A Defence of Common Sense," *Contemporary British Philosophy: Second Series,* ed. J. H. Muirhead (New York: Macmillan, 1925), II, 193–223. Reprinted in *PP,* pp. 32–59.

"Justif."   "The Justification of Analysis," *Analysis,* I (1933–34), 28–30. Lecture notes transcribed by M. McDonald.

PE   *Principia Ethica* (Cambridge: Cambridge University Press, 1903).

PP   *Philosophical Papers* (London: Allen & Unwin, 1959).

PS   *Philosophical Studies* (London: Routledge & Kegan Paul, 1922). Reprinted (Totowa, N. J.: Littlefield, Adams & Co., 1965).

"Prf."   "Proof of an External World," *British Academy Proceedings*, XXV (1939), 273–300. Reprinted in *PP*, pp. 127–50.

"Refut."   "The Refutation of Idealism," *Mind*, XII (1903), 433–53. Reprinted in *PS*, pp. 1–30.

"Reply"   "A Reply to My Critics," *The Philosophy of G. E. Moore*, ed. P. A. Schilpp (Evanston: Northwestern University Press, 1942; 2d ed., New York: Tudor, 1952). All references are to the 1952 edition, now available through Open Court Publishing Company, LaSalle, Ill.

SMPP   *Some Main Problems of Philosophy* (London: Allen & Unwin, 1953). Lectures given in 1910–11.

OTHER WORKS

PAS   *Proceedings of the Aristotelian Society*

PASS   *Proceedings of the Aristotelian Society,* Supplement

PGEM   *The Philosophy of G. E. Moore,* ed. P. A. Schilpp (Evanston: Northwestern University Press, 1942; 2d ed., New York: Tudor, 1952). All references are to the 1952 edition, now available through Open Court Publishing Company, LaSalle, Ill.

PART ONE
Philosophical Method

I

What Is Philosophy?

T HE MATERIAL which I have included under the rubric of philosophical method actually consists of a cluster of philosophical problems, all of which were of especial importance to Moore.

First, what is *philosophy?* What are its sources, tasks, and problems? Second, what are the status and role of *common sense,* particularly as related to knowing? This topic is often confused with a third subject, the status of Moore's appeal to *ordinary language;* hence, I shall consider it next. This will lead to the importance of discussing, fourth, the various meanings of *'meaning'* in Moore's works. And this, in turn, leads to, fifth, the notion of *analysis* and the forms of it which were employed by Moore. The first of these topics—What is philosophy?—will be discussed in the present chapter. The remaining four will be considered in the succeeding chapters of Part One.

First, then, what is Moore's notion of philosophy? This problem may be divided into two parts. (1) What is the source of philosophical reflection: i.e., what presents our philosophical problems to us? (2) What are the tasks of philosophy? Or, what are its chief divisions, fields, or problems? The discussion of these two issues will be followed by (3) some general comments regarding Moore's kind of philosophizing.

I

ARISTOTLE SAID: "It is through wonder that men begin to philosophize"—wonder which is caused by reflection upon the world, its nature and origin.[1] And Plato held that the philosopher is a spectator of all time and existence.[2] The suggestion here is that the philosopher's problems are provided to him (for the most part) directly by the *world*. I think it may be safely said that the world has traditionally been the direct source of the reflective activity of most philosophers. More specifically, this was certainly true of most British philosophers before Moore, whether we mean by the world the world as a whole or certain aspects of it, such as the discoveries of the sciences. The assertions of other philosophers—though seldom or never omitted—have had a subsidiary importance as a source of philosophical activity. With Moore, the situation is reversed. He himself has said:

I do not think that the world or the sciences would ever have suggested to me any philosophical problems. What has suggested philosophical problems to me is things which other philosophers have said about the world or the sciences. In many problems suggested in this way I have been (and still am) very keenly interested—the problems in question being mainly of two sorts, namely, first, the problem of trying to get really clear as to what on earth a given philosopher *meant* by something which he said, and, secondly, the problem of discovering what really satisfactory reasons there are for supposing that what he meant was true, or alternatively, was false. I think I have been trying to solve problems of this sort all my life.[3]

One may say, then, that the source and, in a sense, part of the direct subject matter of Moore's philosophizing have been the assertions which were made by other philosophers. Moore found many of these assertions to be extremely peculiar and perplexing and did his best to understand them, to analyze them, or, where possible, to refute them. Hence, when he encountered the philosophical proposition that everything in the world is

1. *Metaphysics* I, ii. Cf. Plato *Theaetetus*, 155D.
2. *Republic*, VI, 486A.
3. "Autobiography," *PGEM*, p. 14.

4

a mind or a group of minds, he was puzzled, for it certainly seemed to him that the chair in which he was sitting was of a very different nature from his acts of consciousness *about* the chair. Or when he read Berkeley's proposition *'Esse est percipi'* and asked himself whether or not it was true, he found that a direct yes-or-no answer was impossible, for the proposition might mean several things and had, first, to be analyzed into its component meanings. And, finally, when he came across statements in philosophical books such as 'No one can know of the existence of any self other than his own', Moore tried to show that this view was self-refuting, since, in making his case, such a philosopher constantly used phrases like *'We must . . .'* or 'None of *us* can . . .' or 'Every one of *us* is . . .'.

However, even though Moore began with the statements of other philosophers and therefore was somewhat indirect in his approach, he was ultimately interested in saying things about the world (or reality, etc.). This is clearly indicated by the second of the philosophical problems which Moore mentions in the quotation above. Hence, for Moore, the ultimate subject matter of philosophy is the world about which our propositions are true or false. As we shall see, in section II of this chapter, Moore held that one of the most important tasks of philosophy is to give a general description of the world as a whole (metaphysics); and he himself engaged in this task. It is true that his descriptions often seem quite different from those of many of his predecessors. And one is tempted to say that this noticeable feature of Moore's philosophy stems from a certain method—which might loosely be called analysis, as over against synthesis, construction, and speculation (if I may use these generous categories). And to some extent, this generalization is true. One *does* find a unique emphasis upon analysis in Moore's writings. The objects of some forms of analysis are the statements of other philosophers (as mentioned in the preceding paragraph) or certain more commonsensical statements which we all know to be true, even though we do not know precisely *how* we know them to be true. One of the results of this emphasis is that philosophy becomes even more specialized and technical than it had been heretofore. Moore's philosophy is minute philosophy, rather than philosophy in the grand manner. Hence, the layman who reads Moore is apt to become even more confused and bewildered than he was in the past. Moore has rightly been called a philosopher's philosopher. I think that it is plausible to hold that one of the factors which accounts for his having acquired this reputation is the source to which Moore went for his

5

philosophical activity. A philosophy which takes as its point of departure puzzling and problematic utterances of philosophers is apt to be very different from one which begins mainly from, say, wonder about the world.

I have said that Moore often stresses "analysis" rather than "synthesis." I should not, however, wish to give the impression that Moore either (a) minimizes the latter or (b) conceives the two to be radically separate disciplines, after the fashion of some logical positivists. I once made the mistake of believing that Moore did both. Others have held the same erroneous belief. John Wisdom, for example, speaks of "Moore's account of philosophy as analysis."[4] Moore replies: "As if I had somewhere said that philosophy consisted in analysis!"[5] He adds: "It is not true that I have either said or thought or implied that analysis is the only proper business of philosophy! By practicing analysis I may have implied that it is *one* of the proper businesses of philosophy. But I certainly cannot have implied more than that. And, in fact, analysis is by no means the only thing I have tried to do."[6] As we shall see in succeeding chapters, Moore did frequently engage in and worry about analysis. But, as will be evident in the remainder of this work, he did much more. He attempted to say something about what reality is like. But the endeavor to do this did not, for Moore, involve a complete separation of analysis and construction. "If the propositions you choose to analyse are *true* contingent propositions, they can only be true because they tell you something about reality, and, if so, then I think the analysis of them will tell you something about reality too."[7] The discussion in Chapter V will show that some of the forms of analysis in which Moore engaged are manifestations of this view that analysis is not merely linguistic but is informative as to what is real.

II

So much for the source of philosophizing. Next, what are the chief divisions of philosophy? What are its central problems? Just what is philosophy?

Moore does not provide a definition of philosophy. Instead, he charac-

4. *PGEM*, p. 425.
5. *Ibid.*, p. 675.
6. *Ibid.*, pp. 675–76.
7. *Ibid.*, p. 676.

terizes philosophy and its tasks by describing some of the main problems which have engaged philosophers and some of the most important things which they have tried to do.[8] According to Moore, the first and most important and interesting thing which philosophers have tried to do is:

To give a general description of the *whole* of the Universe, mentioning all the most important kinds of things which we *know* to be in it, considering how far it is likely that there are in it important kinds of things which we do not absolutely *know* to be in it, and also considering the most important ways in which these various things are related to one another.[9]

The first and most important problem of philosophy, then, is to give a general description of the whole universe. This problem—called metaphysics—is peculiar to philosophy, since no science, for example, undertakes to give such a general description.

Moore's procedure in characterizing philosophy is this: to begin with the views of common sense and then to see how far philosophical views depart from common sense. According to common sense, says Moore, there are in the universe such substantial kinds of things as material objects and mental acts or acts of consciousness. About such things common sense holds, for example, that acts of consciousness are in some way attached to some material objects and not to others, that material objects continue to exist even when we are not conscious of them, and that there may have been a time when acts of consciousness were attached to no material bodies. Finally, common sense holds that we do know all of these things.[10]

These are, then, *some* common-sense beliefs about the universe. These views, taken together, do *not,* according to Moore, amount to a (general) description of the *whole* universe. They consist merely in saying that there are in the universe certain classes of things and that they are related in certain ways. They allow for the possibility that there may be in the universe (or that there may be known to be in it) *other* classes of things. In order to have a general description of the *whole* universe, we would have to add one or the other of two statements: either (a) everything in the universe belongs to one of these classes; or (b) everything which we

8. *SMPP*, Chap. I. This work consists of lectures which Moore delivered in 1910–11 but which were not published until 1953. I am, at present, dealing only with his chapter, "What Is Philosophy?".

9. *Ibid.*, p. 1.

10. *Ibid.*, pp. 2–16.

know to be in the universe belongs to one of these classes. Statement (b), of course, is not as strong as (a). One obvious modification of the views of common sense is that besides material objects and acts of consciousness, the universe also contains space, in which material objects are situated, and time.

One way, then, to get a general description of the *whole* universe is to make additions of this sort to common sense. But many philosophers have held that even this modified common-sense view is incorrect. Different philosophers have held it to be inadequate in one of three different ways. They have, Moore notes, either added to common sense by holding that there are in the universe substantial things other than those which common sense holds to be in it; or they have contradicted common sense by asserting that some of the things which common sense supposes to be in the world are not in it, or, that if they are we do not *know* it; or they have done both (added and contradicted).[11]

A second major problem or field of philosophy, according to Moore, is the classification of all the different ways in which we can know things or the description of particular ways of knowing them. The question 'How do we know anything?' involves three different kinds of questions. 'How do you know *X?*' may mean: What sort of thing is knowing? What goes on in your mind when you know something? This sort of description, says Moore, is one which philosophy shares with psychology. Second, it may mean: What is meant by saying that any proposition is true? What is truth? This is a question for "logic"—or for what we would call epistemology. Third, 'How do you know *X?*' may mean: What reasons do you have for believing *X?* What else do you know which proves this to be true? This inquiry also belongs to "logic."[12]

A third field of philosophy is ethics. Ethical philosophy tries to classify all the different sorts of things which *would* be good or bad, right or wrong, so as to be able to say: "Nothing would be good, unless it had certain characteristics, or one or other of certain characteristics, and similarly nothing would be bad, unless it had certain properties or one or other of certain properties; and similarly with the question, what sort of actions would be right, and what would be wrong."[13]

---

11. *Ibid.,* pp. 17–23.
12. *Ibid.,* pp. 25–26.
13. *Ibid.,* p. 26.

III

THE GREATER PART of Moore's discussion of "What Is Philosophy?" is devoted to a consideration of the first "department" of philosophy—metaphysics. The second, epistemology, is only touched upon. Ethics is barely mentioned. Elsewhere, of course, Moore wrote considerably on the second and third areas. But in this work he states that metaphysics is the "first and most important" division of philosophy. Its task, we recall, is to give a general description of the whole universe, to establish some general truths about the world as a whole. This view of philosophy—in its most important part—does not differ radically from that of Moore's immediate or distant predecessors. An idealist, for example, would have no quarrel with it. But one is tempted to ask: How far does theory agree with practice, with respect to Moore? The answer to the question depends upon what one is looking for. If one means by a general description of the whole universe a complete, systematic, and interlocking account, such as Hegel's, for example, then one looks in vain for anything like a general description of that sort in Moore's works.

But there is another sense in which if one asks 'Did Moore provide a general description of the whole universe?' the answer is more properly 'Yes'; we know that, for Moore, there are (or were—depending upon when he wrote) in the universe such things as physical objects, sense-data, acts of consciousness, propositions, concepts, etc. Naturally, this sort of description is not that of a consistent and unified *system*. Moore's discussions, after all, frequently took the form of papers which were read at philosophical societies or published in philosophers' journals. Hence, he treated now one topic, now another. He never professed to have treated *all* philosophical problems. He notes (in his "Reply to My Critics") that McKeon and McGill, in the Schilpp volume, pointed out with regret and reproach that there are many philosophical problems with which Moore never tried to deal and replies: "It is, of course, true that there are ever so many intensely interesting philosophical problems on which I have never said a word: if by 'a philosophy' is to be meant a complete philosophy, then there is no such thing as my philosophy." [14] From his writings, however, we can clearly determine what Moore's general description of

14. "Reply," p. 676.

the universe is—or, better, what it is at a particular time, for he provides several alternative general descriptions. The first is that which is deline-ated above, according to which the general kinds of things in the universe are: material objects, minds or acts of consciousness, and space and time. A second alternative is given considerable attention. According to it, the major kinds of things which there are in the universe are: particulars, universals, and facts.[15] According to another alternative, the chief kinds of ontological entities are material objects, mental entities, and sense-data.[16] According to a fourth alternative, everything in the universe is either a proposition or a non-proposition.[17] And so on.

I shall devote attention to some of these alternatives in later parts of this work. If the reader wonders why Moore's metaphysical views receive so much attention in a work which purports to be an examination of Moore's epistemology, I can only say (as I have already emphasized in another way) that, for Moore, as for many philosophers, (1) metaphysics and epistemology cannot be absolutely separated and dealt with in isolation; (2) along with knowing *what it is* to know anything, or *how* can we know, the most important thing to know is *what* can we know? And the question 'What can we know?' breaks down into several questions such as: 'What are the kinds of things that *are*? Are some of these more ultimate or basic than others? If so, does this mean that they are more *real*? And what does that mean?' The providing of possible answers to such questions is, of course, the task of metaphysics.

I have already suggested, in section I, that Moore was not unsympa-thetic toward metaphysics, and I have just reaffirmed this. Perhaps some examples are in order. In "The Refutation of Idealism," he writes:

Whether *esse* be *percipi* or not, I consider it to be the main service of the philosophical school, to which modern Idealists belong, that they have insisted on distinguishing 'sensation' and 'thought' and on emphasizing the importance of the latter. Against Sensationalism and Empiricism they have maintained the true view.[18]

In *Principia Ethica:*

Metaphysicians have . . . the great merit of insisting that our knowledge is not confined to the things which we can touch and see and feel. They have always

15. *SMPP,* pp. 343–52.
16. "The Subject Matter of Psychology," *PAS,* X (1909–10), 36–62.
17. *SMPP,* pp. 56–59.
18. "Refut.," *PS,* p. 7.

been much occupied, not only with that other class of natural objects which consists in mental facts, but also with the class of objects or properties of objects, which certainly do not exist in time, are not therefore parts of Nature, and which, in fact, do not *exist* at all.[19]

And later:

Metaphysicians . . . have indeed recognized and insisted that there are, or may be, objects of knowledge which do not *exist in time,* or at least which we cannot perceive; and in recognizing the *possibility* of these, as an object of investigation, they have, it may be admitted, done a service to mankind.[20]

To be sure, this only shows that Moore approved of metaphysics, or some forms of it; it does not demonstrate that he *was* a metaphysician. That he was a metaphysician at times will be demonstrated throughout this work. At this point, I shall say only two things: (1) Moore was *not* a metaphysician in certain traditional senses. As we shall see, he was too immersed in common sense to be that kind of philosopher. He was too unable to accept statements which seemed to him to be peculiar or to make special use of certain terms, too concerned with the analysis of assertions and with meanings. (2) But he was not a positivist either, nor even a forerunner of positivism, really. First, he does not hold that metaphysics is nonsense, as I already mentioned. He *does* often hold, as G. A. Paul has pointed out, that the claims of metaphysics are complicated, immoderate, and often confused, and that they are sometimes based upon flimsy arguments.[21] But he does not make the typical positivist assertion. Second, he does not try to show that everything that is or that can be talked about in non-tautologous statements is a matter of direct acquaintance. Nor does he suggest that all non-tautologous statements must be empirically verifiable. E.g., a statement of the form 'X is good' is significant, without having to be translated into statements about the feelings, etc., of the person who utters it, even though 'good' stands for a quality which cannot be empirically observed. There are, for him, non-natural as well as natural qualities and objects in the world.[22]

I emphasize this matter of Moore's concern with metaphysics because too many of those who write about Moore tend to overlook it or ignore it.

---

19. *PE,* p. 10.
20. *Ibid.,* p. 111.
21. "G. E. Moore: Analysis, Common Usage, and Common Sense," in A. J. Ayer *et al., The Revolution in Philosophy* (New York: St. Martin's, 1957), p. 60.
22. *PE,* Chaps. I and II.

For example, in *English Philosophy Since 1900,* G. J. Warnock says about Moore: "He seems to have been . . . entirely without any of the motives that tend to make a metaphysician. He was neither discontented with nor puzzled by the ordinary beliefs of plain men and plain scientists." [23] Throughout the rest of the chapter, Warnock tries to construe Moore as having no interest in metaphysics. "Though he did not deny the legitimacy of metaphysical ambitions, he was entirely without them." [24] What then was Moore concerned with? With the "task of unravelling the pronouncements of other philosophers" and "analysis." [25] I have tried to show above that such a view is seriously mistaken and minimizes or ignores some of Moore's most distinguished work. Although Moore did engage in analysis and the unraveling of philosophers' assertions, he did much more. He attempted to do what all metaphysicians have tried, and his way of doing so was not entirely disconnected from that of at least some earlier metaphysicians. To ignore this character of Moore's work is to do a great philosopher a great injustice.[26]

With this brief consideration as to what philosophy is, according to Moore, we may next consider more specific methodological topics, those which are essential features of Moore's epistemology. Four of these stand out: Moore's appeal to common sense, his defense of ordinary language, his concern with meaning, and his emphasis upon analysis.

23. *English Philosophy Since 1900* (London: Oxford Univ. Press, 1958), p. 12.
24. *Ibid.,* pp. 54–55. Cf. pp. 56–58, 61.
25. *Ibid.,* p. 13.
26. Cf. E. D. Klemke, "Mr. Warnock on Moore's Conception of Philosophy," *Philosophical Studies,* XIII (1962), 81–84. For an appraisal of Moore's ontology, see "Moore's Realism," in Laird Addis and Douglas Lewis, *Moore and Ryle: Two Ontologists* (Iowa City: Univ. of Iowa Press; The Hague: Martinus Nijhoff, 1965).

I I

The Appeal to Common Sense

I T IS WELL KNOWN that Moore is a philosopher who has been concerned with defending common sense. But in what, precisely, does this defense consist? I shall first examine what is perhaps Moore's most important instance of appealing to and defending common sense in order to determine what sorts of things he claims to know commonsensically and the way in which he claims to know them. As we shall see, this will lead to such questions as 'How does one know that a given statement *is* a statement of common sense?' and 'How does one know such statements to be *true?*' Secondly, I shall examine Moore's criteria for answering such questions. The discussion will be followed by some comments upon Moore's views.

I

ONE OF THE STRIKING CHARACTERISTICS of Moore's philosophy—in spite of the cumbersome sentences in which it is often expressed—is an apparent straightforwardness and simplicity, almost a naïveté, one is tempted to say (although, to be sure, it is often deceptive). In the works of the philosophers, or in their discussions, Moore encountered various assertions which he could find no good reason to believe, assertions which often denied what every normal man knew very well to be true. For example, he had once heard McTaggart at Cambridge express his view that time is unreal. "This must have seemed to me then (as it still does) a perfectly monstrous proposition, and I did my best to argue against it."[1] After all, Moore reasoned, if time is unreal, am I not forced to *deny* that my going to bed last night occurred *before* my getting up this morning, etc.? Many of Moore's writings point out the strangeness of such "monstrous propositions" as 'Time is unreal', 'Reality is spiritual', 'Material objects do not exist', etc.

Over against the propounding of such strange and paradoxical assertions, Moore often insists upon uttering the statements of common sense and holds such statements to be very *certainly true*. By 'common sense', Moore does not, I think, mean a mental capacity for exemplifying good judgment, as when we say of a wise man that he shows good common sense in his choices. Rather, he means common knowledge or belief, as when we say, 'It's a matter of common sense that New York is farther from Chicago than Milwaukee is, or that water freezes at 32° F.', or he means that which could be a matter of common knowledge if one took the trouble to find out, as in some of the truisms which I shall list below.

Moore's emphasis upon common sense may be seen throughout many of his papers and books but is most clearly exhibited in his celebrated paper, "A Defence of Common Sense," which appeared in 1925.[2] Moore begins by setting forth "a whole long list of propositions, which may seem at first sight, such obvious truisms as not to be worth stating," every one of which, Moore says, "I *know* with certainty to be true."[3] Some of these truisms are:

(I) "There exists at present a living human body, which is *my* body. This body was born at a certain time in the past, and has existed continuously ever since, though not without undergoing changes." "At every moment since it was born, there have also existed many other things, . . . from which it has been at *various distances.*" "Also there have

---

1. "Autobiography," *PGEM*, p. 14.
2. "Def.," *PP*, Chap. 2.
3. *Ibid.,* p. 33.

... existed some other things of this kind with which it was in *contact*." Among these have been "large numbers of other living human bodies . . . and many of these bodies have already died and ceased to exist." "But the earth had existed also for many years before my body was born." Further, "I have at different times since my body was born, had many different experiences . . . e.g., I have often perceived both my own body and other things which formed part of its environment, including other human bodies." Similarly, "in the case of very many of the other human bodies which have lived upon the earth, each has been the body of a different human being who has . . . had many different experiences." [4]

Moore then asserts another "obvious truism": (II) Very many human beings have frequently known (each one, with regard to himself or his own body) everything which Moore claimed to know about himself or his body in the list of truisms in (I) and, hence, have known propositions corresponding to those which Moore had known.[5]

By 'true' Moore means that all the propositions above, and all those corresponding to them, are *wholly* true, not partially true (whatever that means). Furthermore, he means that the statements above express what they would ordinarily be understood to express. "I was not using the expressions I used . . . in any . . . subtle sense. I meant by each of them precisely what every reader, in reading them, will have understood me to mean." [6] The assumption here (which Moore admits) is that there is some meaning which is the ordinary or popular meaning of such statements as 'The earth has existed for many years past', etc. Against the thesis that such statements are ambiguous and problematic—a thesis which some of Moore's predecessors (e.g., Bradley) had defended—depending upon what one means by 'earth', 'exists', 'years', and so forth, Moore maintains that such a view is "profoundly mistaken." An expression like 'The earth has existed for many years past', is, he says, "the very type of unambiguous expression, the meaning of which we all understand." [7] Anyone who takes the opposing view is confusing the question as to whether we understand the meaning of such an expression ("which we all certainly do") with the very different question whether we *know what it means,* in the sense of being able to give a correct *analysis* of its meaning. The question of what

4. *Ibid.,* pp. 33–34.
5. *Ibid.,* p. 34.
6. *Ibid.,* p. 36.
7. *Ibid.,* p. 37.

is the correct analysis of such statements is a difficult one. But to hold that one does not know the correct analysis of statements of this sort does not imply that he does not understand them. On the contrary, whenever we know that anyone is using such an expression in its ordinary sense, we understand its meaning.[8]

Taken as a whole, the list of propositions in (I) and the corresponding propositions which each of us knows imply ("in a certain sense") other propositions: 'Material things are real', 'Space is real', 'Time is real', and 'The self is real'. (No *one* proposition in [I] need imply all of these, of course.) For example, the proposition that I have had different feelings at different times implies that time is real and that at least one self is real. Apparently, Moore believes that these new propositions, taken with the qualification "in a certain sense" (not explained), are just as unambiguous as the truisms in (I). Certain philosophers have at times, however, denied these propositions and, hence, have asserted such things as: 'Material things are not real', 'Space is not real', etc. Such expressions, says Moore, *are* ambiguous. But worse, not only are they ambiguous, and not only do they express views which are incompatible with Moore's truisms, views such as 'No propositions like those in (I) are true', but the propositions expressed by these sentences are "quite certainly false." Moore attempts to demonstrate this in the following way.

The propositions in (I), together with all the corresponding propositions which many of us know to be true, make up certain classes of propositions. This is what Moore means by (II). Take *any* of the classes of such propositions. If *any* of these classes are such that no proposition in that class is true, then it follows that no philosopher has ever existed, and that, therefore, no philosopher can ever have believed with respect to any such class that no proposition in it is true.

In other words, the proposition that some propositions belonging to each of these classes is true is a proposition which has the peculiarity that, if any philosopher has ever denied it, it follows from the fact that he has denied it, that he must have been wrong in denying it. For when I speak of 'philosopher' I mean, of course (as we all do), exclusively philosophers who have been human beings, with human bodies that lived upon the earth, and who have at different times had many different experiences. If, therefore, there have been any philosophers, there have been human beings of this class; and if there have been human beings of this class, all the rest of what is asserted in (I) is

8. *Ibid.* (See below, Chap. V, for Moore's notion of analysis.)

certainly true too. Any view, therefore, incompatible with the proposition that many propositions corresponding to each of the propositions in (I) are true, can only be true on the hypothesis that no philosopher has ever held any such view.[9]

Furthermore, philosophers who have denied some of the truisms in (I) have constantly, even in their writings, expressed views which are inconsistent with their denial. Each of them has, for example, alluded to the existence of other philosophers, or used the term 'we' in 'We do so and so' to assert that not only he but other human beings have done so and so. In so doing, these philosophers have shown that they knew certain propositions corresponding to those in (I)—propositions about other minds—to be true, even though they have elsewhere denied that such propositions are true.[10]

Some philosophers have not asserted that, with regard to any of the classes of propositions in question, no propositions in that class are true but have held a more modest view, namely, that no human being has ever *known* with certainty that any propositions of a certain class (or classes) are true. Moore finds this view to be self-contradictory. These philosophers, too, have spoken about *us* or referred to views commonly held by mankind, etc. Hence, in saying that no human being has ever known that other human beings beside himself exist, such philosophers are saying: "There have been many other human beings beside myself, and none of them (including myself) have ever known of the existence of other human beings."[11]

Moore's conclusion, then, is that he knows all the propositions in (I) to be true and that he knows (II) to be true. In answer to the questions, 'Does he really know all the propositions in (I) to be true? Isn't it possible that he merely *believes* them?' Moore answers: "I have nothing better to say than that it seems to me that I do know them, with certainty."[12] He then admits that he knows some of them, not directly, but only because he has known, in the past, other propositions to be true which were evidence for them. He knows, for example, that the earth existed for years before he was born because he has known other things in the past which were evidence for it. Yet he does not know exactly what that evidence was.

---

9. *Ibid.*, p. 40.
10. *Ibid.*, p. 41.
11. *Ibid.*, p. 43.
12. *Ibid.*, p. 44.

Nevertheless, he finds that this is no good reason for doubting that he knows it. "We are all, I think, in this strange position that we do *know* many things, with regard to which we *know* further that we must have had evidence for them, and yet we do not know *how* we know them; i.e., we do not know what the evidence was." [13]

This, then, is Moore's defense of the "Common Sense view of the world." The pattern runs something like this. A philosopher says, for example, "The proposition that material objects exist is false." Presumably he does not make this statement when he is at home addressing his wife. But he does utter it in his philosophy. It is an *ontological* assertion. Moore reads or hears the statement but does not attempt to refute it on the same grounds. Instead, he says, in effect: "Now look here. Statements like 'Material objects exist' are understood in their ordinary sense by all of us and are known to be true by all of us. Consider, I have a body, and I know that I do. Hence, at least one material object exists. The proof that there is at least one material object lies in the fact that I do have a body. And, really, only a mad man would doubt that. Therefore, since there is at least one material object (and I could in a similar way show you that there are others), your view is wrong." Similarly, if anyone holds that he *believes* that material objects exist, or *tends* to believe it, but claims that we do not know for certain the truth of any statement like 'Material objects exist', Moore simply asserts that, when they are understood in their common or ordinary sense, we do know such statements to be *certainly* true, and, hence, any view which maintains that they are not known to be certainly true is mistaken. And, as we saw, Moore has nothing further to say to anyone who doubts all this, to anyone who questions whether we really know, or know with certainty, such propositions as 'My body has existed for many years past' to be true, than that it seems to him that he *does* know them to be true, and with certainty.

II

I AM SURE that most philosophers do not find this to be quite satisfactory. Yes, one might say, there is a sense in which we all understand such statements as 'My body has existed for many years past' or 'This is a

13. *Ibid.*

hand', and there is a sense in which we know for certain that statements of this sort are true. But this is not the kind of understanding with which, at least, some philosophers have been concerned (or it is not the *only* kind with which they have been concerned) when they questioned various common-sense beliefs. Nor is this the kind of certainty with which they have been content in their search for genuine knowledge or for the ultimate existents of the world. In *one* sense, we understand what it is for tables and chairs to exist, and, in that sense, we know that there are such objects. If you were to ask me what I am doing at this moment, I would not hesitate to say that I am sitting at my desk, pen in hand, filling sheets of paper with statements about the philosophy of G. E. Moore; that there is a lamp on my desk, several books by Moore, a letter to be mailed, etc. And I am sure that you would have no trouble understanding me. And, in our normal, everyday conversation, we would not stop to inquire as to whether I really knew that I had a pen in hand, whether there really is such a thing as a *pen* as over against a collection of sense-data, etc. However, in *another* sense, and in a different context, might one not plausibly hold that it is sometimes appropriate to question various common-sense assertions, since we know, among other things, that common sense is often wrong (Moore admits the latter)? And in this context, I might say very different things. I might suggest, for example, that I am now sensing a red datum which is wholly presented to me is absolutely certain. But I might wonder whether, in this same sense, it is absolutely certain that there is a red *book* on that *table* over there. Might I not find that the book is orange, or that the object is a box and not a book, or that there is, in fact, no object over there at all? Isn't knowledge, then, something much more complicated than Moore takes it to be?

Moore, of course, is not unaware of the possibility of such objections; nevertheless, he thinks (at least, in the "Defence") that there is *never* a problem with respect to either the truth or the ordinary understanding of common-sense statements. The problem, as he sees it, lies elsewhere. Hence, again, he distinguishes understanding what common-sense statements mean (in the sense in which we all do understand them) from knowing *what* they mean, in the sense of being able to give a correct *analysis* of their meanings. Similarly, he distinguishes knowing common-sense statements to be true from being able to know just *how* they are true, or from being able to *say* how they are true. Moore maintains that it is possible to understand common-sense statements about material objects, etc., in their ordinary meaning and to *know them to be true,* without knowing what their correct analysis is. Hence, the plain man knows many things about the world, but he is not able to justify his knowledge claims in any epistemological sense. But to say that because he cannot justify the statements which he purports to know he therefore does not really know them is an unwarranted assumption, according to Moore. And in insisting upon this, Moore is surely right, as long as we remain at a very ordinary common-sense level. And if Moore had merely maintained that, at this ordinary level, we all know certain things to be true, one would have no quarrel. But Moore pushes the issue much further than this. Let me explain. To do so, I shall have to bring up some other matters. After I have done that, I shall return to a continuation of the above comments.

As I mentioned, Moore shows no interest in questioning the *truth* of common-sense statements. He often simply holds that it is perfectly justifiable to take their truth for granted, to take them as being absolutely and indubitably true. In fact, Moore goes even further and holds that the statements of common sense are a "touchstone" of truth.[14] He maintains that a good *reason* for accepting some philosopher's view is that it accords with common sense.[15] Similarly, he holds that a good reason for rejecting a philosophical view is that it "flies in the face of common sense." [16]

One is tempted to ask: Does this imply that common sense may never be mistaken? Moore is not so rash as to suggest that common sense is always right. Not only is it possible for common sense to be mistaken; it has, in fact, often been wrong. We now know that certain views which were once common-sense views, e.g., "That the heavenly bodies were small compared to the earth, and at comparatively short distances from the earth," were very definitely wrong.[17] Since, then, Moore does not maintain that *all* common-sense statements must be true, another question naturally suggests itself: What are Moore's criteria both for deciding when a statement is a *statement* of common sense, in his special sense, and for accepting some of these special common-sense statements as being true? Moore implicitly has such criteria. Let us examine them.

14. A. R. White, "Moore's Appeal to Common Sense," *Philosophy,* XXXIII (1958), 221–39.

15. *SMPP,* p. 156.

16. *PS,* pp. 288–89.

17. *SMPP,* p. 3; cf. p. 7.

III

I SHALL DISTINGUISH FOUR CRITERIA of common sense which are found in Moore's works. I am indebted to Alan R. White for the *second* of these criteria.[18] White lists five criteria, but it turns out that he divides the criterion which I have chosen as my third into two varieties, even though both are criteria of inconsistency. I believe that White is correct in his suggestion that only the first, and possibly the second, of the criteria needs to be satisfied for a statement to be a *statement* of common sense. But for a statement to be a *true* statement of common sense, the situation is more complex. Often Moore seems to hold that all of the criteria must be satisfied for that to obtain. In some cases, however, the last two criteria are employed singly (one or the other) to indicate a true common-sense statement—the first when Moore is refuting the views of some philosopher, the other one in most other cases.

I must make it clear that these criteria are never systematically exhibited and are rarely (I think) *intentionally* appealed to by Moore as being *criteria*. Hence, formulating a list of them may be somewhat misleading, as it may be interpreted as a suggestion that Moore had a clear *doctrine* of the criteria. This is not the case. Moore *uses,* on occasion, now one, now another of the criteria. At times, one is led to believe that they were simply *assumptions* which Moore cared neither to doubt nor to systematically affirm. But then this is an occurrence common in philosophy as elsewhere. A philosopher may often adhere to certain principles, criteria, or methodological devices, simply because they are so basic or so much a part of the framework within which he operates that it never occurs to him that any scrutiny or systematic delineation of them should be made. This is certainly the case with Moore's criteria. As far as I know, he never called them criteria of common sense, even though he did appeal to one or the other of them on different occasions.

1. There is, first, the criterion of *universal acceptance.* This criterion serves a double function, remember. A statement which is universally accepted is a statement of common sense.[19] Moore frequently appeals to the fact that certain views are generally or universally *assumed* to be true.

18. "Moore's Appeal to Common Sense," pp. 228 ff. Cf. A. R. White, *G. E. Moore: A Critical Exposition* (Oxford: Blackwell, 1958), pp. 11 ff.
19. "Def."; cf. also *SMPP, passim.*

He follows this procedure, for example, in connection with the existence of physical objects.[20] We saw examples of this in discussing Moore's "Defence," above. But he often refers to views which "we all do, in ordinary life, constantly believe." [21]

Now it would be appropriate to use the criterion of universal acceptance for determining whether or not a statement is a *statement* of common sense, although how one would ever attain to knowledge that a statement was absolutely universally accepted is somewhat of a problem. But it would be positively shocking to some if Moore used universal acceptance as a criterion of the *truth* of common-sense statements for reasons I mentioned at the end of section I. There are some occasional hints that he may have been using it in this way.[22] However, for the most part, I do not find that he ever relied upon this criterion by itself for determining the truth of statements. He, after all, did at times suggest that it would be appropriate to question whether universally accepted beliefs were true.[23] But, then, as readers of Moore so well know, Moore often said that something was the case, but also that it was not the case, and again, that he was not sure whether it was the case, or that he had good reasons to believe that it was the case, or that, for all he knew, it might be the case, and so on—each statement in different essays; so that it is often impossible to determine just what he really did believe. His view on sense-data is a prime example, as we shall see later. Here too there is no consistent view.

2. The second criterion has been called (by White) *compulsive acceptance*.[24] Moore sometimes points to the fact that certain beliefs are such that, not only do we all hold them, but "we cannot help believing them," even if they seem paradoxical or inconsistent with other beliefs of ours.[25] I have found very few passages which suggest this criterion; hence, I shall not linger over it.

3. The third criterion is *inconsistency upon denial* (of a statement). There are several forms of this criterion. I think that three of them especially stand out. In all cases, Moore uses this criterion to show that

20. *SMPP*, pp. 21, 116, 139.
21. *Ibid.*, pp. 182–86.
22. "Prf."; cf. also *SMPP, passim*.
23. "Are the Materials of Sense Affections of the Mind?", *PAS*, XVII (1916–17), 424–25.
24. White, *G. E. Moore*, p. 12.
25. *SMPP*, pp. 342; cf. *PS*, pp. 164–65.

where a statement leads to an inconsistency, its denial may be *held* to be acceptable or true, or, even, *is* true.

(A) One type of inconsistency is that of presupposing the truth of what one is supposedly trying to disprove. We see this in the case of philosophers who deny that time is real. These philosophers often say things which show that they know very well that time is real; for example, they sometimes say that we *constantly* believe or do so and so. By so doing, they presuppose that things happen in time. In this case, inconsistency is not a criterion of the certain truth of the statement which the philosopher denies—call it *p*—but it does point out that the philosopher actually believes *p* to be true.[26]

(B) Another type of inconsistency involves conflicting views, both of which are held. Moore says that any assertion may be held to be true if its denial is incompatible with other views which the person denying it explicitly holds to be true.[27] We show such a person that our view is consistent with something else which he holds to be true, whereas his view contradicts it. But Moore surely knows that systems or beliefs can be totally consistent yet totally false! Yes, he escapes by saying that this argument does not *prove* that the statements in question are *true* but it does justify our *holding* them to be true. Moore says:

I could only point out as clearly as possible what it means, and how it contradicts other propositions which appear to be equally true. My only object in all this was, necessarily, to convince. But even if I did convince, that does not prove that we are right. It justifies us in *holding* that we are so; but nevertheless we may be wrong.[28]

Obviously, this type of criterion would not always be philosophically relevant. For we are often interested not merely in what we may *hold* to be true but what *is* true.

(C) A third kind of inconsistency is one which Moore makes much of in his "Defence of Common Sense." Moore holds that there is such a thing as the "Common Sense view of the world." What this common-sense view of the world is, Moore does not explicitly say. One might be led to think that, by the common-sense view of the world, Moore means that view which holds such propositions as Moore has stated ("There exists at

26. SMPP, p. 202.
27. *Ibid.*, pp. 284–87.
28. PE, p. 145.

present a body which is my body', etc.) to be true. That this list of truisms which Moore presents cannot be the *whole* of the common-sense view of the world follows from his assertion that these truisms are or state only *certain features* of the common-sense view of the world. So, then, we do not know precisely what *else,* for Moore, the common-sense view includes. But let us assume that we have some notion as to what this phrase means. Moore says that he is one of those philosophers who have maintained that the common-sense view of the world is, "in certain fundamental features, wholly true"; and, further, that *all* philosophers have agreed with him in holding this, although some of them have *also* held views inconsistent with these features of the common-sense view of the world.

Now for Moore's argument. The features of the common-sense view which, according to Moore, he and *all* philosophers have known to be true are those propositions in the classes of truisms which were mentioned above. I say *classes* of truisms, because we are here to include not only Moore's assertions like 'There is a body which is my body', etc., but also those assertions of each individual that correspond to those of Moore's. Now Moore maintains that these features (the classes of propositions in question) have a peculiar property, namely, that *"if we know that they are features in the 'common sense view of the world,'* it follows *that they are true."* It is self-contradictory to say that *we* know them to be features in the common-sense view and yet hold that they are *not* true, for "to say that we know this, is to say that they are true." [29] Furthermore, many of these propositions have an even more peculiar property: *"If they are features in the common sense view of the world (whether 'we' know this or not) it follows that they are true,* since to say that there is a 'common sense view of the world' is to say that they are true." [30] Now, as long as we remain at the level of common sense, Moore's argument seems to be acceptable. But as we shall see shortly, this does not prevent us from raising certain questions on matters which Moore glides over too easily.

4. Now for the criterion upon which Moore relies most. The ultimate criterion for holding the statements of common sense to be true is that *they are self-evidently true.* I have often referred to the fact that, in his "Defence of Common Sense," Moore said, with respect to his common-sense statements: "I have nothing better to say than that it seems to me

---

29. "Def.," *PP*, pp. 44–45.
30. *Ibid.,* p. 45.

that I do know them with certainty." [31] He often follows this practice: e.g., "The only proof that we do know external facts lies in the simple fact that we do know them." [32] Again: "What are we to say of these two principles? They do seem to me to be self-evident." [33] "In the end, all we can do is to say that something is self-evidently true without being able to give any method of arguing that this is so. 'It is simply a matter of inspection.'" [34]

Certain statements, then, are, according to Moore, self-evident. What does this mean? "The expression self-evident means that the proposition so-called is evident or true by *itself* alone; that it is not an inference from some proposition other than itself." [35] We cannot, then, prove self-evident statements. Rather, the proof of other statements rests upon these. Well, then, what basis do we have for accepting such statements? Do we perform some test in order to verify them? Moore suggests that we somehow just see or intuitively apprehend that such statements are self-evident and that, therefore, we do not need a *basis,* i.e., evidence, grounds, etc., for accepting them. For example, in his "Proof of an External World," Moore gives what he calls a conclusive proof of the existence of "things outside us." He first shows that, if he can prove that the statement, 'Two human hands exist at this moment', or a similar statement, is true, then he will have also proved that 'Things outside us exist'. The premiss which he adduces for his conclusion is: 'Here is one hand, and here is another'. But did he really *know* that the premiss is true? "How absurd it would be to suggest that I did not know it, but only believed it, and that perhaps it was not the case! You might as well suggest that I do not know that I am now standing up and talking—that perhaps after all I'm not, and that it's not quite certain that I am!" [36] Hence, a statement like 'Here is one hand, and here is another' may be called self-evident. It is neither proved (derived as a conclusion from other premisses) nor verified (Moore holds that the only time where the latter would be appropriate would be the case, say, in which Moore had a wooden hand). [37]

But how do we know whether or not statements are really self-evident?

31. *Ibid.,* p. 44.
32. "Hume's Philosophy," *The New Quarterly* (Nov., 1909), reprinted in *PS,* p. 160.
33. *SMPP,* p. 191; cf. "External and Internal Relations," (*PAS,* XX (1919–20), reprinted in *PS,* p. 306.
34. White, *G. E. Moore,* p. 233. Cf. *SMPP,* p. 357.
35. *PE,* p. 143.
36. "Prf.," *PP,* pp. 146–47. Cf. my discussion of 'knowledge that' in Chap. VI, sect. I.
37. "Prf.," *PP,* p. 149.

I do not know exactly how to set about arguing that they are self-evident. The chief thing to be done is, I think, to consider them as carefully and distinctly as possible, and then to see whether it does not seem as if they *must* be true; and to compare them with other propositions, which do seem to be certainly true, and to consider whether you have any better reason for supposing these other propositions to be true than for supposing this one to be so.[38]

IV

WHAT ARE WE TO THINK OF THIS? There are some who may still think that it will not do, that *there is a sense* in which 'This is one hand, and this is another' is not absolutely known to be true on various occasions, and that it will not help our doubt any by trying to bamboozle us with 'How absurd to suggest that . . . etc.'

Someone may raise an objection: "But you are making this too much of a philosophical matter. When Moore is talking about the knowledge of common-sense statements, he only means the plain, ordinary knowledge which the plain, ordinary man has about plain, ordinary things." To which one might answer: This is only part of the story. If this were all that Moore were doing, one could hardly quarrel with him. But Moore's appeal to common sense is sometimes employed in very different circumstances from "plain, ordinary" ones, and, at such times, is, many would believe, hardly appropriate. Let me explain.

As I already indicated, Moore claims that, with respect to the long list of truisms which were stated earlier, and with respect to some similar statements, he *knows* every one of them to be true, and with certainty. And if anyone doubts that he really knows such statements to be true, Moore simply keeps asserting that he, in fact, *does* know them to be true and that that's all there is to say on the matter. The defense of the truth of such statements is at these times presented solely at a very ordinary, commonsensical level. If someone asks, say, "Is time real?" Moore answers: "Of course it is. You know very well it is. You had your breakfast before your lunch, didn't you? And you got out of bed before you entered the bathroom, didn't you?" Hence, we are here operating on the level of plain, ordinary, common-sense talk. No epistemological issues are raised.

I suppose that, taken on the commonsensical level and limited to it,

38. *SMPP*, p. 191.

nearly all philosophers would agree that Moore's truisms and perhaps other common-sense statements in *this* sense of 'know' are known to be true. But there is another sense of 'know' in which some philosophers have held that statements concerning the existence of physical objects, for example, are false, or are false in certain respects, or may be false, or cannot be known to be true, or cannot be known to be true with absolute certainty. Statements of this kind involve both ontological and epistemological considerations. They involve ontological considerations because philosophers who have denied the existence of physical objects (or whatever it may be) have used 'exist' in a special sense. They involve epistemological considerations because these philosophers, in saying that we do not know that certain objects, such as material things, exist, are using 'know' in a technical sense. As I showed in sections I and II, and as we shall very clearly see again in Chapter III, Moore, when making the plain, ordinary ploy and attempting to refute various philosophers, completely ignores these points. He does this by refusing to argue on metaphysical and epistemological grounds and by transferring the discussion from the level of ontology and epistemology to the level of vulgar, common sense. His technique is that of an appeal to the fact that such statements as he is defending are understood by all of us and are known to be true by all of us at the level of common sense, whereas the statements of the philosophers whom he is attacking are not. Here, Moore's whole argument for the statements which he is concerned to defend consists in saying that these statements are true because he simply knows them to be true; and because, even when philosophers are led to deny them, in the very process of denying them they show that they themselves hold the statements to be true and, hence, contradict themselves.[39] I think that all philosophers would, without question, grant that Moore has scored on *this* shot, once for all (or they should agree). But many might argue that what Moore has not done, however, is to show that, at a very different level, the level of ontology and epistemology, the statements of the philosophers who deny the existence of material objects or the knowledge of the existence of material objects are false. That is to say, he has not refuted the philosophers upon their grounds at all. They could, for example, grant everything that Moore has said about having lunch *after* breakfast and still insist that, because of the special meanings which they have in mind, a

39. "Def.," *PP*, pp. 38–43.

sentence such as 'Time is real' is false. Moore's refutation, then, is a refutation only by virtue of a transfer from the level of ontology and epistemology to that of plain, ordinary common sense. And, really, on *that* level, why argue? For everyone, or nearly everyone, would admit that on the level of common sense Moore is surely right. The problem, I repeat, is: What about the other level? Moore bypasses this issue when appealing to common sense either to effect his refutations or to maintain his own doctrines.

For example, Moore often says that he knows some statement of common sense to be "certainly true" or that he knows it "with certainty." [40] What kind of certainty is this? The only kind of certainty which he considers when talking about common-sense statements is the sort which is intended in ordinary discourse. On *this* level, it would be appropriate, when one is confronted with the question 'Do you know for certain that that is a chair?' to answer, 'Yes'. That there is such a notion of certainty as this, I should not wish to dispute. In this sense, we all know many statements regarding the existence of chairs, tables, coffeepots, ourselves, other selves, etc., with certainty. But if one attempts to give a philosophical explication of certainty, he may find that some statements which are commonsensically certain are by no means epistemologically certain. In this epistemological sense, some would suggest that there are only two kinds of certainty. One kind is seen in the explication of analyticity. When we know a proposition to be analytic, we know it to be certain. And, in order to substantiate the fact that we here have a case of certainty rather than probability, some have proposed an explication of analyticity—Carnap's notion of L-truth, for example. A second kind of certainty is obtainable with regard to certain classes of statements, such as those about sense-data, which it makes no sense to doubt. If anyone senses a red patch, or even a chair-percept, it hardly makes sense to wonder if he is sensing them. Such things we know, whenever we do know them, with certainty. But is it clear (one might ask) that, in this sense of 'certain', we are equally certain that we are perceiving a red apple or a chair at all times when we believe that we are perceiving them? Is it not the case that we have frequently been wrong on such matters? And does it not make sense on some occasions to doubt whether it is a real chair that we are perceiving? Moore ignores all these factors when defending or appealing to his

40. *Ibid.*, p. 43.

common-sense certainty. Hence, many would be inclined to hold that his certainty becomes basically psychological in nature. As we saw in section II, he often says about various propositions that they just *seem* to him to be certainly true, that they are self-evident, that they are such that he cannot doubt them, that he *must* accept them, etc. But even his list of truisms contains statements which may not seem to be so certain to everyone.

The point which I am trying to establish, then, is this: Moore's defense of common sense is a defense which is valid only within a very limited area and which triumphs outside of this area only by virtue of excluding from consideration a whole vast range of problems and distinctions. This is not to say that, at the level on which it succeeds, it has no value. On the contrary, we may be grateful to Moore for having reminded us of what we all do in fact know (in one sense of 'know'). And if there are any philosophers who have *commonsensically* denied Moore's truisms (I have never met any who have positively denied them at this level, but there may be some), then Moore has conclusively shown that such philosophers are wrong, or silly, or mad. But what one might equally insist upon is this: Moore's defense does not either defend or refute anything with respect to peculiarly philosophical problems. More specifically, his defense does not establish that what we all know commonsensically to be true may be known to be true in an epistemological sense, where grounds, evidence, verification, etc., enter in. But, then, Moore surely knows that the two are different. Otherwise, why would he have gone to the pains, in *other* contexts, of specifying various ways of knowing, in the philosophical sense (ways which I shall consider in Chapter VI), and why would he have brought, in those contexts, his epistemological findings to various problems in an effort to solve them? Yet, though Moore was aware of the difference in levels, he often neglected to make the distinction when considering the statements made by other philosophers and when showing them to be absurd from the viewpoint of common sense. Hence, it might be suggested that he comes out the victor, but only by virtue of playing in a different game.

But if one grants that Moore may have erred in appealing to common sense for refutational purposes, in certain contexts, can one still admit a positive value to Moore's appeal to common sense? Furthermore, since Moore himself realized that certain philosophical inquiries went beyond matters of common sense, does there remain any point to Moore's strong emphasis on common sense? I think that one might give an affirmative answer to both questions. For one could say that what Moore is maintaining is simply this. Our philosophical inquiries must start from common sense—after all, what else is there to start from? Thus there is a sense in which common sense needs no defense. And, indeed, any effort to either defend or refute common sense is in error. However, when we engage in philosophical investigations, we soon find that many problems and questions arise and many distinctions must be made. The result of such analytical probings can never oppose or refute common sense in the sense of showing the *common-sense view of the world* to be false. What it can show is that the *analysis* of such common-sense statements is much more difficult and complex than it appears to be prior to such dialectical probings. Thus again, Moore's point is: We all know various common-sense truisms to be true, and we all understand them in the ordinary sense, but what we often do not know is their correct analysis. One of the tasks of philosophy is to seek their correct analysis. Whatever the results of such analysis may yield, there is one thing which it may not do: it cannot falsify all those common-sense truisms which we *all* hold to be true, i.e., it cannot refute the *common-sense view of the world* from which we must all start, because there is no other place from which to begin.

III

Ordinary Language

I T WOULD HARDLY BE APPROPRIATE to omit consideration of a topic which has often been confused or coalesced with Moore's appeal to common sense—namely, his appeal to *ordinary language*.

The controversy apparently began with an early article by Norman Malcolm,[1] in which Malcolm says that he is going to talk about an important feature of Moore's method, "his way of refuting a certain type of philosophical proposition." Malcolm presents a list of such propositions, all of which, he holds (rightly), would be rejected by Moore as *false*. Some of these are:

> (a) There are no material things.
> (b) Time is unreal.
> (c) Space is unreal.
> (d) No one ever perceives a material thing.
> (e) There are no other minds . . .[2]

1. "Moore and Ordinary Language," *PGEM*, pp. 345–68.
2. *Ibid.*, p. 345.

31

He then presents the "sort of argument" which he believes Moore would give in order to "attack these statements." Some of these arguments are:

(a) You are certainly wrong, for here's one hand and here's another; and so there are at least two material things.

(b) If you mean that no event ever follows or precedes another event, you are certainly wrong; for *after* lunch I went for a walk, and after that I took a bath, and after that I had tea.[3]

At the end, Malcolm correctly notes that all of these philosophical statements which Moore is attacking "go against 'common sense'. This fact plays an important part in the explanation of the nature of Moore's attack upon these statements."[4] But a few paragraphs later, Malcolm adds: "The essence of Moore's technique consists in pointing out that these statements *go against ordinary language*."[5] Malcolm's identification of the two appeals is made even more explicit in a later article.[6] Speaking this time of some statements of Moore's which Malcolm regards as a *misuse* of ordinary language, he writes: "Moore's assertions do not belong to 'common sense'; i.e., to ordinary language, at all."[7]

The first assertion of Malcolm's, then, to which I wish to call attention is this: 'According to Moore, common sense and ordinary language are the same'. I shall call the view which identifies common sense and ordinary language, or which identifies the two appeals, the *ordinary language identification principle*. Of course, Malcolm not only holds that ordinary language and common sense are identical for Moore; he also holds that they are the same for himself. But since I am not discussing Malcolm's philosophical views, the assertion to which I am calling attention is not 'Ordinary language and common sense are the same', but 'Moore holds that ordinary language and common sense are the same', i.e., the assertion that Moore makes the ordinary language identification. I hope to show below that this assertion is false.

But Malcolm also makes two other assertions. Both of them are slightly more elaborate than the first.

In the first of his articles, referred to above, Malcolm also maintains that when Moore was replying to the philosophical propositions ('There are no

3. *Ibid.*, p. 346.
4. *Ibid.*, p. 348.
5. *Ibid.*, p. 349.
6. "Defending Common Sense," *The Philosophical Review*, LVIII (1949), 201–20.
7. *Ibid.*, p. 219. But see below, n. 11.

material things', 'Time is unreal', etc.) he was merely making a certain linguistic recommendation. His reply was a misleading way of saying, 'It would be an improper way of speaking to say that there are no material things', etc.

Let us consider an example of what Malcolm means in more detail. I take the example from his essay. A philosopher—i.e., someone who utters strange and paradoxical assertions—says: "We do not know for *certain* the truth of any statement about material things." Moore's supposed reply is: "Both of us know for *certain* that there are several chairs in this room, and how absurd it would be to suggest that we do not know it, but only believe it, and that perhaps it is not the case—how absurd it would be to say that it is highly probable, but not certain!" [8]

But Malcolm goes on. He suggests that Moore holds that we are entitled to say in some particular cases that a person who says that he knows for certain the truth of a material-thing statement is mistaken. For example, Jones might say that he knows for certain by the smell that carrots are cooking. But I know that it is turnips, not carrots, because I looked. Hence, it would be appropriate for me to say that Jones does not know the truth of *that particular statement*. But when the philosopher asserts that we can never know for certain *any* material-thing statements, he is not asserting an empirical fact. The reason why he says that no one can ever say "I know for certain that *p*," where *p* is a material-thing statement, is that "he regards that *form of speech as improper*." He holds that "the phrase 'known for certain' is not properly applied to material-thing statements." [9] "Moore's reply," on the other hand, is, according to Malcolm, a "misleading" way of saying: "It is a proper way of speaking to say that we know for certain that there are several chairs in this room, and *it would be an improper way of speaking* to say that we only believe it, or that it is only probable!" (italics added) [10] Both the philosopher's statements and Moore's, then, are, according to Malcolm, "disguised linguistic statements." Malcolm maintains that Moore actually held this view and concludes: "In this as in all the other cases Moore is right." [11]

---

8. *PGEM*, p. 351. These are Malcolm's words, attributed to Moore. I am not denying, here or elsewhere, that this answer is like statements which Moore actually made.

9. *Ibid.*, pp. 353, 354.

10. *Ibid.*, p. 354.

11. *Ibid.* In all fairness, I should say that the concluding two paragraphs of a later paper of Malcolm's suggest a less extreme view. See "Philosophy for Philosophers," *The Philosophical Review*, LX (1951), 340.

I shall call this view that it is a proper way of speaking to say 'so and so', whereas it is an improper way of speaking to say 'such and such', where 'such and such' is a philosophical proposition *of the sort* which Malcolm lists, the *ordinary language linguistic recommendation principle*. The second assertion of Malcolm's to which I want to call attention is: 'Moore holds the ordinary language linguistic recommendation principle'. I hope also to show that this second assertion of Malcolm's is false.

Malcolm also makes a third assertion. In the same article, he maintains that, with respect to each of the philosophical propositions which he lists, Moore's (sometimes imagined) reply is "perfectly true," and that "what he says is in each case a *good* refutation, a refutation that shows the *falsity* of the statement in question" (italics added).[12] Later Malcolm says that Moore "takes his stand upon ordinary language and defends it against every attack, against every paradox. The philosophy of most of the more important philosophers has consisted in their more or less repudiating ordinary language. Moore's philosophizing has consisted mostly in his refuting the repudiators of ordinary language."[13] But in what does the refutation consist? "Moore's great historical role consists in the fact that he has been perhaps the first philosopher to sense that *any philosophical statement which violates ordinary language is false,* and consistently to defend ordinary language against its philosophical violators" (italics added).[14]

I shall call this view that any philosophical statement which violates ordinary language *is false* the *ordinary language refutational principle*. The third assertion of Malcolm's to which I want to call attention is this: 'Moore holds the ordinary language refutational principle', i.e., 'Moore maintains that any philosophical statement which violates ordinary language is false'. I also hope to show that this third assertion of Malcolm's is false.

I wish to distinguish both Malcolm's second and third assertions from a more modest assertion. I shall call the view that ordinary language may be appealed to as a preliminary to the solving of philosophical problems; that it may be instrumental for certain refutational purposes; that it may be an indicator of what we *believe* to be the case, and even of what *may* be the case, but that it cannot be appealed to in order to determine what *is* the

12. *PGEM*, p. 349.
13. *Ibid.*, p. 365.
14. *Ibid.*, p. 368.

case; and that ordinary language ought, where possible, to be defended, but that it does not merit slavish obedience—the *ordinary language partial adherence principle*. Now, the more modest assertion to which I am referring is: 'Moore holds the ordinary language partial adherence principle'. Whereas I wish to show that Malcolm's three assertions are false, I wish to demonstrate that *this* more modest assertion is certainly true. For brevity, I shall, in the following, call anyone who holds *either* the ordinary language identification principle *or* the ordinary language linguistic recommendation principle *or* the ordinary language refutational principle, *or* any two of them, *or* all three, an *ordinary language proponent*. I shall *not* use this expression to refer to anyone who merely holds the ordinary language partial adherence principle.

I shall go about the task in the following way. *First,* I wish to show that, according to Moore's views and in accordance with his method, the following three things *should be true* for Moore:

1. Common sense and ordinary language are separate notions.
2. The appeal to ordinary language is subsidiary to the appeal to common sense.
3. An appeal to *common sense* in order to refute (show the falsity of) statements like 'There are no material things', etc., has some plausibility, whereas an appeal to *ordinary language* in order to prove such statements false is (whatever other values it may have and functions it may perform) implausible, ineffective, and indeed, ridiculous.

Second, I want to demonstrate that (1), (2), and (3) *are* true for Moore. It can be demonstrated very briefly that Moore *did* hold (3) to be true, and hence, that (2) is true for him; and thus, that (1) is true for him since (2) follows from (3), and (1) from (2). By showing that Moore held (3) to be true, I shall have shown that Malcolm's first and third assertions are false.

Third, I wish to show that, when Moore replied to the paradoxical statements of philosophers, he was not making linguistic recommendations, i.e., that Malcolm's second assertion is false. This can be demonstrated even more briefly.

II

FIRST, IS THERE ANY GOOD REASON why Moore should have held that (3) is true? Let us remember the method which Moore often employed. He constantly came across statements in philosophical works of the following sort: 'Time is not real', 'Physical objects do not exist', etc. He was perplexed by such "monstrous assertions," and he tried to discover just what such statements could possibly mean. And very often, in order to determine what they could mean, he "translated" them into statements of ordinary language, that is, the language which most of us use on most occasions to address our friends while eating dinner, loafing by the fireside, etc. Then he tried to show that such statements are in conflict with the views of *common sense,* i.e., with views which most of us generally hold to be true as we go about our everyday activities, and that such statements as conflict with common sense are false. He attempted to indicate just what these common-sense views are, and, in stating them, of course, employed ordinary language again. For example, a philosopher says: 'Space is unreal'. Moore replies: "If you mean that nothing is ever to the right of, or to the left of, or behind, or above anything else, then you are certainly wrong; for this inkwell is to the left of this pen, and my head is above them both." [15] Now, if common sense is to be equated with ordinary language, then whenever Moore translated a philosopher's statements into ordinary language, he was merely showing that his statements were not statements of ordinary language. But surely he was doing more than this! One ought, at least, to look for some indication that he was doing more. And it is not too hard to find. As Malcolm himself notes, Moore was concerned to show that the philosophers' peculiar statements are *false.* And they are false, not by virtue of being in conflict with ordinary language—that is hardly a criterion of truth and falsity—but by virtue of being in conflict with common sense, that is, with views which "we all know to be true." 'Time is unreal' is *false,* not because it is the sort of thing which we would ordinarily not say; it is false because I have often, for example, put the kettle on the stove, *then* waited for the water to boil, and *after* that made my tea. If statements of the form, 'First I did so and so, and after that I did thus and thus, and still later I . . .' are true, then the statement 'Time is unreal' is false. Such statements as the former are statements of common sense which we know to be true, in Moore's view. Statements which are incompatible with them must, therefore, be false. Hence, (3) is true: one can reasonably appeal to *common sense* in order to show that statements like 'Time is unreal' are false, but one

15. *Ibid.,* p. 346. These are Malcolm's words, not Moore's. But again, they are very similar to utterances which Moore actually made.

cannot plausibly appeal to *ordinary language* in order to show that they are false. One cannot do the latter because there can be many arguments of the form, '*p* is false because it is incompatible with *q, r,* and *s*', where *q, r,* and *s* are all statements of ordinary language, yet one of them (*q* or *r* or *s*), or any two of them, or all three of them, are false! In such cases, where any one or any two or all three are false, one can hardly demonstrate that *p must be* false.

Does the statement that "one can reasonably appeal to common sense in order to show that statements like 'Time is unreal', etc., are false" contradict my statement in Chapter II in which I protested against that very thing? Here I am omitting from consideration the peculiar philosophical sense whereby such statements ('Time is unreal', etc.) might conceivably be true. There is a plain, ordinary sense in which we all admit that they are false. This all that I am concerned to defend at this point, for this is all that Moore's appeal to common sense provides for.

Second, Moore should have held, therefore, that (3) is true. Did he hold it to be true? Of course. He was very explicit in his "Reply":

A man may be using a sentence perfectly correctly, even when what he means by it is false, either because he is lying or because he is making a mistake; and, similarly, a man may be using a sentence in such a way that what he means by it is true, even when he is not using it correctly, as, for instance, when he uses the wrong word for what he means, or by a slip or because he has made a mistake as to what the correct usage is. Thus using a sentence correctly—in the sense explained [that is, 'in accordance with the best English usage,' explained a few lines above]—and using it in such a way that what you mean by it is *true,* are two things which are completely logically independent of one another: either may occur without the other.[16]

Similarly, in the second of his three articles on Wittgenstein's 1930–33 lectures, Moore refers to some views of Wittgenstein which he seems to support. They agree with the passage just quoted. Moore writes:

From the fact that you are using language correctly, in the sense of 'in accordance with an established rule,' it by no means follows that what you assert, by this correct use of language, is 'correct' in the very different sense in which 'that is correct' = 'that is true,' nor from the fact that you are using language incorrectly that what you assert by this incorrect use of language is 'incorrect' in the very different sense in which 'that is incorrect' = 'that is

16. "Reply," p. 548.

false.' It is obvious that you may be using language just as correctly when you use it to assert something false as when you use it to assert something true, and that when you are using it incorrectly, you may just as easily be asserting something true by this incorrect use as something false.[17]

I have fulfilled my first and second tasks. I have shown, first, that Moore ought to have seen that (3) is true. I have shown, second, that Moore did hold (3) to be true. Hence, I have shown that Malcolm's first and third assertions are false.

Third, I now turn to Malcolm's second assertion, namely, the assertion that Moore holds the ordinary language linguistic recommendation principle. My third task was to show that this assertion is false.

In his "Reply" Moore refers to an essay by M. Lazerowitz [18] in which the latter advocates the view that what philosophers have meant by such statements as 'Material objects are unreal', 'Time is not real', etc., is merely a recommendation that "we should not use words in the way we do," and, more specifically, that when Moore replied to philosophers, he was making such recommendations (this is the same charge as Malcolm's). Moore explicitly says that it would be incorrect to say that when he tried to show that time is *not* unreal, "all I was doing was to recommend that we should use certain expressions in a different way from that in which we do. If this is all I was doing, I was certainly making a huge mistake, for I certainly did not think it was all. And I do not think so now." [19]

Of course, Moore's "Reply" was written *after* Malcolm's and Lazerowitz' charge that Moore held the ordinary language linguistic recommendation principle. Hence, it is possible that Moore held it without being aware of it. As he himself has said, philosophers often assume or believe views of which they are not conscious. But neither Malcolm nor Lazerowitz cites any evidence for his charge. Nor can I, after reading all of Moore's published works, find any such evidence. I think that since no contrary evidence is available, it is true to say that Moore was right in stating in his "Reply" that he did not hold the ordinary language linguistic recommendation principle and that, therefore, Malcolm's second assertion is false.

I also mentioned above a fourth, more modest, assertion which is true.

---

17. "Wittgenstein's Lectures in 1930–33," *Mind*, LXIII (1954), 308, reprinted in *PP*, pp. 252–324.
18. "Moore's Paradox," *PGEM*, pp. 371–93.
19. *PGEM*, p. 675.

This is the assertion that Moore holds the ordinary language partial adherence principle, i.e., that Moore appeals to ordinary language as a preliminary to the solving of philosophical problems, that he believed that ordinary language indicates what we believe to be the case and what may be the case, and that Moore maintained the desirability of defending ordinary language where possible, without giving slavish allegiance to it. I am concerned to show that this more modest assertion *is* true, and to that task I now turn. But this involves us in a complete examination of the nature and extent of Moore's appeal to ordinary language.

III

WHAT, THEN, IS THE ROLE of ordinary language in Moore's philosophy? Before I can discuss this, some distinctions are necessary. I believe, for reasons which will be evident, that one must distinguish the following:

1. An expression of a non-technical language;
2. An expression of a technical language;
3. Common usage of (1);
4. Common usage of (2);
5. Proper usage of (1);
6. Proper usage of (2);
7. An ordinary *use* of (1);
8. An ordinary *use* of (2).

By 'expression' I mean a word, phrase, or sentence; by 'non-technical', the vernacular language we use in everyday life. A technical language, on the other hand, is the specialized language of a science or of a philosophical system, etc. 'Common usage' and 'proper usage' refer to the material with which philologists and lexicographers deal. The two differ because what has become common usage may not always be proper, and vice versa. An ordinary use of an expression is a use which is, in fact, generally made. Hence, it is a use which is either in accordance with common usage or in accordance with proper usage. Unless I specify otherwise, I shall mean the former. The opposite of an ordinary use is, thus, a misuse. How does a proper or common usage differ from an ordinary use? Through a study of usage, we learn, e.g., that 'street' rather than *'Strasse'* or 'house' is properly or commonly used in our language to refer to certain "objects" for conveying vehicles, etc. That certain words are used in certain ways and what words are used in what ways are philological and lexicographical questions. On the other hand, Jones's and Smith's *use* of 'street' or 'tree' on various occasions is quite a commonsensical matter and is now, in certain quarters, believed to be a philosophical matter. This is especially held to be so if, instead of 'tree' or 'street', Jones or Smith uses words such as those which worried Wittgenstein in the *Philosophical Investigations*. I believe that ordinary uses are of some relevance to philosophy (and so is usage), but I doubt whether they constitute its entire subject matter.[20]

All of these terminological distinctions are, of course, not Moore's. Occasionally, he uses 'usage' where he means 'use', but it is usually apparent which he means. After making such adjustments, one can, I think, say the following (omitting from consideration, for the time being, [2], [4], [6], and [8]): Moore is *not* concerned with (3) or (5). In *Principia Ethica* he tells us that he is not going to discuss the proper meaning of the word 'Ethics', "for verbal questions are properly left to the writers of dictionaries and other persons interested in literature; philosophy . . . has no concern with them."[21] Again: "My business is not with proper usage, as established by custom." He is not concerned with "how people generally use the word."[22] On the other hand, Moore *is* concerned with (7), and hence with (1), to some extent. The qualification is important. But to what extent? Let us now see precisely what Moore's appeal to ordinary language consists of.

First, Moore makes a *practical* appeal to ordinary language. He wants to be understood, and he fears that if he does not use expressions in their ordinary sense, he won't be understood. In one essay he writes: "I have hitherto used the word 'existence' pretty freely, and I think that when I used it, I used it in its ordinary sense. . . . If I am not using the word in its ordinary sense, then I shall not be understood by anyone."[23] Moore nearly always takes excruciating pains to communicate. The opening pages of almost all of his longer essays and of many of the 1910–11 lec-

---

20. It is not necessary to limit 'an ordinary use' to mean the specific occasion on which a term is uttered or written. If Jones uses 'see' in an ordinary way at 10 A.M., 1 P.M., and 8 P.M., these are all occasions when Jones makes an ordinary use of 'see'. The same goes for Smith. But one might interpret 'use' in such a way that the term—here, 'see'—need not have been uttered or spoken. And one might hold that it need not even have been thought; it might merely be what Jones or Smith would have said, had they used the term in an ordinary way.

21. *PE*, p. 2.

22. *Ibid.*, p. 6.

23. "The Nature and Reality of Objects of Perception," *PAS*, VI (1905–6), reprinted in *PS*, pp. 72, 73.

tures (published as *Some Main Problems of Philosophy*) reveal this concern. One of the aspects of this effort to get across precisely what he means is that in order to be understood he must use ordinary language, i.e., he must make an ordinary use of the expressions of our everyday non-technical language.

But what is an ordinary use of such expressions? (A) An ordinary use of an expression is one which we all constantly make.[24] (B) An ordinary use of an expression is one which is understood by anyone who knows the language in which it occurs.[25] (C) An ordinary use of an expression is one which is in accord with common usage.[26]

Second, Moore appeals to ordinary language for *refutational* purposes, or, at least, as a preliminary to refutation. As we have seen, he delighted in pointing out that philosophers often use lofty or vague generalities which provided most of his philosophical problems. They spoke of "Time with a big *T*," of reality being spiritual. They made assertions like 'All that we know of material objects is the orderly succession of our own sensations', assertions which may seem plausible at first, but which, says Moore, lose their plausibility when we consider them in particular instances. For example, this assertion, when concretely translated, means that we can't know that the train coach in which we are riding is running on wheels or coupled to other coaches.[27] "Mistakes are, I think, very apt to happen if one talks merely in generalities; and moreover one is apt to overlook important points."[28] Hence, Moore appealed to ordinary language as a preliminary to philosophical refutation. As I have pointed out above, appealing to ordinary language or making a linguistic translation is not in itself the refutation of a philosophical assertion. The crucial point, for Moore, is to show that the translations of the philosophers' generalizations conflict with *common sense,* i.e., with beliefs which all of us hold or views which we know to be true. Nevertheless, we must (in most cases) first make the translation to ordinary language; we must make ordinary use of expressions of our common language.

Moore employs a second kind of refutational appeal to ordinary language. He points out that philosophers often use certain terms in a way which is inconsistent with their ordinary use. That is, they commit

24. "The Subject Matter of Psychology," *PAS*, X (1909–10), 41; *PE*, p. 151.
25. *SMPP*, pp. 216–17.
26. "Imaginary Objects," *PASS* XII (1933), 59, reprinted in *PP*, p. 105.
27. *SMPP*, p. 135.
28. *Ibid.*, pp. 29–30.

misuses.[29] Or they introduce technical terms which are inconsistent with their ordinary use or use technical terms of some standing in ways which are inconsistent with their common technical uses.[30] As we shall see, Moore did not object to introducing a technical term as long as it was a new term or a term used in a precisely defined and limited way. But he did object to using an ordinary term, say 'time', in a technical way, since it often led to confusion and obscurity.

Third, Moore appeals to ordinary language[31] in a more positive way. What he says here has, I believe, misled some people. It is important to see just what Moore is and is not saying.

Ordinary language, he maintains, is sometimes indicative of what we *believe* to be true. In the 1910–11 lectures, Moore speaks of recognizing an "enormous class of things" called 'truths'. He admits that he may be wrong.

Possibly there really are no such things at all. Many philosophers don't seem to recognize them. But I think we can't help all of us constantly talking as if there were such things. And for my part, I can't help thinking, in the first place, that there are such things as true beliefs; and, in the second place, whenever I consider a true belief . . . I can't help thinking that there is always in the Universe one of these peculiar things which I call 'truths' corresponding to it.[32]

Very often, then, ordinary language suggests something which we believe to be the case. But, of course, this does not mean that it *is* the case.

Also, ordinary language often indicates something which *may* be true. In "The Subject Matter of Psychology," Moore speaks of an important characteristic of mental acts: namely, that any given mental act is an act *"of the same person* or *of the same mind"* as another mental act. By speaking of *my* mental acts, I indicate an important characteristic, one which distinguishes them from other mental acts (of other people). "The language we use," says Moore,

constantly implies that one respect in which two mental acts may resemble one another is by the fact that one of them is the mental act of one person and the

29. *Ibid.*, Chaps. 7, 11, *passim*.

30. "Are the Characteristics of Particular Things Universal or Particular?", *PASS*, III (1923), 97, reprinted in *PP*, p. 18.

31. It should now be clear that whenever I say 'ordinary language', I mean the ordinary use of expressions of our vernacular, everyday language.

32. *SMPP*, p. 311.

other the mental act of another person; and that one respect in which two mental acts may resemble one another is by the fact that both of them are mental acts of the same person. And that something important is meant by this language seems to me to be quite certain. As to *what* exactly is meant, I confess I cannot be sure.[33]

In this case, ordinary language indicates what may be the case, although by itself it cannot establish that it *is* the case.

Similarly, in the 1910–11 lectures, Moore writes:

Let us call the existence of the world at any one moment a different *fact* from its existence at any other moment, no matter whether *what* exists at the one moment is different from *what* exists at the other, or not. To speak in this way is, you see, quite in accord with our ordinary use of language; for even if absolutely the same thing does exist at both of two different moments, we should yet say that its existence at the one moment was a different fact from its existence at the other.[34]

Moore suggests here that if we use a certain expression in a certain way, we are not merely conforming to customary or proper usage; we also hold that something or other may be or very likely is the case which this usage indicates. Of course, this is no foolproof method. For example, we might have used language in such a way that we would not have called the existence of the world at one moment a different fact from its existence at another. Suppose that we had used language in that way. I am quite sure that Moore would have shown us that in this case our ordinary use of language was incorrect—something which he often did, as we shall see shortly.

I have shown the limited ways in which Moore often appeals to ordinary language: (1) One must employ ordinary language in order to be understood; (2) an appeal to ordinary language is helpful as a preliminary to philosophical refutation; and (3) ordinary language indicates what we *believe* to be the case and what *may* very well be the case. It would be a mistake to think that in (3) Moore becomes an ordinary language proponent, for clearly one can admit (3) without admitting that ordinary language indicates what actually *is* the case. The latter is unreasonable, whereas (3) seems perfectly plausible. I have tried, then, to show

---

33. *PAS*, X (1909–10), 41; cf. "Is Existence a Predicate?", *PASS*, XV (1936), 178–79, reprinted in *PP*, pp. 118–19; "Professor James' 'Pragmatism,' " *PAS*, VIII (1907–8), 33–77, reprinted in *PS* as "William James' 'Pragmatism,' " p. 133.
34. *SMPP*, p. 169.

some of the reasons why it is true to say that Moore appeals to ordinary language yet false to say that he is an ordinary language proponent. But even this is not the whole story.

IV

THE ABOVE CONSIDERATIONS show that, while Moore had a healthy respect for ordinary language, he was not an ordinary language proponent, as Malcolm and others have believed him to be. But even his healthy respect, like our respect for most prescriptions or principles, was tempered by notable exceptions, either by way of *departing* from ordinary use of language, or by *adding* to it, or by *correcting* it.

1. In the 1910–11 lectures, Moore distinguishes several kinds of "mental attitudes": feeling sure, being sure, knowing, believing, being inclined to believe, etc. He suggests that believing is an attitude of mind which is present in knowledge and in many different degrees of awareness from feeling sure to merely imagining, even where the degree of belief is so slight that we would not usually call it believing.

Where a man says 'I am inclined to believe,' and implies therefore that he *doesn't* actually believe, I think he really has towards the thing he says he is inclined to believe, exactly the same attitude of mind *in a very slight degree,* which, if it were a little stronger, he would express by saying that he 'believed.' I am, therefore, going to depart from common usage so far as to call such cases, cases of a very slight degree of belief; and also so far as to say that we *do* believe, though we don't *only* believe, but something else as well, even when we know. But these are, I think, the only departures from common usage in my use of the term.[35]

Here Moore is not correcting the ordinary use of language, but merely departing from it by way of extending it.

2. Sometimes Moore adds to ordinary language by introducing new technical terms. The most notable instance is 'sense-datum'. Since the whole problem of sense-data will be dealt with later, I shall not discuss his introduction of the term at this point.[36] In introducing this term and others, Moore deals with the distinctions numbered (2), (4), (6), and (8),

---

35. *Ibid.*, pp. 274, 299; "The Character of Cognitive Acts," *PAS*, XXI (1920–21), 137–38.

36. See "Is There Knowledge by Acquaintance?", *PASS*, II (1919), 180–81; "Reply," pp. 680–81.

which have been listed above at the beginning of section III, or with combinations of these.

There are also cases where Moore does not himself introduce a new technical term but justifies the use of one, even though it is not in accordance with ordinary uses of ordinary language. One such term is 'mind' in 'in my mind' or in 'in mind'. He recognizes the ordinary use of 'mind' in these phrases which is such that we often say, for example, 'I had you in mind when I bought that'. He then emphasizes that *philosophers* have also spoken of such things as bodily pains and images as being 'in my mind'; that the use of 'mind' when it is said that the bodily pains which I feel are 'in my mind' is not an ordinary one. For

nobody, I think, would say that bodily pains which I feel are 'in my mind' unless he was also prepared to say that it is *with* my mind that I feel bodily pains; and to say this latter is, I think, not quite in accordance with common non-philosophic usage. It is natural enough to say that it is with my mind that I remember, and think, and imagine, and feel *mental* pains—e.g., disappointment, but not, I think quite so natural to say that it is with my mind that I feel *bodily* pains, e.g., a severe headache.[37]

Here is then a well-established philosophical use which differs from ordinary use, and Moore, it turns out, accepts this special philosophical use.

3. Sometimes Moore corrects ordinary use of language. In "The Refutation of Idealism," he states that the existence of a sensation must be distinguished from the existence of the object of a sensation: e.g., the sensing of blue from blue. He notes that most philosophers have not distinguished the two and hence have held propositions like *'Esse est percipi'*. He then points out that ordinary language provides no means of referring to such objects as *blue, sweet*, etc., except by calling them sensations, that "it is an obvious violation of language to call them 'things' or 'objects'. Similarly, ordinary language offers us no means of referring to objects like 'causality' or 'identity' except by calling them ideas or conceptions." He then suggests that, in every sensation or idea, we must distinguish the two elements: the object of sensing from sensing.[38] This is a case not merely of departing from ordinary language, by extending it, for example, or of introducing a new technical word, but of correcting

37. "Prf.," *PP*, p. 141.
38. *PS*, pp. 19–20.

ordinary language so that it corresponds with some fact which we know to be the case.

It is evident then that Moore makes exceptions to the ordinary use of ordinary (non-technical) language, either by merely departing from ordinary use, or by adding to it, or by correcting it. He sometimes departs from the ordinary use of technical language too. And sometimes he indicates that he is going to use a term which is often used in both ordinary and technical language in some special sense. For example, in *Principia Ethica,* he states that he is going to call ethical propositions of his first class (propositions regarding what kinds of things are good in themselves) 'Intuitions', since they are incapable of proof or disproof. "But I beg it may be noticed that I am not an 'Intuitionist' in the ordinary sense of that term." The difference is that "the Intuitionist proper" holds that the propositions of Moore's second class (propositions stating that a certain action is right or a duty) are incapable of proof or disproof. "I . . . am no less anxious to maintain that propositions of *this* kind are *not* 'Intuitions' than that propositions of my *first* class *are* Intuitions." [39] Again, in *Principia Ethica,* he writes: "I shall, where it seems convenient, take the liberty to use the term 'organic' with a special sense. I shall use it to denote the fact that a whole has an intrinsic value different in amount from the sum of the values of its parts. I shall use it to denote this and only this." [40]

Here then are cases which show that, while Moore respected ordinary language, he did not revere it. The latter fact may be seen both in his departing from, adding to, or correcting the ordinary use of ordinary language, and in his departing from the ordinary use of technical language, or specifying a certain sense in which he plans to use a term which is used in both ordinary and technical language.

V

I HAVE TRIED TO SHOW that Moore, while he appeals to ordinary language for certain limited purposes, is by no means an ordinary language proponent. I suggested that, for him, *common sense* takes precedence over ordinary language. It does so because the appeal to common sense can, for

---

39. *PE*, Preface, p. x; see also next paragraph for a further distinction in the use of 'Intuition'.
40. *Ibid.*, pp. 35–36.

example, determine truth or falsity—if one does not raise certain types of epistemological questions—whereas the appeal to ordinary language is merely preliminary to the determination of truth or falsity. In addition to the matter of truth and falsity, there is another area of philosophical concern which greatly interests Moore and which takes precedence over an appeal to ordinary language, and this is *meaning*. In one of his earlier papers, "Necessity," Moore writes:

> My primary object in this paper is to determine the *meaning* of necessity. I do not wish to discover what things are necessary; but what that predicate is which attaches to them when they are so. Nor on the other hand, do I wish to arrive at a correct verbal definition of necessity. That the word is commonly used to signify a great number of different predicates, which do actually attach to things, appears to me quite plain. But this being so, we shall be using the word correctly, whenever we apply it to any of these; and a correct definition of necessity will be attained if we enumerate all those different predicates which attaches to them when they are so. Nor on the other hand, do I wish to correctly defined is common usage. The problem which I wish to solve is different from either of these. It is a problem which resembles them in its universal application. There is a solution of it not only for necessity but for everything that we can think of; and in many cases the discovery of this solution appears to me to be of fundamental importance for philosophy.[41]

Moore then distinguishes three ways in which anyone who says '*A* is necessary' or 'red' or 'round', etc., may be wrong: (1) "He may be using the word 'necessary' in a sense in which it is not commonly used." For example, if he wants to convey the thought that *A* is red, then, whether or not *A* is red, he is "committing a verbal error" in saying '*A* is necessary'. (2) He may be using the word 'necessary' in a way in which it *is* commonly used, but "he may be mistaken in supposing that *A* really has the predicate, which he rightly denotes by that word." (3) He may be using the word correctly and be rightly supposing that *A* has one of the predicates denoted by the word, "and yet he may be wrong in a different way. For while rightly thinking that it [*A*] has one of these predicates he may be mistaken in supposing that it also has some other of them." Confusions of this sort, says Moore, are "a frequent source of fallacy in reasoning." [42] The mistake is not one about the use of a word nor about a factual question. Hence:

41. "Necessity," *Mind,* IX (1900), 289.
42. *Ibid.,* pp. 289–90.

The question which we must answer . . . is quite different from either of these two questions: Is he using the word correctly? or Has the thing in question that predicate? For there may be no doubt at all that we should answer yes or no to either of these questions. . . . My main object is not to discover whether any propositions of the form '*A* is necessary' are true or false, nor yet whether they are clearly expressed; but what their *meaning* is.[43]

Moore here clearly distinguishes three things: (1) correct use, (2) truth (and falsity), and (3) meaning. He tells us that his main concern is with (3). I believe that this emphasis is quite consistent throughout his works. Before I show why, I must answer some objections which disciples of the post–1929 Wittgenstein might like to bring up at this point.

A. "Of course, Moore was primarily interested in *meaning*. But, after all, 'meaning is use'. The meaning of a term is its use in our language." I am well aware that the slogan is Wittgenstein's. We shall see whether it is Moore's. Use is *one* of the meanings of 'meaning' for Moore (as we shall see in Chapter IV), though not the most important one. However, when Moore speaks of meaning *in the above passage,* he does not mean use. After all, he distinguishes (1) correct use from (3) meaning.

B. "But by (1) Moore means *usage*. Hence, this still allows us to suspect that by (3) he means *use*." First, again, whatever he means by (1) he does *not* mean use by (3), as we shall see. Second, he does not mean usage in (1). Or, at least, since his terminology was not always consistent, and since he may have fused the meanings of 'use' and 'usage', (1) certainly does not refer solely to usage, but refers to use as well, and primarily to use. This may be seen by the following. Moore (in the above passage) distinguishes three questions, corresponding to (1), (2), and (3). These are:

1. Is he using the word correctly?
2. Has the thing in question a certain predicate?
3. What is the meaning of the word?

'Is he using the word correctly?' may be paraphrased: 'Is he *using* the word according to correct *usage?*' (that is, is he performing an ordinary use?). Hence, Moore is referring to use in (1). And, again, he makes it clear that he is not now interested in (1) or (2), but in (3).

We have then, according to Moore, three things to consider. In order to keep distinctions clear, it would be better to phrase the questions as:

43. *Ibid.,* p. 290.

1. What is the use of an expression? (And is it used in accordance with correct—or common—usage, etc.?)

3. What is the meaning of an expression?

And, in the case of statements:

2. Is the proposition expressed by the statement true or false?

The answer to the first question is determined by examining what people say. The third question, on the other hand, is a philosophical one. Answering it requires tools of distinction and analysis. The second question may be partly a philosophical matter, or a matter of scientific inquiry, or a matter of plain common sense. Hence, the following statements are known to be true by common sense, scientific examination, and philosophical inquiry, respectively:

Here is a hand, and here is another.

The anatomical structure (or chemical composition) of a human hand is such and such.

'Here is a hand, and here is another' implies that material objects do exist.

A philosopher who holds that (2) and (3) are genuinely philosophical matters (at least, in part), whereas (1) is not (it is at most preliminary); that (2) is a matter of common sense; and that (1), (2), and (3) may be considered separate inquiries can hardly be called an ordinary language proponent. I have tried to show that Moore is not one.

I have cited various passages which make it clear that he ought not to have been an ordinary language proponent and that he was not one. But let us consider just one more, part of which I quoted earlier.

In *Principia Ethica* Moore says that the most fundamental question in ethics is how 'good'—or good—is to be defined.[44] He says that he is not asking for a verbal definition. "Such a definition can never be of ultimate importance in any study except lexicography. If I wanted that kind of definition I should have to consider in the first place how people generally use the word 'good'; but my business is not with its proper usage as established by custom."[45] This takes care of *usage*. He goes on: "I shall ... use the word in the sense in which it is ordinarily used; but at the same time I am not anxious to discuss whether I am right in thinking that

44. Moore often asks the question in two forms: How is 'good' defined? and How is *good* defined?

45. *PE*, p. 6.

it is so used." [46] That takes care of *use*. In short, verbal matters are not a philosophical issue. "When A says 'Good means pleasant' and B says 'Good means desired', they may merely wish to assert that most people have used the word for what is pleasant and for what is desired respectively. . . . This is quite an interesting discussion; only it is not . . . an ethical discussion." [47] We want something else from philosophy. "What we want to learn . . . from ethical teachers, is not how people use a word; it is not even, what kind of actions they approve, which the use of the word 'good' may certainly imply; what we want to know is simply what *is* good." [48]

So much for the ordinary language controversy. The quotation from Moore which appears near the beginning of this section has brought a new topic into discussion. Moore says that his main object is to determine the *meaning* of necessity. What does Moore mean by 'meaning'? This is a whole problem in itself, and an enormously complicated one. The topic is one which relates to philosophical method, and to Moore's discussion of analysis as well, and I shall turn to it now.

46. *Ibid.*
47. *Ibid.*, pp. 11–12.
48. *Ibid.*, p. 12.

IV

The Meanings of
'Meaning'

I N HIS "REPLY" during the discussion of the various ways of "expressing an analysis" Moore points out an "important thing to notice"
about them: namely, that they all avoid the use of the word, 'means'. He
then adds: "It is, in my view, very important to avoid the use of this
word . . ."[1] Would that he had—not only in his discussion of analysis,
but elsewhere. He admits that he has often given "false impressions" by
using it; to which one might add that he has provided an extremely difficult task for his interpreters, that of distinguishing his various kinds of
meaning.

One faces a problem in writing about meaning, and it should be
acknowledged right from the start. I am about to discuss the various
meanings of 'meaning' which are found in Moore's works. But what
about this first term in that phrase—the word 'meaning' which occurs
directly before the word 'of' in the expression 'the meaning of

1. *PGEM*, p. 664.

"meaning"'? Obviously, this is a meta-use of 'meaning' or rather, since discussion of meanings is already at the meta-level, a meta-meta-use. What does it mean? Someone might suggest that, if one attempted to answer the question, he could then go on to ask what, in turn, *it* means. This looks like an infinite regress, a difficulty which can be avoided, I think, by the notion of explication. I am about to give an explication of the various uses of 'meaning' in Moore. There is no greater difficulty in giving an explication of 'meaning' than in giving one of any other term. Just as we might be concerned to explicate 'causality', 'universal', 'induction', so we are now concerned with an explication of 'meaning' as it occurs in Moore's works.

I

IN CHAPTER II, I listed some of Moore's truisms, every one of which, he says, "I know with certainty to be true." These, one may remember, are commonsensical statements like: 'There exists at present a living human body which is my body', 'The earth has existed for many years past', etc. Any proposition of this sort, Moore said, is an unambiguous expression, the meaning of which we all understand. Anyone who denies this is confusing the question as to whether we understand the meaning of such an expression with the different question "whether we *know what it means,* in the sense that we are able to *give a correct analysis* of its meaning." [2] Here, then, Moore clearly refers to two different kinds of meaning: one an ordinary, commonsensical sort of meaning, the other a technical one which involves analysis. We can, and often do, know the meaning of an expression in the first sense, even though we do not know the meaning in the second sense.

One might be led to believe that a consideration of Moore on meaning would merely involve discussion and elaboration of these two meanings of 'meaning'. This would be an erroneous opinion. There is a lot of ground to cover between ordinary meaning and analysis. A close scrutiny of Moore's works reveals at least *seven* meanings of 'meaning'. Two of these are seldom employed and rarely mentioned. The other five are constantly employed; one or more of them are always presupposed; and most of them are, at some time or other, specifically mentioned and discussed.

2. "Def.," *PP*, p. 37.

The latter group of five meanings will be discussed in some detail. But first it is well to deal briefly with the two kinds of meaning which receive less emphasis in Moore's works.

1. The first of these is that in which 'meaning' is synonymous with, or very similar to, 'importance', 'significance', 'value', etc. We often speak of some thing or state of affairs or condition as either having or lacking meaning, in the sense of significance. "To have meaning or significance is commonly used in the sense of 'to have importance'; and this again means 'to have value either as a means or as an end'." [3] This passage is the only one which I have found where Moore mentions this meaning of 'meaning', although, when translated to mean 'having value either as a means or as an end', Moore makes use of it throughout *Principia Ethica* and *Ethics*.

2. The second kind of meaning which is seldom discussed by Moore and which plays a minor role in his writings is *emotive meaning*. The only passage where Moore directly discusses emotive meaning is in his "Reply," in answer to C. L. Stevenson's charge that Moore had "an exaggerated emphasis on the purely cognitive aspects of ethical language." [4] Moore spends several pages in elaborating what the cognitive-emotive distinction might plausibly be taken to mean. He suggests that we might say that a sentence has cognitive meaning "if and only if it is both true that it can be used to make an assertion, and also that anyone who was so using it would be asserting something which might be true or false." [5] Emotive meaning, on the other hand, is such that if a man said, for example, that it was right of Brutus to stab Caesar, "(1) the man *would* be asserting that he, at the time of speaking, approved of this action of Brutus' and (2) would *not* be asserting anything, which might conceivably be true or false, *except* this or, possibly also, things entailed by it, as, for instance, that Brutus did stab Caesar." [6] Moore accepts the cognitive meaning criterion and suggests that he always accepted it, but he denies that, in his ethical writings, he ever employed a uniquely emotive meaning criterion. He says that it would be paradoxical to hold that, when a man asserts that Brutus' action was right, he is asserting nothing whatever that could be true or false, that his words have no cognitive meaning,

3. *PE*, p. 35.
4. *PGEM*, p. 82.
5. "Reply," p. 539.
6. *Ibid.*, p. 540.

except, perhaps, the assertion that Brutus did stab Caesar.[7] Nevertheless, paradoxical as it is, Moore says that he is *now* partly inclined to think that the view may be true.

I have some inclination to think that in *any* 'typically ethical' sense in which a man might assert that Brutus' action was right, he would be asserting nothing whatever which could conceivably be true or false, except, perhaps, that Brutus' action occurred—no more than, if he said, 'Please, shut the door.' I certainly have *some* inclination to think all this. . . . But I also still have *some* inclination to think that my former view is true. And, if you ask me to which of these incompatible views I have the stronger inclination, I can only answer that I simply do not know.[8]

(There is perhaps a third sense of 'meaning' which is sometimes used by Moore but which has no philosophical importance *in his use of it.* According to this use, 'mean' means 'intend', as in 'I intend, next, to do so and so'. Though it has superficial similarities, this is not the philosophical use of 'intend'.)

II

I SHALL TURN NOW to the five kinds of meaning which are given more attention by Moore, either because he merely mentions them oftener or because he employs or presupposes them throughout his works. This group is divided into two sub-groups, but it is almost impossible to know which of the five fall under which of the two sub-groups! It is easy to see that there must be two groups, but it is not so easy to know exactly how the classification should be made. The two major categories are: (A) common or ordinary, and (B) special or technical, meanings of 'meaning'. Of the five types which I shall discuss, it is pretty certain that the first belongs under (A). It is also clear that the last belongs under (B). Where the other three properly belong is the problem. The difficulty is even heightened because, of *these* three, the third is so distinct from the others that it seems as if my twofold classification were not adequate. Well, perhaps the categorizing is not the important thing. Let us turn to a

7. *Ibid.*, pp. 541–42.
8. *Ibid.*, p. 545.

consideration of the five kinds of meaning or, if you will, the five meanings of 'meaning'.

1. *The sense of an expression in ordinary parlance* [9]

In ordinary language we often use a sentence of the form (a) 'Do you know what *p* means?' in such a way that (b) 'Do you understand *p*?', or even (c) 'Do you get the sense of *p*?', would be acceptable substitutions. For example, I certainly do know what Jones means when he says 'The distance between my two stereo speakers is nine feet'. I not only "get the sense" of his statement; I understand it perfectly well. I might even have an image "in my mind" of laying out a yardstick to measure the distance when I say that I understand the sentence. Similarly, I understand what Jones means when he says 'The distance between the earth and the sun (at *t*) is 93,000,000 miles'. I *understand* it, even though my mental imagery is not nearly so vivid. Finally, when Jones talks about gene-mutations, or the displacement of electrons during bombardment, I somehow at least get the sense of what his statements mean, although I may not be willing to say that I understand them in quite the same way I did his former statements. There are occasions, then, when we might find one of the three expressions to be more adequate, but there are others when the three turn out to be nearly synonymous.

This seems to be the meaning of 'meaning' which Moore had in mind when he said that we certainly do understand the meaning of such propositions as 'The earth has existed for many years past' (although we may not know precisely *what* it means). The same point is made in the 1910–11 lectures when he says that we can all understand what is meant by the statement 'No such person as Waverley, the hero of Scott's novel, ever did *really exist*—Waverley was not a *real* person'. We can understand this assertion (and know that it is true) even though we cannot give an account of what we mean by some of the expressions within it, the expressions 'really exist' and 'real'. Although we may not know exactly what these expressions mean, we can easily understand the meanings of the sentences in which they occur and know them to be true or false. "We may, therefore, know quite well, in one sense, what a word means, while at the same time, in another sense, we may not know what it means. We

9. By 'expression' I mean: word, phrase, or sentence. Usually, when referring to the latter, I specifically use 'sentence', or, when appropriate, 'statement', i.e., a sentence which asserts something to be the case.

may be quite familiar with the notion it conveys, and understand sentences in which it occurs, although at the same time we are quite unable to define it." [10] Moore further illustrates this situation by means of the words 'life' and 'alive'. We all know what is meant by saying that some men are alive and others dead. We know it sufficiently well to be able to say in many cases '*A* is alive', '*B* is dead', etc. Yet if we try to define 'life' and give some account of the differences between life and death, which apply to all cases, we find it extremely difficult. "Well, in the same way, it seems to me that we do usually understand quite well the meanings of these much more fundamental expressions 'real,' 'exists' . . . even though we do not know their meaning in the sense of being able to define them." [11]

2. *The use of an expression*

A second meaning of 'meaning' is very similar to the first, in some respects. Often, we are not only able to *understand* an expression of which we do not know its meaning in the sense of being able to give an analysis or definition of it; but we are also able to *use* the expression intelligently or in accord with common usage. We generally hold that someone knows the meaning of various expressions (including sentences) if he is able to use them in ways in which they are ordinarily used. If I consistently use 'pentagon' when speaking of five-sided figures, then my hearers know that I know what 'pentagon' means. This is the meaning of 'meaning' "in the sense in which a Polynesian who knew no English might want to discover it," [12] but the meaning which those of us who know English do not need to discover, because we already know it and use it in accordance with common usage. In a lecture note of 1933 Moore is reported to have said: "Philosophy only analyses words of which we already know the meaning, in the sense that we can use the word right, although we could not perhaps *say* what it means." [13]

In this second sense, to know the meaning of an expression is to be able to use it in the way it is generally used, or according to correct usage; to be able to use it when it is appropriate and refrain from using it at other times. Here the meaning of a term is its use. [14]

10. *SMPP*, p. 205.
11. *Ibid.*, p. 206.
12. *Ibid.*, p. 217.
13. "Justif.," p. 28.
14. See also *PE*, p. 6; "Def.," p. 36; "Reply," p. 548. The inclusion of *use* as one of the meanings of 'meaning' may seem inconsistent with Moore's views as expressed in the last

3. *The verbal definition of an expression*

On many occasions Moore confuses or equates the use of an expression
with its verbal definition. Nevertheless, I believe that he wishes to distinguish the two and for an obvious reason. We can often use an expression
without being able to give its verbal definition. Indeed, in some cases, a
verbal definition is impossible. Hence, we speak of primitive or undefined
terms which, for Moore, include 'yellow' and 'good', for example. We
certainly can use these terms, and even use them in accordance with
common or correct usage, even though we can give no verbal definitions
of them. With respect to other terms, however, we can provide verbal
definitions, and this yields another meaning of 'meaning'.

Moore barely mentions this kind of meaning in a few passages.[15] That
he did not emphasize it is due, I believe, to the fact that verbal definition
is, or seems to be, the linguistic counterpart of one form of analysis:
namely, definitional analysis, which for Moore is not linguistic, since the
objects of analysis in this case are objects, notions, concepts, etc., and not
verbal expressions. Furthermore, Moore held pure verbal definitions to be
a philological and lexicographal matter and not one which is of central
concern to philosophy.

4. *The referent of an expression*

The fourth meaning of 'meaning' which is found in Moore's works
requires a more lengthy discussion. Here, the meaning of an expression is
its referent. But the referent may be (and is, in Moore's writings) of two
kinds: (a) the *object* to which the expression refers, or (b) the *concept*
which it expresses. I shall call the two resulting theories the *object theory*
and the *concept theory* of meaning. Sometimes, when making remarks
that apply to both, I shall simply speak of the *reference theory*. Moore is
not always consistent in his use of 'object' as against 'concept'. Sometimes
he speaks of the concept as being an object too. But when he specifically
employs the object theory, the object in this sense is different from the
sense in which a concept is held to be an object. I shall separate the two
theories, to the extent that it is possible. There are passages, however, in
which Moore uses 'object' and 'concept' indiscriminately and seems to

---

section of Chap. III; however, when Moore distinguished meaning from use, he was referring
to only one kind of meaning, i.e., the concept theory, and in that sense, use and meaning are
distinct.

15. "Necessity," *Mind,* IX (1900), 289; *PE,* p. 6.

hold that they are alternative expressions. Here, again, one wishes that Moore had been clearer and more consistent in his use of terms.

a. *The object theory*

This is the theory that the meaning of an expression is the object which the expression refers to, stands for, signifies, or designates. Take the sentences:

> This is a chair.
> That is green.

'Chair' refers to an object which can be ostensibly "defined." 'Object' *here* is used in a commonsensical, ordinary way. It is not quite as ordinary a way of speaking to call the referent of 'green' an object. It is, perhaps, a bit more natural to speak of it as a property or quality. Nevertheless, an instance of it can be pointed to; one can become acquainted with it. We can, as it were, "tie up" 'green' with a "thing" (quality) in the world, and thereafter use the word to refer to many similar things. 'This' and 'that', in the above two sentences, are somewhat more difficult to tie to objects. There is a sense in which, if 'chair' refers to a physical object of a certain shape, etc., to which I am (say) pointing, and if 'green' designates a quality of a momentary patch with vague boundaries, then there is nothing over and above *chair* and *green* (the objects, not the words). Nor is the situation really helped if we use 'John' and 'Paul' in place of 'this' and 'that'. In certain cases the idea of there being two kinds of entities, one which particular terms ('this', 'John') refer to, and one which quality terms (in the wide sense—'chair' and 'green') refer to, *seems* more plausible. Suppose, for example, that I sense a phenomenal datum which is red and square. I want to describe it, so I call it *a* and say '*a* is red and square'. At first it certainly seems proper to say that '*a*' refers to this particular object and 'red' and 'square' to two of its obvious properties. However, I think that the following is a quite plausible objection: "I can see that, in this case, 'red' and 'square' refer to objects—in this wide sense—but I fail to see, once you have labeled all the qualities (and relations, where there are such), what there is left for '*a*' to refer to." And I must confess that experientially, I cannot find any object for '*a*' to uniquely refer to. Whether this entails that what at first *seems* to be the case *is not* the case I shall not attempt to say just now, as I am merely trying to describe the object theory of meaning in the form in which it has commonly been held.

The object theory of meaning has sometimes been called the *naming* theory, since some have thought of (general) words as naming their bearers, after the fashion of proper names. With the latter qualification, "naming theory" has seemed, to some, to be a misnomer, since, due to the fact that there are many instances, 'red' does not name in the same sense in which '*a*' or 'John' or 'Winston Churchill' does or might. However, the object theorist would, I think, retort that the naming relationship is essentially the same but the kinds of objects named are different. A particular term names a unique, unrepeatable individual, whereas a predicate term names a repeatable character (either a quality or a relation).

An objection has often been raised against the object theory of meaning: Not *all* words name or designate. Of course, they don't. Object theorists knew this all along. They were aware of the fact that logical words, the copula, etc., do not refer.[16] These words were given meaning in some other way. Some thought that the logical connectives, for example ('and', 'or', etc.), are defined by such devices as truth tables; others held that their meaning in use is indicated or explicated by truth tables.

Moore seems to have held the object theory of meaning at various times. In *Principia Ethica* he briefly mentions the object theory and then says that he is not concerned with the mere use of 'good'; rather: "My business is solely with that object or idea which, I hold, rightly or wrongly, that the word is generally used to stand for."[17] But, since Moore here says "object or idea," it is not clear that he is using 'object' in the stricter sense. In later pages he sometimes does so. For example, several paragraphs after the passage last referred to, he states that what we mean by a horse is "that a certain object, which we all of us know, is composed in a certain manner: that it has four legs, a head, a heart, a liver, etc., etc., all of them arranged in definite relations to one another."[18] Furthermore, he often says things like " 'Good' denotes some property."[19] On the whole, Moore is not concerned to defend the object theory, although he often employs it. Most of his discussions are of the concept theory or are such that the object theory and concept theory are intermingled.

16. L. Wittgenstein, *Tractatus Logico-Philosophicus,* trans. D. F. Pears and B. F. Mc-Guinness (London: Routledge & Kegan Paul, 1961), 4.0312; cf. Bertrand Russell, "The Philosophy of Logical Atomism," *Logic and Knowledge,* ed. R. Marsh (New York: Macmillan, 1956).

17. *PE,* p. 6.
18. *Ibid.,* p. 8.
19. *Ibid.,* p. 2.

There are reasons other than those mentioned why some have held the object theory to be inadequate. Take the two sentences:

> Rover is a dog.
> Oswald is a centaur.

In the first, there is no problem about the referent of 'dog'. But what about the referent of 'centaur'? 'Dog' names something, namely, this hunk of protoplasm, etc., which I call 'Rover'. Or, at least, Rover is an instance of dog. But what about 'centaur'? Even though I tell you all about what Oswald is like, it seems peculiar to say that 'centaur' refers, because there are no centaurs. Some have thought that it names a mental entity, that a centaur is "something in my mind." Now if I am thinking about a centaur, then my act of thinking may truly be said to be mental or in my mind. But, clearly, in this sense, a centaur isn't mental, because it is what my mental act is *about,* and my act of awareness is different from its object: whereas the former is mental, the latter is not. Others have thought that 'centaur' names an image which I have before my mind. But a centaur cannot be an image because a centaur is *what* I imagine. Hence, a centaur is different from the image of a centaur. Furthermore, we all certainly do agree that there are *no* centaurs, but there very definitely *are* images of centaurs.[20]

Because of problems of this sort—more often the controversy has been over Pegasus—many philosophers have adopted one of four alternatives. The first preserves the object theory but widens its scope. The others preserve it in part or reject it. (i) According to the first view, we can keep the object theory because 'object' is more inclusive than 'existent'. Only *some* objects exist, e.g., Rover. Others, e.g., Pegasus, do not exist but they nevertheless are real or have being. (ii) The second alternative preserves the object theory for most (non-logical) terms but adds the theory of descriptions to take care of sentences involving Pegasus (as well as other cases where the object does exist). Instead of saying 'Pegasus is white', we say 'There is an x, such that x is a winged horse, unique, and white'. (iii) The third alternative holds that the referents of many expressions are concepts or notions or objects of thought, instead of objects in the strict sense (chairs and tables). The proponent of this view maintains that, although 'Pegasus' does not name an object (strict sense), it certainly does

20. *SMPP*, pp. 226–28, 264–65, 290.

name an object of thought, because I *am* now thinking of Pegasus, and I can tell you many things about him. (iv) The fourth alternative suggests that we stop looking for objects for words to refer to and talk about the *use* of expressions.

When Moore was dissatisfied with the object theory, he occasionally approved of (ii) in a modified form;[21] he sometimes moved to (iv);[22] he sometimes adopted (i);[23] he more often adopted (iii); and this leads to a second form of the reference theory of meaning.

b. *The concept theory*

The second version of the reference theory might be called the concept theory of meaning. This is the view that the meaning of an expression is the concept (notion, etc.) which the expression stands for, refers to, or designates; in the case of statements, the meaning is the proposition which the sentence expresses. The passage in *Principia Ethica,* to which I have already referred, makes use of the concept theory.[24] Moore said that the meaning of 'good' is the object or idea which the word stands for. 'Idea', 'notion', 'concept', 'object of thought' are often used as synonyms through-out Moore's works.

In the 1910–11 lectures Moore discusses some questions regarding the word 'real'. He asks us to "call up before your minds the notion or idea which is suggested by the word."[25] "I am solely concerned with the object or property or idea, which is what is called up to your mind by the word 'real,' if you understand the English language: it is solely some questions about this object or property or notion or idea that I wish to investigate."[26] He discusses certain objections to calling this object an object or property and then goes on: "What, then, are we to call it? . . . One very natural way of naming it is to call it the meaning of the word 'real'—'meaning' in the sense of *what is meant;* for in fact the thing I want to talk about *is* the object or property or notion or idea which is conveyed or meant by the word real and is in that sense, its meaning."[27]

21. "Russell's 'Theory of Descriptions,'" *The Philosophy of Bertrand Russell*, ed. P. A. Schilpp (Evanston: Northwestern Univ. Press), 1944, pp. 175–225, reprinted in PP, pp. 151–95.
22. See above, p. 56.
23. SMPP, Chap. XVI.
24. PE, pp. 6–8.
25. SMPP, p. 217.
26. *Ibid.*
27. *Ibid.*, p. 218.

The concept theory appears and is elaborated in one of Moore's earliest papers, "The Nature of Judgment." [28] He here equates 'meaning', 'universal meaning' (Bradley), and 'concept'. "A concept" he writes, "is neither a mental fact nor any part of a mental fact." [29] It is the *object* of our thinking, of a mental act, but it exists independently of our thinking. If it did not exist independently of our awareness, there would be nothing for us to think about. Hence, like a Platonic Form, a concept is immutable and eternal.[30] For example, when

I say 'This rose is red,' I am not attributing part of the content of my idea to the rose, nor yet attributing parts of the content of my ideas of rose and red together to some third subject. What I am asserting is a specific connexion of certain concepts, forming the total concept 'rose' with the concepts 'this' and 'now' and 'red'; and the judgment is true if such a connexion is existent. Similarly when I say 'The chimera has three heads,' the chimera is not an idea in my mind, nor any part of such an idea. What I mean to assert is nothing about my mental states, but a specific connexion of concepts. If the judgment is false, that is not because my *ideas* do not correspond to reality, but because such a conjunction of concepts is not to be found among existents.[31]

In this view, then, to know the meaning of an expression is to be familiar with the notion it conveys.[32] It is to apprehend concepts as the objects of knowledge.[33]

5. *Analysis*

I have discussed four of Moore's five main meanings of 'meaning', according to which the meaning of an expression is its sense, its use, its verbal definition, and its referent (object or concept). In Moore's fifth view, meaning is analysis. I cannot preserve the symmetry and say that the meaning of an expression is its analysis, because it is not only (or mainly) expressions which are analyzed. In fact, in his "Reply," Moore states that he seldom thought of the objects of analysis as being expressions. More often they were things or concepts.[34]

Moore frequently held that one of the meanings of 'meaning' is analysis.

28. "The Nature of Judgment," *Mind*, VIII (1899), 176–93.
29. *Ibid.*, p. 179.
30. *Ibid.*, pp. 180, 192.
31. *Ibid.*, p. 179.
32. *SMPP*, p. 205.
33. "The Nature of Judgment," p. 182.
34. "Reply," p. 661.

In the case of *words,* he writes: "For by knowing what they mean is often meant not merely understanding sentences in which they occur, but being able to analyse them." [35] And a few lines later, with respect to concepts or notions, he writes: "We may be quite familiar with a notion itself . . . even though we cannot analyse it." [36] Hence, we may know the meaning in one sense, but not in another sense; we may not be able to give an analysis. Here, to know what X means is to analyze X, or to give a correct analysis of its meaning.

But what Moore means by analysis is a very difficult and complicated subject in itself. Hence, it deserves a special chapter.

35. SMPP, p. 205.
36. *Ibid.*

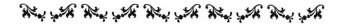

V

Analysis

I HAVE FREQUENTLY REFERRED to passages in which Moore stresses that he is not at all in doubt as to the meaning of various assertions—'meaning' in this sense refers to an ordinary understanding of the assertions. Nor is he in doubt as to the truth of many such statements. But what he *is* in doubt about is their correct *analysis* ('meaning' in another sense). For example, in the latter part of "A Defence of Common Sense," Moore says:

I am not at all sceptical as to the *truth* of such propositions as 'The earth has existed for many years past,' 'Many human bodies have each lived for many years upon it,' i.e., propositions which assert the existence of material things: on the contrary, I hold that we all know, with certainty, many such propositions to be true. But I am very sceptical as to what, in certain respects, the correct analysis of such propositions is.[1]

And later he states that the proposition 'There are and have been many

1. "Def.," *PP*, p. 53.

Selves' is "quite certainly true," but, again, all the analyses which have been suggested of such a proposition are highly doubtful.[2] With respect to such propositions (as well as to all his truisms, some of which I listed in Chapter II) Moore holds that it would be the height of absurdity to wonder whether they are true. Nevertheless, it would be quite proper to be puzzled as to what is their correct analysis, since this is a much more complicated matter. Indeed, "no philosopher, hitherto, has succeeded in suggesting an analysis of them, as regards certain important points, which comes anywhere near to being certainly true."[3]

Similarly, in his "Proof of an External World," Moore considers Kant's view that if someone doubts the existence of "things outside us," we are not able to counter his doubts by a satisfactory proof. Moore probes the meaning of "things outside us" and affirms that there are many things which, if they existed, would be things of that kind: e.g., dogs, planets, hands, etc. Then he offers a "proof" that such things do exist outside us. "Here is one hand," he says, "and here is another." Therefore, at least two things outside us exist; and many similar proofs are possible. The premisses quite certainly are true, Moore says, and the conclusion quite certainly follows from them. Hence, the proof is "perfectly conclusive." Again, however, he admits that the analysis (of premisses and conclusion) is quite problematic and doubtful. One might very well be perplexed as to how such propositions are to be analyzed. The absurd thing would be to wonder if the propositions are true.[4]

According to Moore, then, knowing the *truth* of a proposition is one thing, and being able to give an *analysis* of it is another; one may very well know its truth without being able to provide its analysis. Similarly, as has already been pointed out, *understanding* a proposition, in the ordinary sense, and *knowing what it means,* in the sense of being able to give a correct analysis of its meaning, are two different things; and, again, one may be able to understand a proposition without being able to give an analysis of its meaning. In other words, anyone who knows English will be able to understand 'This is a table', yet he may not be able (without a certain training or intellectual ability) to *say* precisely what it means. The meaning of the proposition is not in doubt (in the sense that it is easily

2. *Ibid.*, p. 59.
3. *Ibid.*, p. 53.
4. "Prf." *PP*, pp. 146–50. It should be pointed out that what Moore *calls* the proof is only part of the actual proof, which concerns the entire essay. See Chap. IX.

understood), but the analysis of its meaning may be very doubtful and extremely problematic.

I shall turn now to a detailed consideration of what Moore means by analysis. Again, this is a highly complex matter. Just as there were many kinds of meaning (or, if you will, uses of 'meaning'), so are several forms of analysis distinguishable in Moore's writings. He does not, himself, seem to always be aware that he has used 'analysis' in many ways. Even his remarks in the reply to his critics indicate that he was not always clear as to what he has meant by analysis.

That he was frequently concerned with analysis (among other things), however, is certain. Even in his earliest writings we see this concern manifested. Many passages of *Principia Ethica,* for example, exhibit it. In that work he points out the ambiguity in saying 'Such and such is good'. 'Good' may mean 'good as means' or 'good as end'.

It is plain that these are very different assertions to make about a thing; it is plain that either or both of them may be made, both truly and falsely, about all manner of things; and it is certain that unless we are clear as to which of the two we mean to assert, we shall have a very poor chance of deciding rightly whether our assertion is true or false. It is precisely this clearness as to the meaning of the question asked which has hitherto been almost lacking in ethical speculation.[5]

A few lines later he writes: "Ethical questions are commonly asked in an ambiguous form. It is asked 'What is a man's duty under these circumstances?' or 'Is it right to act this way?' or 'What ought we to aim at securing?' But all these questions are capable of further analysis."[6]

In considering Moore's views on analysis, I shall devote attention to the following questions:

A. What is analyzed in an analysis?
B. What kinds of analysis are there?
C. What are the criteria of a good analysis?

II

I SHALL, IN THIS SECTION, merely state summarily what the objects of analysis are, for Moore. The discussion in the next section will indicate which *kinds* of analysanda are correlated with which kinds of analysis.

5. *PE,* p. 24.
6. *Ibid.*

What, then, is analyzed in an analysis? What is the analysandum? There seem to be three main kinds of analysanda for Moore. These are:

1. expressions (words, groups of words, sentences);
2. objects or entities;
3. concepts and propositions.

1. In his "Reply" Moore says that he never intended to use the word 'analysis' in "such a way that the analysandum would be a verbal expression."[7] What he intended and what he did often seem to be different, for as we shall see, some forms of analysis *do* employ expressions as the objects to be analyzed. It is only when we consider certain forms of analysis that the object definitely is not an expression. And in spite of his protest, there are many explicit passages in which he clearly holds verbal expressions to be the objects of analysis. In *Some Main Problems of Philosophy,* after saying that we can understand the meaning of sentences which employ certain words ('real', etc.) and can be certain that some of these sentences are true and others false, Moore goes on to say: "We can do both these things, without, in a sense, knowing exactly what these words mean. For by knowing what they mean is often meant not merely understanding sentences in which they occur, but being able to analyze them."[8] And in the 1953 Preface to the book, he continues to speak of expressions which "can be correctly analyzed in a certain way."[9] Again, in "The Justification of Analysis," we are told that philosophy "analyses words."[10] But one need not stay with explicit references of this sort. An examination of Moore's actual practice shows that he often holds expressions of all sorts to be the analysanda (as we shall see, in more detail, in the next section).

2. Sometimes entities or objects are the analysanda. Occasionally Moore merely refers in a general way to entities as the objects of analysis.[11] Sometimes he specifies the sorts of entities. *Principia Ethica* suggests that physical objects are among the entities which are analyzed.[12] Other passages indicate that mental entities are being analyzed: for example, "the occurrence which I mean here to analyse is merely the *mental* occurrence

7. *PGEM*, p. 661.
8. *SMPP*, p. 205.
9. *Ibid.*, p. xii.
10. "Justif.," p. 28.
11. "Facts and Propositions," *PASS*, VII (1927), 171, reprinted in *PP*, p. 61.
12. *PE*, pp. 7–8.

—the act of consciousness—which we call seeing." [13] But, in other places, he speaks of the analysis of facts,[14] properties,[15] and relations.[16]

3. There are numerous passages which state that the objects of analysis are concepts or notions and propositions (what sentences express). Both of these are also called 'meanings'. In one passage, immediately after speaking of the analysis of sentences, Moore speaks of analyzing notions.[17] In *Principia Ethica* he says that he is concerned with the analysis of the *idea* which the word 'good' generally stands for.[18] Other passages state that the concept is the analysandum.[19] And others indicate that propositions are the objects of analysis.[20]

I believe that this is sufficient for a preliminary discussion. I shall turn now to a consideration of the main kinds of analysis employed by Moore. This will require a rather lengthy exposition.

III

SINCE SOME FORMS OF ANALYSIS are divided into sub-species, it will be desirable to list them all first and then discuss them in detail, in the same order. The kinds of analysis which I have distinguished in Moore's writings are:

    1. Refutational analysis:
        (a) Showing contradictions;
        (b) Translation into the concrete;
    2. Distinctional analysis;
    3. Decompositional analysis:
        (a) Definitional;
        (b) Divisional;
    4. Reductional analysis.

'Translation into the concrete' is Moore's phrase. The rest are not, but

13. *SMPP*, p. 29; cf. pp. 307, 309.
14. *Ibid.*, p. 265.
15. *Ibid.*, p. 309.
16. *Ibid.*, p. 276.
17. *Ibid.*, pp. 205, 206.
18. *PE*, p. 6.
19. "Reply," p. 661.
20. "Are the Characteristics of Particular Things Universal or Particular?", *PASS*, III (1923), 102, reprinted in *PP*, p. 17; see also "Reply," p. 661.

they have been chosen in order to suggest the peculiarity of each kind of analysis.

1. *Refutational analysis*

Two forms of refutational analysis were employed by Moore, one of which consists of pointing out contradictions, primarily in the writings of other philosophers, the other of which has as its essential feature the process of "translating into the concrete" in order to show that a proposition is incompatible with something we know to be true. Both of these forms, as the name I have chosen indicates, were employed by Moore for the purpose of analyzing the assertions made by philosophers and showing these views to be wrong or self-contradictory. The first of the refutational forms of analysis points out obvious, or, more likely, hidden, contradictions in those views. The form of the argument sometimes is:

View A asserts p (plus something else); view A asserts *not-p* (plus something else); therefore, view A is self-contradictory.

Or the form may be:

p implies q, and p implies *not-q;* therefore, p implies $q . not-q$.

But there is no one unique form here. The second refutational form of analysis shows *in a special way* that assertions of some philosophers imply statements which are incompatible with those assertions. The form of the argument here is:

P is concretely translated by p; if p is true, then q and r and . . . are false; but q and r and . . . *are true;* therefore, p is false; and, hence, P is false.

(a) *Showing contradictions*

Moore is a master at laying bare the contradictions which occur in or are implied by the theories and assertions of other philosophers. In "A Defence of Common Sense," Moore shows that a view which is in opposition to his regarding the *certain* knowledge of the truisms which he there stated is self-contradictory. According to this view, put forth by some philosophers, none of us knows for certain any propositions which assert either the existence of material objects or the existence of other selves. As I already mentioned, Moore points to the fact that any philosopher who holds this view always makes assertions about *us*. Hence, when he says 'No human being has ever *known* of the existence of other human beings', he is saying: 'There have been many other human beings beside myself, and none of them (including myself) has ever known of the existence of other human beings'. Hence, the philosopher claims to know the very thing which he also claims cannot be known.[21]

Again, in *Principia Ethica,* Moore points to the contradiction which lies in the philosophical theory that 'Each man's happiness is the sole good' by showing that this theory equates the concept 'the good' with the concept 'each man's happiness' and that this "leads to the consequence that something which is only one thing is also a plurality of things, or 'that several things are *each* of them the *only* thing desirable.' "[22]

(b) *Translation into the concrete*

Moore refers to a special form of refutational analysis as "translation into the concrete." It is similar to (a) but is distinctive enough to merit discussion by itself. The technique here is to "translate" a philosophical assertion into some concrete substitute, a clear statement or conjunction of statements. If the translation yields a statement which implies other statements which are inconsistent with the truisms of common sense, which we "know to be true," then the original philosophical assertion may be rejected as false. Let us see how Moore used this technique.

In "The Conception of Reality" Moore tries, at great length, to discover what Bradley meant by the assertion 'Time is unreal'.

What would most people mean by this proposition? I do not think there is much difficulty in discovering what sort of thing they would mean by it. Of course, Time with a big T, seems to be a highly abstract kind of entity, and to define *exactly* what can be meant by saying of an entity of that sort that it is unreal does seem to offer difficulties. But if you try to translate the proposition into the concrete, and to ask what it *implies,* there is, I think very little doubt as to the sort of thing it implies.[23]

For, once you translate the proposition into the concrete, i.e., into propositions like 'There are no temporal facts', then the result clearly is: "Nothing ever happens before or after anything else; nothing is ever simultaneous with anything else; it is never true that anything is past; never true

21. "Def.," pp. 42–43; Cf. "The Nature and Reality of Objects of Perception," *PAS*, VI (1905–6), pp. 68–69, reprinted in *PS*, pp. 31–32; "Hume's Philosophy," *The New Quarterly* (Nov., 1909), reprinted in *PS*, p. 158; *SMPP*, p. 19.

22. M. Lazerowitz, "Moore and Philosophical Analysis," *Philosophy*, XXXIII (1958), 195. Cf. Moore's "Four Forms of Scepticism," *PP*, pp. 208–10.

23. *PS*, p. 209.

that anything will happen in the future; never true that anything is happening now; and so on." [24] That is,

    (*P*) Time is unreal.

when translated yields, e.g.,

    (*p*) There are no temporal facts.

which implies, among other things,

    (*q*) Although I did, when my alarm went off, (1) shut it off, (2) get out of bed, (3) put my slippers on, (4) go downstairs, (5) enter the bathroom, (6) leave the bathroom, (7) have my breakfast; I did not *first* do (1), and then *after* that do (2), and still *later* do (3), and so on; nor did I even do any of these in any sequence whereby any one of them occurred *after* another of them.

    (*r*) I am not now holding my pen *at the same time* as I am writing on this paper.

But (*q*) and (*r*) are decidedly false. For I did *first* shut off the alarm, and *then* get out of bed, and *after* that put on my slippers, etc., etc. And I am holding my pen *at the very same moment* as I am writing. Therefore, since (*q*) and (*r*) are false, (*p*) is false; and, since (*p*) is a translation of (*P*), (*P*) is false. Hence, Mr. Bradley's proposition has been shown to be false.

A similar sort of analysis can be performed with respect to numerous philosophical propositions. Take the view that "All that we know of material objects is the orderly succession of our own sensations." [25] We must, says Moore, see what this means "in particular instances." Suppose that you are traveling in a railway train. You sense various sense-data, colors, shapes, shakings, etc., and you know that if the train stopped, and you got out and examined it, you would apprehend still others. According to the view in question, this is *all* that you can know about the existence of the train in which you are traveling. And when you believe that the *train* exists, this is all you believe. While you are riding in it, you cannot know that the train is on wheels, or that the car is coupled to other cars. But this clearly is false, says Moore. We do know that "there really are wheels on which your carriage is running at the moment, and couplings between the carriages." [26] Yet this view

24. *Ibid.*, p. 210.
25. *SMPP*, pp. 132–44.
26. *Ibid.*, p. 135.

really has been seriously held by many philosophers. . . . So long as it is merely presented in vague phrases such as: All that we know of material objects is the orderly succession of our own sensations; it does, in fact, sound very plausible. But, so soon as you realize what it means in particular instances like that of the train—how it means that you cannot possibly know that your carriage is, even probably, running on wheels, or coupled to other carriages—it seems to me to lose all its plausibility.[27]

Similarly, with respect to another view regarding our knowledge of the existence of material objects, the view that "all that we know of material objects is that they are the unknown causes of our sensations." About this view, Moore says: "Many philosophers have, I think, really believed the theory, and it also may seem very plausible so long as you merely state it in abstract terms. . . . But it also seems to me to lose its plausibility, so soon as you consider what it implies in particular concrete instances."[28]

So much then, for the two forms of refutational analysis. Two points should be mentioned. First, the objects of analysis, in both cases, appear to be linguistic, i.e., sentences. Yet Moore would not always agree that they are such. Rather, he would probably hold that it is what sentences express —propositions—that is being analyzed. Second, in these two varieties of analysis, the analysandum-analysans distinction is not quite appropriate; that is, we do not, in these cases, seek an analysans which explicates, defines, or in some other way characterizes an analysandum. Rather, we point out that certain views or propositions are self-contradictory or lead to contradictory consequences, or we show that certain propositions imply other propositions which we know to be false.

2. *Distinctional analysis*

The chief feature of this form of analysis is the discrimination or distinguishing of several meanings which a term, phrase, statement, or question may have. In the preface to *Principia Ethica,* Moore writes: "It appears to me that in Ethics, as in all other philosophical studies, the difficulties and disagreements, of which its history is full, are mainly due to a very simple cause: namely to the attempt to answer questions without discovering precisely *what* question it is which you desire to answer."

27. *Ibid.*
28. *Ibid.*, pp. 136–37; for further cases of or references to this refutational device, see "Kant's Idealism," *PAS,* IV (1903–4), 135–36; "The Character of Cognitive Acts," *PAS,* XXI (1920–21), 132–33; for cases similar to it, "Kant's Idealism," p. 131; "Some Judgments of Perception," *PAS,* XIX (1918–19), reprinted in *PS,* pp. 227–28.

Very often, moral philosophers have before their minds "not one question, but several." What is needed is "the work of analysis and distinction," which, however, "is often very difficult." [29] And later: "This, then, is our first question: 'What is the good?' . . . But this is a question which may have many meanings." [30] Moore goes on to discuss some of them. Similarly, in "The Refutation of Idealism," Moore disputes Berkeley's proposition that to be is to be perceived. "This is a very ambiguous proposition." [31] And later: "But now: Is *esse percipi?* There are three very ambiguous terms in this proposition, and I must begin by distinguishing the different things that may be meant by some of them." [32]

Let us look at another example of distinctional analysis in somewhat greater detail. For this purpose *Principia Ethica* provides a good illustration. Moore distinguishes two kinds of ethical judgments: those "which state that certain kinds of things have good effects," and judgments "which state that certain kinds of things are themselves good." [33] The first are false if they claim to be universally true, and, even if uttered as generalizations, they are only true of certain periods in history. The second, however, if true at all, must be universally true. "It is, therefore, extremely important to distinguish these two kinds of possible judgments. Both may be expressed in the same language." In both cases, we usually say 'Such and such a thing is good'. But in the one case, 'good' means 'good as means', and in the other it means 'good as end'.

It is plain that these are very different assertions to make about a thing . . . and it is certain that unless we are clear as to which of the two we mean to assert, we shall have a very poor chance of deciding rightly whether our assertion is true or false. It is precisely this clearness as to the meaning of the question asked which has hitherto been almost entirely lacking in ethical speculation.

Again: "A great part of the vast disagreements prevalent in Ethics is to be attributed to this failure in analysis."

In almost every one of Moore's papers or books one can find the work of discriminative, distinctional analysis exhibited. In "External and Internal Relations," Moore says, with respect to Bradley's assertions that all

29. *PE*, p. vii.
30. *Ibid.*, p. 3.
31. *PS*, p. 5.
32. *Ibid.*, p. 7.
33. These quotations and all subsequent ones in this paragraph appear in *PE*, pp. 23–24, 26.

relations are "intrinsical" (i.e., none are "purely external") : "I shall try to make clear the exact meaning of this proposition . . . and to distinguish it clearly from certain other propositions which are, I think, more or less liable to be confused with it." [34] Later, he emphasizes the need to distinguish relations from relational properties. [35] In the same essay, he distinguishes "two different senses" of the statement that *A* is different from *B*. [36] In "The Nature of Moral Philosophy" Moore emphasizes that the expression 'moral obligation' may stand for "two different ideas" [37] and stresses the need "to distinguish clearly between the different meanings of the word 'good'. [38] In "The Implications of Recognition" Moore asks: "What is meant by saying that a sense-datum has been 'modified' by past experience?" and answers: "There are . . . two different things that may be meant which it is important to distinguish." [39] In another paper he shows how the 'is' of predication has been confused with the 'is' of identity. [40] The first ten pages of "The Refutation of Idealism" and the first ten or so of "Proof of an External World" are packed with numerous discriminations. [41] And so on. [42]

The objects of distinctional analysis appear to be linguistic entities— terms, phrases, and sentences. However, I again think that Moore means the referents of all of these and not merely the expressions themselves to be the objects of analysis. He is distinguishing various *meanings* which some expression or other expresses. Most of the passages which exhibit the use of distinctional analysis are similar to the following: "You will understand at once what question I mean to ask. But, for all that, the words which I have used are highly ambiguous. If you begin to ask yourselves what I do mean by them, you will find that there are several quite different things which I might mean." [43]

34. *PAS*, XX (1919–20), 40–62, reprinted in *PS*, p. 277.
35. *Ibid.*, p. 282.
36. *Ibid.*, p. 285.
37. *Ibid.*, p. 323.
38. *Ibid.*, p. 328.
39. *PAS*, XVI (1915–16), 208.
40. "Is the 'Concrete Universal' the True Type of Universality?", *PAS*, XX (1919–20), 140.
41. "Refut.," pp. 5, 7, 8, 9; "Prf.," pp. 3–13.
42. See also: "Are the Characteristics of Particular Things Universal or Particular?", p. 100; "Are the Materials of Sense Affections of the Mind?", *PAS*, XVII (1916–17), 418–20; "The Nature and Reality of Objects of Perception," *PS*, pp. 33, 36–38, 40, 53, 84; *PE*, p. 69; "Justif.," p. 29; "Four Forms of Scepticism," *PP*, p. 224.
43. "The Nature and Reality of Objects of Perception," *PS*, pp. 32–33.

3. *Decompositional analysis*

The distinctive feature of decompositional analysis is that something complex is "decomposed" into its component parts or elements. As Moore says, we analyze something "down to its simplest terms." [44] There are two forms of decompositional analysis. In the case of *definitional* analysis, either expressions, or, as Moore prefers to say, concepts, meanings, etc., are the objects of analysis. In the case of *divisional* analysis, meanings or objects (in the broad sense) are the analysanda.

(a) *Definitional analysis*

At first sight it seems that Moore means by 'definition' verbal paraphrase. One is led to suspect this by the examples which Moore chooses, of which his favorite and his paradigm, '*X* is a brother', is analyzed into '*X* is a male sibling'.[45] It certainly seems that the result of analysis here is the mere clarification of a term. The analysans simply states in other terms an expression synonymous to the analysandum. Whereas the analysandum is a complex term, the analysans consists of two or more simple, or at least less complex, terms. One might thus argue: (*P*) the analysans does not reveal any new properties of the analysandum. Nor do we learn anything by this form of analysis. When we learn that to be a male sibling is what it means to be a brother, we do not learn any new facts about brothers or about being a brother. Rather, we find that some expression may be used synonymously with some other expression (in this case, 'brother'). Therefore: (*C*) Definitional analysis is merely linguistic. It consists in verbal paraphrase. The analysandum is a verbal expression.

What would Moore say to this? Let us take (*C*) first. In his "Reply" he is very explicit. "I think I can say quite definitely that I never intended to use the word in such a way that the analysandum would be a verbal expression. When I have talked of analysing anything, what I have talked of analysing has always been an idea or concept or proposition, and *not* a verbal expression." [46] Hence, Moore denies that, in his case at least, (*C*) is true. What about (*P*)? Moore denies that (*P*) is a true characterization of analysis. He explicitly states that when we say " '*X* is a brother' means the same as '*X* is a male sibling,' " we are not giving an *analysis* of the concept 'being a brother'. Rather, we are

---

44. *SMPP*, p. 268.
45. "Reply," pp. 662 ff.
46. *Ibid.*, p. 661.

merely asserting, with regard to two verbal expressions, that they have (to use an expression of Mr. W. E. Johnson's) *some* the same [*sic*] meaning, or at best, that they each have only one meaning, and that the meaning they have is the same. You are not *mentioning* the meaning of either, or saying *what* the meaning of either is; but are merely making a statement which could be completely understood by a person who had not the least idea of what either expression meant.[47]

Hence, (*P*) cannot be an adequate characterization of what analysis is. For if I discover merely that two expressions have the same meaning, then I do not learn anything about any concept or idea which the expressions express. Therefore, anyone who showed me that two expressions had the same meaning would "certainly *not* have been giving me an analysis of any *concept,* just as, also, he would certainly *not* have given me an analysis of any expression."[48] Hence, (*P*) does not entail (*C*). Definitional analysis then is not merely linguistic for Moore. It involves the decomposition of concepts or objects. I shall return to this matter in section IV.

(b) *Divisional analysis*

In spite of Moore's protests, synonymity seems to be the distinguishing feature of definitional analysis. There is a second kind of decompositional analysis in which the breaking up of a complex into simple parts is still retained but the synonymity feature is not. Furthermore, whereas one might be led to suspect that definitional analysis is merely linguistic, that it appears to be verbal paraphrase, one would never make this accusation with respect to divisional analysis. The analysanda in divisional analysis may be objects or entities, in a sense of 'object' which excludes linguistic expressions. Finally, we may learn something new in divisional analysis. We may learn, for example, that some concept or object is really complex, although we had not heretofore been aware of it; and divisional analysis may make clear just what the component parts are.

The fact that it is objects or entities which are being analyzed is clearly seen in Moore's analysis of a sensation. Moore points out that discussions of sensations have been unfortunate in the past because philosophers have failed "to distinguish between a sensation or idea and what I call its object." Moore at great length isolates these "two distinct elements, consciousness and the object of consciousness."[49] "In every sensation or idea

47. *Ibid.,* p. 662.
48. *Ibid.*
49. "Refut.," p. 17.

76

we must distinguish two elements, (1) the 'object,' or that in which one differs from another; and (2) 'consciousness,' or that which makes them sensations or mental facts." [50]

In the 1910–11 lectures numerous entities are (divisionally) analyzed: e.g., beliefs. "The answer as to the analysis of beliefs is this. . . . In the case of every belief without exception, whether it be true or whether it be false, we can always distinguish two constituents—namely, the *act* of belief, on the one hand, and the *object* of belief or what *is* believed on the other." [51] Facts are also analyzed. Take, for example, the fact that my right hand is near my left hand. "This fact seems plainly capable of being analyzed into the following constituents. . . . This right hand—this sense-datum—is one of them—and the other is *what* we assert of this sense-datum, the property which we attribute to it—namely, the property *of being near the left hand*." [52]

In *Principia Ethica* Moore performs an analysis of instances of esthetic appreciation. Any such instance includes "not merely a bare cognition of what is beautiful in the object, but also some kind of feeling or emotion." [53]

Sometimes Moore is concerned to show that certain objects *cannot* be analyzed: i.e., that they are simples. For example, in *Principia Ethica* he emphasizes that, whereas *horse* is a complex notion or object, *good,* like *yellow,* is a simple one. By simple he means absolutely unanalyzable, indefinable, undecomposable. It is interesting that Moore's view of definition here includes the defining of objects. "You can give a definition of a horse, because a horse has many different properties and qualities, all of which you can enumerate. But when you have enumerated them all, when you have reduced a horse to his simplest terms, then you can no longer define those terms." [54] Similarly, we can "define" non-existent complex objects: e.g., a chimera. "It is an animal with a lioness' head and body, with a goat's head growing from the middle of its back, and with a snake in place of a tail." In this case too the object is a complex one; "It is entirely composed of parts, with which we are all perfectly familiar." All complex objects, then, are analyzable, definable, decomposable. But yellow

50. *Ibid.,* p. 20.
51. *SMPP,* p. 258.
52. *Ibid.,* p. 303.
53. *PE,* pp. 189 f.; see also p. 192.
54. *Ibid.,* p. 7.

77

and good, for example, are not complex; "they are notions of that simple kind, out of which definitions are composed and with which the power of further defining ceases." [55]

4. *Reductional analysis*

The term 'reductional analysis' was applied to the kind of analysis which philosophers like Russell, Wisdom, Stebbing, etc., engaged in during the heyday of Logical Atomism. It was also called new-level, philosophical, or distinctional analysis.[56] Russell, in the *Monist* lectures, held a highly metaphysical view of the nature of reductional analysis. Logical Atomism, he said, is the view "that you can get down in theory, if not in practice, to ultimate simples, out of which the world is built, and that these simples have a kind of reality not belonging to anything else." [57] These simples included such things as sense-data, but not physical objects. Hence, a statement referring to a physical object is required to be reduced to a statement, or set of statements, referring to sense-data (or sense-data and universals) but not to physical objects. Thus, for Russell, sense-data are among the ultimate simples of the world, and physical objects are, in some sense, "built out" of them.[58]

Later analysts shunned this tendency towards a rather traditional phenomenalism and spoke of logical constructions. If y is a logically proper name or a description of something which could be named, then if x's are logical constructions out of y's, then every statement about x's can be replaced by an equivalent statement about y's. For example, 'average man' neither names nor describes what can be named (in the theory). Hence, the average man is a logical construction out of ordinary men. That is, for every sentence about the average man an equivalent one can be found about ordinary men. But 'Caesar', 'Eisenhower', etc., do not name either. Thus, the need for the use of definite descriptions arises. Similarly, 'table' neither names nor describes what can be named. Hence, tables are logical constructions out of sense-data. But this did not mean that, for these analysts, there are no tables: i.e., no physical objects. It merely meant that

---

55. *Ibid.*, pp. 7–8; for other negative cases, see *SMPP*, pp. 265, 344. Cf. G. J. Warnock, *English Philosophy Since 1900* (London: Oxford Univ. Press, 1958), Chap. II.

56. For a history of this movement, see J. O. Urmson, *Philosophical Analysis* (Oxford: Clarendon Press, 1956), especially Parts I and II.

57. See beginning of Lecture VIII, "The Philosophy of Logical Atomism," in *Logic and Knowledge*, ed. R. Marsh (New York: Macmillan, 1956), pp. 269–70.

58. *Ibid.*

for every *sentence* employing the *term* 'table', an equivalent one can, in principle, be found which does not use 'table' but which does use terms referring to sense-data. The phenomenalism remains, but it is a reconstructive version, not a traditional theory.[59]

Is Moore a reductional analyst? G. J. Warnock holds that Moore definitely is one. Moreover, he construes Moore to be a traditional phenomenalist. He writes:

Moore took very seriously a suggestion that is implicit in his metaphorical name for his enterprise. The use of the word 'analysis' carries the suggestion that something complex, something constructed, is to be decomposed—that its component elements or parts are to be distinguished, and its mode of construction from these elements or parts made clear. . . . A cube, for example, can be thought of naturally enough as a geometrical complex of planes in three dimensions; the proposition 'This is a cube' seems likely, accordingly, to be susceptible of analysis in terms of these planes, their numbers, their shapes, their mutual relations. . . . But now what of the proposition 'This is a hand'? Is the notion of *being a hand* absolutely simple, a notion so basic and elementary as to be incapable of any analysis? It hardly seems quite so simple as that. But if not, what elements are they into which it can be analysed? What entities are they that are simpler, more basic, than hands, of which hands could be said to be, in some strange sense, constructed or composed? Moore had no doubt that there were simpler entities of some sort on which our knowledge of hands (and of other such things) was in some way based, and which were indeed what we always directly referred to in uttering such propositions as that this is a hand. But certainly these entities have no familiar name. . . . Moore employed for referring to them the technical term 'sense-data.' [60]

This description of Moore's philosophy is a surprising one. Warnock makes it seem as if it were quite obvious that Moore is both a reductional analyst and a traditional phenomenalist. I should suggest that it is not quite that obvious. What, then, led Warnock to make such assertions as he did? I suspect that the source of Warnock's charge lies in certain passages like that in section IV of Moore's "Defence of Common Sense." Let us turn to that passage.[61]

Take a proposition like 'Material objects exist'. As we have seen, Moore has no doubt about the truth of this proposition, nor does he find any difficulty in understanding it. But again he is skeptical as to what the

---

59. For further details see Urmson, *Philosophical Analysis*, especially pp. 22–44.
60. Warnock, *English Philosophy Since 1900*, pp. 25–26.
61. "Def.," *PP*, pp. 53–58.

correct *analysis* of such propositions is. He thinks, however, it is quite evident that the question how propositions of this type are to be analyzed depends on how propositions of a *simpler* type are to be analyzed. For example, I know at this moment that I am perceiving a pen, a sheet of paper, a hand, etc. It seems to Moore that we cannot know how the proposition 'Material things exist' is to be analyzed until we know how these simpler propositions—'I am perceiving a human hand', etc.—are to be analyzed. But, he says, even these are not simple enough.

It seems to me quite evident that my knowledge that I am now perceiving a human hand is a deduction from a pair of propositions simpler still—propositions which I can only express in the form 'I am perceiving *this*' and '*This* is a human hand.' It is the analysis of propositions of the latter kind which seems to me to present such great difficulties; while nevertheless the whole question as to the *nature* of material things obviously depends upon their analysis.[62]

What about the analysis of propositions like 'This is a hand', 'That is the sun', 'This is a dog', etc.?

Two things only seem to me to be quite certain about the analysis of such propositions . . . namely that whenever I know, or judge, such a proposition to be true, (1) there is always some *sense-datum* about which the proposition in question is a proposition—some sense-datum which is *a* subject (and, in a certain sense, the principal or ultimate subject) of the proposition in question, and (2) that, nevertheless, *what* I am knowing or judging to be true about this sense-datum is not (in general) that it is *itself* a hand, or a dog, or the sun, etc., etc., as the case may be.[63]

(2) may be dealt with quite briefly. That what Moore knows regarding the sense-datum is not that it is *itself* a hand seems certain because he knows that his hand has many other parts (the bones inside it, etc.) which certainly are not parts of the sense-datum which he now sees in looking at a human hand.

As to (1): That there are sense-data, Moore did not doubt. He thought he was helping the reader to agree that there is no doubt about their existence by saying:

In order to point out to the reader what sort of things I mean by sense-data, I need only ask him to look at his own right hand. If he does this he will be able to pick out something (and, unless he is seeing double, *only* one thing) with regard to which he will see that it is, at first sight, a natural view to take

62. *Ibid.,* p. 53.
63. *Ibid.*

that that thing is identical, not, indeed, with his whole right hand, but with that part of its surface which he is actually seeing, but will also (on a little reflection) be able to see that it is doubtful whether it can be identical with the part of the surface of his hand in question. Things *of the sort* (in a certain respect) of which this thing is, which he sees in looking at his hand, and with regard to which he can understand how some philosophers should have supposed it to *be* the part of the surface of his hand which he is seeing, while others have supposed that it can't be, are what I mean by 'sense-data.' [64]

But, as his critics have pointed out, this is a very puzzling passage. Furthermore, it does nothing to show in what sense, whenever I know a proposition like 'This is a hand' to be true, there is always some sense-datum which is "in a certain sense, the principal or ultimate subject" of the proposition in question. As we have seen, such a proposition does not state that the sense-datum which I see is itself a hand. Well, does it assert that the sense-datum is part of the (front) surface of the hand, or what? In what way is the sense-datum the ultimate subject of perceptual propositions?

Let us, following Moore, try an analysis of the proposition 'This is a human hand'. Its analysis, according to Moore, is roughly of the form: 'There is one thing, and only one thing, of which it is true both that it is a human hand and that *this surface* is a part of its surface'. In other words, Moore holds that I do not *directly* perceive *my hand* and that when I am (correctly) said to perceive it what is meant is that I perceive in a more fundamental sense something which is representative of it: i.e., a certain part of its surface. This Moore holds to be certain about the analysis of propositions like 'This is a human hand'. As we have seen, the analysis includes a proposition of the form 'This is a part of the surface of a human hand', where *this* now means something different from what it meant in the original proposition. But, Moore holds, this new proposition, as well as the original, is also about the sense-datum which I see and which is a sense-datum *of* my hand. Granting, for the time being, that there are sense-data, another question arises: When I know that 'This is part of the surface of a human hand', what am I knowing about the sense-datum? Am I knowing that the sense-datum is *itself* a part of the surface of a human hand?

Or, just as we found in the case of 'This is a human hand,' that what I was knowing about the sense-datum was certainly not that it *itself* was a human

64. *Ibid.*, p. 218.

hand, so is it perhaps the case, with this new proposition, that even here I am not knowing, with regard to the sense-datum, that it is *itself* part of the surface of a hand? and, if so, what is it that I am knowing about the sense-datum itself? [65]

Moore finds that three alternative types of answers are possible and that to any answer which has been suggested of any of these types there are "grave objections." One might hold that what I am knowing is that the sense-datum itself is part of the surface of a human hand. Although I do not directly perceive my hand, I do directly perceive part of its surface, in this view. Or one might hold that the sense-datum is related in some representative way to the surface. What I know here is that there is some relation, *R,* and some one thing or set of things which is part of the surface of a hand and which has *R* to the sense-datum I see. According to a third view, what I know is a set of hypothetical facts of the form 'If certain conditions had been fulfilled, I should have been perceiving a sense-datum intrinsically related to the sense-datum I now see, in a certain way, *X,* and if others had been fulfilled, I should have been perceiving a sense-datum intrinsically related to the sense-datum I now see, in another way, *Y,* etc'.[66]

Moore finds objections to all of these alternatives. I shall not rehearse them here since I shall consider them again in Chapter X. Furthermore, as we shall also see, he never found good reason to embrace one of these alternatives. Because of this fact alone, it would certainly be inaccurate to portray Moore as definitely being a traditional phenomenalist in the way that Warnock has done. For Moore was fairly explicit in denying such a view (although he may not have consistently denied it). "No sense-datum, or part of a sense-datum, or collection of sense-data, can possibly be a material object. . . . Many philosophers have spoken as if certain collections of sense-data or 'sensations' *were* material objects." [67] Later he argues *against* the views that the existence of physical objects consists in the existence of the sense-data which subjects are directly apprehending or which they were to apprehend, and that the existence of physical objects consists in the existence of sense-data which really exist now even though no one is apprehending them.[68]

65. *Ibid.,* p. 219.
66. *Ibid.,* pp. 219–22.
67. SMPP, p. 130.
68. *Ibid.,* pp. 134–45, 137–38.

Finally, evidence to show either that Moore is or is not a reductional analyst is very scanty. He tried to analyze propositions like 'Material objects exist' into simpler ones like (among others) 'I am perceiving a hand', and to analyze these in turn into still simpler ones such as 'This is a hand'. And he did maintain that some sense-datum is always, in a certain sense, the ultimate subject of all such propositions of the latter two types, but he never did explain what that assertion means. All of this is insufficient to demonstrate that Moore is clearly a reductional analyst in the sense in which Russell and others were, but it does show that Moore was, on occasion, interested in a program very similar to that of the reductional analysts.

IV

IN A PAPER entitled "The Notion of Analysis in Moore's Philosophy" [69] C. H. Langford rightly charges that "Moore has not attempted to apply his method of analysis to the notion of analysis itself," that he "has not . . . attempted to examine systematically the question what relation it is that must hold between an analysandum and analysans in order that the latter should correctly analyze the former." He goes on to say that he wants Moore to "state more explicitly his own position regarding the nature of analysis." [70]

Moore takes up the challenge in his "Reply." He there formulates two separate sets of necessary conditions or criteria for a correct analysis. It seems perfectly clear that Moore holds both sets to be essential. Hence, both sets may be discussed conjointly. Of the eight criteria which follow, the last three are found in Moore's first set, and the first five occur in his second set. He devotes more space to the first five. Hence, I shall reverse the order and take them up first.

First, "both *analysandum* and *analysans* must be concepts or propositions, not mere verbal expressions." [71] As I have already indicated, Moore holds concepts and propositions to be meanings. They are what expressions express. Sometimes, in the case of concepts, he thinks of them as being "abstract" entities, self-substantial and even eternal, which the mind can inspect. But in order to perform an analysis we cannot get at or peer

69. *PGEM,* pp. 321–42.
70. *Ibid.,* p. 323.
71. "Reply," p. 664; cf. p. 661.

at the concepts and meanings apart from language. Hence, Moore writes: "Of course, in order to *give* an *analysis,* you must *use* verbal expressions." [72] Is there then a single, *proper* way of expressing an analysis? No, there are alternatives. Suppose we are analyzing the concept *brother*. One can say any of the following:

A. The concept 'being a brother' is identical with the concept 'being a male sibling'.

B. The propositional function 'X is a brother' is identical with the propositional function 'X is a male sibling'.

C. To say that a person is a brother is the same thing as to say that that person is a male sibling.

D. To be a brother is the same thing as to be a male sibling.[73]

All of these are equally correct ways of expressing an analysis. All of the assertions, (A) through (D), contain the terms 'brother' as analysandum and 'male sibling' as analysans. Yet none are *about* these expressions; they are all about the concepts expressed by the verbal expressions. That is, the concepts are what are being analyzed, not the expressions. Of course, we could give an analysis of an expression as well as of a concept. But it would be rather trivial. The following is an example of an analysis of the expression 'X is a brother'. 'The expression contains the letter "X," the word "is," the word "a," and the word "brother"; and it begins with an "X," "is" comes next in it, then "a," and then "brother." '

I think that the rest of the first five criteria may now be given with little exegesis, since they are clearly stated.

Second, "both *analysandum* and *analysans* . . . if the analysis is a *correct* one, must in some sense, be *the same concept.*" [74] This criterion seems fairly plausible if we think of concepts as being the *meanings* of expressions. For then it would seem quite natural to hold that the criterion states something commonsensical: the meaning of one expression ('brother') is the same as the meaning of the second ('male sibling'). However, we have seen that Moore wants the analysis to do more than this. But what that more is, he does not say.

Third, "the *expression* used for the *analysandum* must be a different *expression* from that used for the *analysans.*" [75] It will be noticed that the

72. *Ibid.,* p. 664.
73. *Ibid.,* pp. 664–65.
74. *Ibid.,* p. 666.
75. *Ibid.*

second and third criteria might be those of a correct definition. And I have already called attention to the fact that analysis, in one of its forms, is very nearly equated by Moore with definition, providing that definition is not merely verbal: i.e., that entities, meanings, etc., and not words are defined.

Fourth, "the expression used for the *analysandum* must not only be different from that used for the *analysans,* but they must differ in this way, namely, that the expression used for the *analysans* must explicitly *mention* concepts which are not explicitly mentioned by the expression used for the *analysandum.*" [76] In the example given by Moore the expression 'X is a male sibling' (says Moore) "explicitly mentions the concepts 'male' and 'sibling', whereas the expression 'X is a brother' does not." [77] The expression of the fourth criterion is rather peculiar. I think Moore means to say: The expression used for the analysans must explicitly employ terms which refer to or express concepts, terms that are not explicitly employed by the expression used for the analysandum.

Fifth, "the *method of combination* should be explicitly mentioned by the expression used for the *analysans.*" [78] That is, the expression 'X is a male sibling' not only "mentions concepts" (male and sibling) which are not mentioned by 'X is a brother', but it mentions the way in which the two concepts are combined in the concept brother. According to Moore, the method of combination in this case is that of mere conjunction. What Moore means by conjunction he does not say. Certainly he cannot mean conjunction in the sense in which two apples (or one orange and one apple) are conjoined to make up a group of two objects. The conjunction is of concepts and must form some sort of unity. But, again, he cannot have in mind the unity in which two halves of a circle are conjoined to form a whole. For male and sibling are *different* concepts, yet when "conjoined," they form the concept of brother, or in the other direction, the analysis of *brother* yields two components, *male* and *sibling*. Hence, all this is problematical. Moore never clarified, in the few papers which were written after the "Reply," just what he meant by this fifth point, or by any of the others for that matter.

Moore tersely states three more criteria for a correct analysis. These are: *Sixth,* "nobody can know that the *analysandum* applies to an object without knowing that the *analysans* applies to it."

76. *Ibid.*
77. *Ibid.*
78. *Ibid.*

Seventh, "nobody can verify that the *analysandum* applies without verifying that the *analysans* applies."

Eighth, "any expression which expresses the *analysandum* must be synonymous with any expression which expresses the *analysans*." [79]

The sixth and seventh criteria are rather odd. 'Nobody can know that *x* without knowing that *y*' may mean either: (a) as a matter of psychological fact, whenever I know *x* obtains, I know that *y* obtains (this is an empirical generalization which, to date, has not, as far as we know, been disproved, but it may be); or (b) 'p entails q': i.e., knowing that the analysandum applies to an object entails knowing that the analysans applies to it. It is not clear whether Moore means (a) or (b) to be the explication of the sixth criterion. A similar objection applies to the seventh criterion.

The synonymity criterion leads to many difficulties, as Quine has so vividly pointed out.[80] I shall not review them here.

V

A COUPLE OF GENERAL COMMENTS about Moore's criteria for a correct analysis are in order.

First, it is clearly evident that the criteria are applicable to only one form of analysis—definitional analysis. They do not, as a whole, apply to any of the other kinds of analysis. Nor do most of the criteria singly apply to other forms. Am I wrong then in calling the other activities analysis? No, Moore's language indicates that he held what I have called refutational, distinctional, divisional, and his version of reductional analysis to be genuine forms of analysis. Why then did Moore limit the discussion in his reply to definitional analysis? I have noted that Langford charged that Moore has never attempted "to examine systematically the question what relation it is that must hold between an analysandum and an analysans in order that the latter should correctly analyze the former." [81] The analysandum-analysans distinction reminds one of the definiendum-definiens pair. Was Moore misled to believe that the two must be very much the same? Or was his discussion of analysis limited by the way in which Langford

79. The sixth, seventh, and eighth criteria are all found in a single paragraph on p. 663 of the "Reply."
80. W. V. Quine, "Two Dogmas of Empiricism," *From a Logical Point of View* (Cambridge: Harvard Univ. Press), 1953.
81. *PGEM*, p. 323.

put the challenge? I do not know. The only thing that is clear is that Moore's criteria apply only to definitional analysis and not to other forms. It is true that his explicit discussions of analysis refer more often to definitional analysis than to other kinds. But it is also true that he referred to the other forms as analysis too, as I have shown. Hence, his treatment of analysis in his "Reply" is too restrictive.

Second, leaving aside the other forms of analysis, what about Moore's discussion of the criteria of definitional analysis? Is the discussion adequate? More specifically, does not this form of analysis lead to a paradox, as many have pointed out? The "paradox of analysis" is precisely this: "If the verbal expression representing the analysandum has the same meaning as the verbal expression representing the analysans, the analysis states a bare identity and is trivial; but if the two verbal expressions do not have the same meaning, the analysis is incorrect." [82] Moore's attempt at a solution is not very helpful. He admits: "I am not at all clear as to what the solution of the puzzle is." [83] He mentions one possibility. According to it, if you say 'To be a brother is the same thing as to be a male sibling', you are making a statement both about the concept brother *and* about the two verbal expressions which occur in the analysis. That is, in this view, 'to be a brother is the same thing as to be a male sibling' is a conjunction of two assertions: the first, 'the verbal expression "X is a brother" has the same meaning as the expression "X is a male sibling"'; the second, an assertion about the concept 'X is a brother', and not about a verbal expression. Moore concludes: "But I do not think that this can possibly be the case: what would the second assertion in this conjunction be?" [84] Hence, he leaves the issue without any solution.

Thus, in spite of his attempt at clarification, the whole problem of analysis persists in Moore's philosophy. We learn no more at the end than we did at the beginning, in a sense. One is reminded of Omar Khayyam:

> Myself when young did eagerly frequent
> Doctor and Saint, and heard great argument
>   About it and about: but evermore
> Came out by the same door where in I went.

82. *Ibid.*
83. "Reply," p. 665.
84. *Ibid.*, p. 666.

PART TWO
Knowing about Knowing

VI

The Ways of

Knowing

I HAVE NOTED ALL ALONG that it is often very difficult so say just what Moore holds with respect to a given issue. This was especially evident in my consideration of what Moore means by *meaning* or *analysis*. There is no single, unique meaning of 'meaning' and no one form of analysis in Moore's writings. Similarly, we now find that there are several kinds of *knowledge* for Moore. It is not simply the fact that there are several kinds of meaning, analysis, knowledge, etc., which makes it difficult to read Moore. Philosophy has been called (rightly, I think) the art of making distinctions. What provides the difficulty is the fact that what Moore says about, say, one kind of analysis, does not always fit with what he says about another kind, or what he says about the same kind on some other occasion. He nowhere brings together all of the kinds of meaning or analysis which he has distinguished. When we turn to his discussion of various kinds of knowledge, the situation is, fortunately, not quite as bad. (Nevertheless, it is not unproblematic.) Moore maintains that there are four main kinds of knowledge, one of which has sub-species. These four are: (i) dispositional knowledge, (ii) apprehension, (iii) propositional knowledge (or knowledge proper), and (iv) indirect knowledge. Or one might call the four: (i) knowing how, (ii) being acquainted with, (iii) (directly) knowing that, and (iv) indirectly knowing that. As one might suspect, Moore's discussion of (i) is minimized. Hence, I shall treat it briefly first and then give more space to a consideration of (ii), (iii), and (iv).

I

WE SOMETIMES USE 'knowledge' in a common, nonphilosophical sense, in such a way that a man may be said to know some thing at any given moment, even though he is not at that very moment thinking of the thing or conscious of it in any way whatever. In fact, in this sense of 'know', a man need not be, at the moment, conscious at all. Thus, at any moment over a period of many years I have known that 2 plus 2 equals 4 and that the Pilgrims landed in 1620, although at the majority of these moments, I was not thinking of these "facts" and, at many of them, I was not conscious at all. In this common-sense use of 'know', what we mean by saying that Brown at time *t* knows something is: If at *t* Brown had been asked 'How much is 2 plus 2?' or 'When did the Pilgrims land?' he would have answered '4' or '1620'. It has been quite common to call such knowledge *dispositional knowledge,* and it seems to be the mission of certain philosophers to remind us constantly of it. The term is used by Moore in a paper written in 1929,[1] although the kind of knowledge to which it refers was clearly distinguished as early as the 1910–11 lectures.[2] In the 1929 paper Moore's discussion, although longer, is limited to what might be called *propositional* cases: i.e., cases like the two which are mentioned above, one a mathematical identity, the other the statement of a historical fact. But, obviously, we have dispositional knowledge of more than just propositions or facts. We may also have dispositional knowledge of what red is, or of how to swim. Again, to say that we know what red is means that when asked to select the red piece in a collection we are able to do so; it does not imply that we are always conscious of red. Similarly one can know how to swim, even though he is not swimming at the time or

1. "Indirect Knowledge," *PASS,* IX (1929), 21.
2. *SMPP,* pp. 79–80.

thinking about swimming. We hold that Maggie knows how to swim if, when she is thrown into a pool, she can make it to the edge, etc. If the first form of dispositional knowledge is propositional in character, the essential marks of the latter two forms are: being acquainted with (and perhaps recognizing) something and possessing an ability or skill. (Some might want to construe the former as an instance of the latter.) Undoubtedly, there are other forms. In the extremely brief passage in the 1910–11 lectures Moore realized and suggested that some of these other forms existed, but he gives no indication of them in the 1929 paper.[3]

Moore makes two main points with respect to dispositional knowledge: (A) I have already mentioned the first: In the dispositional sense of 'know', we may know an object (in the wider sense) even at times when we are neither directly nor indirectly apprehending that object,[4] indeed, at times when we are not conscious at all. (B) No one can dispositionally know an object unless he has previously apprehended that object, either directly or indirectly.[5] In order to dispositionally know that 2 plus 2 equals 4, or what red is, I must at some earlier time have apprehended the truth of the proposition *2 plus 2 equals 4* or apprehended a red sense-datum.

It is somewhat surprising that Moore holds (B) to be true. He overlooks the possibility that one might dispositionally know an object when he has previously apprehended "parts" or aspects of that object (and of others), but not the very same object. For example, it seems plausible to hold that I dispositionally know what a red circle is on the basis of having previously apprehended a red square and a white circle, but never a red circle. (Many similar illustrations might be given.)

As I have already suggested, Moore does not make much fuss over dispositional knowledge. Hence, I shall say no more regarding it and turn to the remaining kinds of knowledge. Moore also referred to dispositional knowledge as *non-actualized knowledge.* He calls all the other forms *actualized knowledge,* meaning by this that, in all of these cases of knowing, when I know something I actually know it; that is, I know it *at that time;* it is *then* present to my consciousness or "before my mind."[6]

3. *Ibid.,* p. 79.
4. I shall discuss apprehension below. Generally, apprehension refers to the way of knowing sense-data, images, propositions, etc.
5. *SMPP,* pp. 79–80.
6. "Indirect Knowledge," pp. 21–22.

II

AMONG THE THREE KINDS of actualized knowledge which Moore discusses, the first is *apprehension*. It is, as we shall see, what Russell has called knowledge by acquaintance. Or at least one form of Moore's *direct* apprehension is identical with Russell's knowledge by acquaintance. For Moore has two forms of apprehension, direct and indirect. Let us consider direct apprehension first.

1. *Direct apprehension*

(A) Moore says that *direct apprehension* is a "way of perceiving things," in fact, "one of the most important ways we have of perceiving things." [7] We must not be misled by the word 'perceiving' here. By perceiving Moore means such things as the sensing of sense-data or the perceiving of percepts. He does *not* mean the perception of physical objects. We do not get at the latter by direct apprehension. There are, for Moore, at least three kinds of entities which are perceived by direct apprehension. (1) The first kind consists of sense-data. Moore writes:

I want you to realize as clearly as possible what sort of a thing *this* way of perceiving which I call 'direct apprehension' is. It is . . . that which happens when you actually see any colour, when you actually hear any sound, when you actually feel the so-called 'sensation' of heat, as when you put your hand close to the fire; when you actually smell a smell; when you feel the so-called sensation of hardness, in pressing a table; or when you feel the pain of a toothache, etc., etc. In all these cases you *directly apprehend* the sense-datum in question. [8]

(2) The second kind of entity which is directly apprehended consists in images. The direct apprehension of these occurs, or may occur, in cases of remembering. Suppose that you first directly apprehend a particular color and then turn your eyes away so that you no longer directly apprehend it but are still conscious "of it," by thinking of or remembering it. In a sense, says Moore, you may still have the color "before your mind," but you are no longer *directly* apprehending *it*. However, you may be directly apprehending *something*, namely, an *image* of it—"one of those faint copies of sense-data." Moore holds that the relation which you now have to the image, i.e., that of directly apprehending it, is the very same relation

7. *SMPP,* p. 46.
8. *Ibid.*

which you earlier had to the sense-datum itself (although, of course, the two *objects* are different). "You directly apprehend the image *now* in exactly the same sense as you just now directly apprehended the sense-datum, *of* which it is an image: but you are no longer now directly apprehending *the* sense-datum which you were directly apprehending a moment ago."[9] (3) A third kind of entity which may be directly apprehended, according to Moore, consists of direct apprehensions themselves. These too are "objects" which may be directly apprehended by a "higher-order" apprehension. Suppose that one looks at an envelope and apprehends its whitish color. Moore writes:

It seems to me that if I try to observe what is happening in my mind, I can *also* directly apprehend not only the whitish colour but *also* my own direct apprehension of it . . . I think, therefore, we certainly sometimes apprehend not only sense-data and images, but also our own acts of consciousness.[10]

In a paper entitled "Is There Knowledge by Acquaintance?" Moore holds acquaintance to be the very same relation as the one which he has called direct apprehension in the 1910–11 lectures. And his answer to the question asked in the title is: "Undoubtedly there is, and . . . nobody has ever doubted that we have it; . . . what those who have raised the question have really meant to dispute is not the existence of acquaintance, but merely the truth of some of Mr. Russell's theories about it."[11] Here again he stresses that we are indeed acquainted with such things as sense-data. "I quite certainly am at this moment acquainted with many different sense-data; and in saying this, I am merely using this language to express a fact of such a kind, that nobody has ever thought of disputing the existence of facts of that kind."[12]

Similarly, in "The Implications of Recognition"[13] Moore, speaking of Russell's views "(a) that we often are, at a given time, acquainted with a thing, which we are not at that time knowing by description; and (b) that we often are, at a given time knowing a thing by description, which we are not, at that time, acquainted with," adds: "These two views of his are views which I, for my part, firmly believe to be true."[14]

9. *Ibid.*, p. 47.
10. *Ibid.*, p. 49.
11. *PASS*, II (1919), 184.
12. *Ibid.*, p. 180.
13. *PAS*, XVI (1915–16), 201–23.
14. *Ibid.*, p. 203.

But in a footnote appended in 1952 to the expression 'knowing things' in the 1910–11 lectures, Moore says that he no longer thinks sensing and perception are ways of knowing things and that he now believes that "what Russell, in *The Problems of Philosophy* (Chapter V), calls 'knowledge by acquaintance,' has no right to be called 'knowledge' at all (nor 'acquaintance' either, for that matter)."[15] Since Moore never defended this later view, I have not thought it desirable to give it much weight in my presentation of his views, even though it reverses the opinions which he held throughout most of his philosophical career.

Moore also briefly mentions that we are acquainted with universals as well, but he says that he is "inclined to think that the sense in which we are acquainted with universals (though there is one) is essentially different from that in which we are acquainted with sense-data."[16] This sense of acquaintance seems to be, or to be akin to, that form of direct apprehension which I shall take up in the next paragraphs.

(B) In all three cases with which we have been concerned our direct apprehension was of things or objects or particulars, using these nouns in such a way that sense-data, images, acts of awareness are things (objects, etc.), but physical objects, truths, facts, etc., are not. But Moore also maintains that there is a type of direct apprehension which is not of sense-data, images, or direct apprehensions. This is direct apprehension of *propositions*. To distinguish the two forms of *direct* apprehension I shall speak of the former (discussed in [A]) as direct apprehension of *things* (using 'things' in the specific sense which I have indicated above), and I shall call the latter direct apprehension of *propositions*. (May I remind the reader that we now have two kinds of direct apprehension, and that direct apprehension is itself only one form of apprehension? The other form, to be discussed later, is indirect apprehension.)

A proposition, one may remember, is, for Moore, that which a sentence (if it is a statement) expresses. It is not the collection of words, but what these words *mean*. Now suppose, says Moore, that I utter the sentence 'Twice 2 are 4'. When I say these words, most people who speak English not only hear certain sounds but also understand what the spoken words *mean*. Hence, they do not merely directly apprehend things, in this case, auditory sense-data; they also apprehend a proposition or meaning which is expressed by the words, the same meaning which slightly different

15. *SMPP*, p. 77 n.
16. "Is There Knowledge by Acquaintance?", p. 183.

combinations of words (e.g., '2 times 2 are 4', etc.) express. This way of apprehending a proposition—the way in which you apprehend one when you read a sentence or hear one uttered and understand its meaning—Moore also calls *direct* apprehension.[17] But, as Moore recognizes, a question immediately arises. He has given the name 'direct apprehension' to the relation which we have to such things as sense-data when we actually sense them, etc. The question is: Is the former kind of direct apprehension (the direct apprehension of things) the same as the present kind (the direct apprehension of propositions)? In Moore's words: "Is the relation which you have to a proposition, when you hear the words which express it uttered, and understand the meaning of these words, the same relation as that which you have to a colour, when you actually see it?" He answers: "I confess I cannot tell whether this is so or not."[18] He says that he thinks there are reasons for supposing that the two relations are different, but he cannot tell what the difference is.[19]

I ought to emphasize that, for Moore, the direct apprehension of propositions, while it involves the understanding of a proposition, does not involve knowing the proposition to be true or false. I can, for example, understand the proposition that Wittgenstein weighed over 175 pounds. I have not the slightest idea as to whether or not it is true. Knowledge of truth and falsity enters into knowledge proper, which will be discussed in section III and again in Chapter VIII.

2. *Indirect apprehension*

I have so far under the major heading of the kinds of knowledge or ways of knowing discussed, first, dispositional knowledge and, second, apprehension in one of its forms—namely, direct apprehension. The latter was divided into two kinds: direct apprehension of things and direct apprehension of propositions. I now turn to the other form of apprehension, *indirect apprehension*.

What is indirect apprehension? Moore gets at the issue by first calling our attention to the aboutness feature of propositions. All propositions are about some thing or things. Take 'Twice 2 are 4'. The proposition expressed by this sentence is, according to Moore, about the number 2 and the number 4. In apprehending this proposition, says Moore, we not only directly apprehend the proposition; we also directly apprehend those

17. *SMPP*, p. 67.
18. *Ibid.*
19. *Ibid.*, p. 68.

objects the proposition is about, i.e., two and four. However, Moore notes, in the case of many propositions which we directly apprehend, we do *not* directly apprehend all of the things the proposition is about. While I am looking at a specific patch of color and thus directly apprehending it, I may also directly apprehend a proposition about it: e.g., that it is white. In this case I directly apprehend the proposition and again, directly apprehend the thing the proposition is about. But, of course, I can also directly apprehend propositions *about* the color patch when I am not directly apprehending *it*. For example, now when I am no longer directly apprehending that specific color patch or any which is similar to it, I can still directly apprehend propositions about it—say, that it was, or that I just directly apprehended it, etc. "It is," says Moore, "obvious that we are constantly thus directly apprehending propositions *about* things, when we are *not* directly apprehending these things themselves." [20] This relation which we have to a *thing,* when we directly apprehend a proposition *about* it but do *not* directly apprehend the thing itself, Moore calls indirect apprehension.[21] If a moment ago in looking at an envelope, I directly apprehended a patch of color, then now while I am thinking about the color patch, or remembering it, but not directly apprehending it, I am (1) directly apprehending a proposition *about* it, and (2) indirectly apprehending the color patch *itself*.

Moore anticipates that one might object to this name, 'indirect apprehension', "on the ground that I am not now really apprehending the patch of colour at all: on the ground that to say that I have to it any relation at all, which can be called *apprehension,* is misleading." [22] His defense is as follows:

So long as I am directly apprehending a proposition about a thing, I *am* in a sense conscious of that thing—I am *thinking of it or about it,* even though I am not directly apprehending it, and there is quite as great a difference between *this way* of being related to it, the apprehending of a proposition about it, and what happens when I am *not* thinking of it in any sense at all—when it is utterly out of my mind, as between *this* way of being related to it and that which I have called direct apprehension. Some name is, therefore, required for *this* way of being conscious of a thing—this way which occurs when you do directly apprehend some proposition about it, though you do not

20. *Ibid.,* p. 69.
21. *Ibid.*
22. *Ibid.,* pp. 69–70.

directly apprehend it; and I cannot think of any better name than indirect apprehension.[23]

III

I TURN NOW to the third major kind of knowledge. Moore calls it *knowledge proper*.[24] It is *knowledge that such and such is the case*. Moore characterizes it as "a relation, which while it includes direct apprehension also includes something more besides," [25] or "a kind of relation which never holds between a person and an object, except at a moment when he is directly apprehending the object, but which also never holds unless, *besides* merely apprehending the object, he is also at the same moment related to it in another way as well." [26] It is "the relation which we commonly mean to express when we say without qualification that we *know* a proposition to be true—that we *know* that so and so is the case." [27] But what is the *more* that is involved?

Moore points out that, in a sense, one may be said to know a proposition simply by virtue of directly apprehending it, whether or not the proposition is true or false. For example, if I believe that my hat is hanging in the hall when in fact it is *not,* I am, in believing it, *both* directly apprehending the proposition that my hat is hanging in the hall, that is, understanding it, *and* having the attitude of belief towards it. But if the proposition is false because my hat is *not* in the hall, then I believe falsely or erroneously. However, directly apprehending the proposition, i.e., understanding it, is as we have already seen *a* form of knowing. Hence, there is a sense in which I can know a proposition even if it is false. Moore adds: "But obviously, only in a sense." [28] In a more general sense, when we speak of propositional knowledge, we are concerned with knowing propositions to be *true,* and in *this* sense of knowing propositions, we do not, of course, know them if they are false. Hence, there is a more important sense of 'know', as applied to propositions, whereby in order to know a proposition to be true one must directly apprehend it, to be sure; but several other conditions must be fulfilled. What are some of these conditions? As

23. *Ibid.*, p. 70; cf. pp. 74 ff.
24. *Ibid.*, p. 81.
25. *Ibid.*, p. 79.
26. *Ibid.*, p. 80.
27. *Ibid.*
28. *Ibid.*

Moore points out, one must first also *believe* the proposition. Furthermore, in order to have knowledge that the proposition is true, the proposition must, obviously, *be true* and not false.[29] But even these extra conditions are not sufficient to constitute knowledge. One may directly apprehend a proposition and believe it, and the proposition may be true, and yet he may not really *know* the proposition to be true. Moore illustrates: Suppose that a man now believes that it will not rain on June 20 of next year. And suppose that when the time comes, it *does not* rain. Hence he *now* believes what is true. Yet, says Moore, we would not admit that he now really *knows* that it will not rain on June 20 of next year. Even if he apprehends and believes the proposition that it will not rain, and even if it does not rain, yet we could certainly doubt whether he now *knows* the proposition to be true. Hence, X's claim to have knowledge proper, knowledge that so and so is the case, involves:

(1) X directly apprehends a proposition *p;*
(2) X believes *p;*
(3) *p* is true; and
(4) "some fourth condition." [30]

What is this fourth condition? Exactly what it is, says Moore, is "extremely difficult to discover." One might be tempted to believe that the fourth condition is:

(4′) *p* follows from some *other* proposition or set of propositions which X knows to be true.

'Follows from' here means: has the logical relation of conclusion to premisses, so that if *p* follows from *q,* then *q* entails *p.* But this will not do. We cannot accept (4′) as the sought-after fourth condition. For, as Moore says, if I cannot know any proposition *p* to be true unless I have first known some other proposition, say *q,* from which it follows, to be true; then I cannot have known *q* to be true unless I have first known some other proposition *r* to be true; nor can I have known *r* to be true unless I have first known *s* to be true; and so on, *ad infinitum.* In other words, it would follow from the view that (4′) is the fourth condition "that no man has ever known any proposition whatever to be even probably true, unless he has previously known an absolutely infinite series

29. *Ibid.* These two conditions are discussed in detail in Chap. VIII.
30. *Ibid.*, p. 81.

of other propositions. And it is quite certain that no man ever has thus known a really infinite series of propositions." [31]

But what then *is* the fourth condition? Before turning to Moore's "answer" let me review precisely what it is that Moore is seeking. He is seeking for a criterion (constituted by the four conditions, whatever they will be) for *immediate, empirical* knowledge. I say *immediate* because the criterion is not one for determining when a proposition follows from some other proposition or propositions, when it follows in the relation of conclusion to premisses. In other words, conditions (1) through (4) are not meant to constitute the criteria for a valid argument. The latter might be called a criterion for *mediate* knowledge. Moore is clearly not stating any such criterion. He is, rather, concerned to know what the conditions are for immediately knowing an empirical proposition to be true, for knowing it to be true *without* knowing that it follows from some other proposition or propositions. I say *empirical*—meaning 'empirical' in the sense in which propositions about chairs, etc., are empirical—because Moore is here *not* concerned with criteria for any of the following:

(a) direct apprehension of sense-data, etc.;
(b) direct apprehension of propositions
    (no criteria are needed for [a] or [b]);
(c) possession of a disposition
    (to find out if X has the disposition, we perform a simple, practical test);
(d) logical truth.

Moore is concerned with a criterion for knowing the truth of propositions like 'This pencil exists', or 'I know that this pencil exists'. And, as we have seen, in order to know the truth of 'This pencil exists', the three conditions (1) through (3) mentioned above must hold, plus (4) some fourth condition. Our present problem is: What is the fourth of the conditions which must hold before one can be said to know empirical propositions like 'This pencil exists', to be true, to be *immediately,* not mediately, true?

Moore's answer is alarming. After three arduous chapters he seems to suggest that the fourth condition is:

(4″) X must immediately know the proposition to be true.[32] But this is

31. *Ibid.*, p. 122–23.
32. *Ibid.*, p. 125.

precisely what we were looking for—the conditions of immediately know-ing a proposition to be true: i.e., the conditions of knowledge proper! What we wanted to find out is: When can we immediately know a proposition like 'This pencil exists' to be true? It will not do to tell us that, in addition to the fact that conditions (1) through (3) must hold, we must immediately know the proposition to be true. Someone might maintain that Moore's position can be made plausible by distinguishing two kinds of immediate knowledge: direct immediate knowledge and derived immediate knowledge. Then by (4″) Moore would mean 'X must directly immediately know the proposition to be true'. That is, a proposition or act of apprehension would have to be construed as having a certain feature of "givenness." Finally, upon the basis of (4″) plus (1) through (3), we would have criteria for derived immediate knowledge. There are no textual references or even suggestions by which to support this interpretation. Hence, one is led to believe that Moore is involved in the circularity shown above.

I said that Moore seems to suggest that (4″) is the fourth condition. Actually, Moore does not *say* that (4″) is the fourth condition. But he does not say or even suggest that anything *else* is. And the object of his long discussion was to find the fourth condition. Hence, it is reasonable to believe that he really does mean (4″) to be the fourth condition. This much is certain: he does claim to know the truth of propositions like 'This pencil exists' or 'I know that this pencil exists', etc., *immediately*.[33]

I should like to suggest that with a *suitable* fourth condition Moore's four-condition-schema is a good one. And I believe that there is such a suitable fourth condition which, along with the other three, constitutes a tenable criterion for the knowledge of empirical propositions. I shall, however, defer discussion of it until section V. Before turning to it I shall deal with Moore's fourth major kind of knowledge, *indirect knowledge*.

IV

MOORE'S PAPER, "Indirect Knowledge," [34] on which this section is largely based, is an extremely difficult one and lacks a clear structure. I am not sure that I totally understand some of its subtleties. However, for the

33. *Ibid.*
34. *PASS*, IX (1929), pp. 19–50.

present purpose it is sufficient to see what sorts of knowledge are indirect. And Moore's illustrations are perfectly clear, although in one instance somewhat odd. He cites as examples of indirect knowledge: knowledge by *inference* and knowledge by *testimony*. Suppose, he says, that by adding a column of figures I get to know that their sum is 62. This is "a case in which I learn a fact *by inference*." [35] Or suppose that in some particular year I learn by reading the newspapers that Cambridge won the Boat Race. This is an instance in which "I learn a fact by testimony." In both cases my knowledge of the "fact" learned—that the sum is 62, or that Cambridge won the race—is *based* or *grounded* or *founded* upon knowledge which I had at the time, or knowledge I had just previously of some *other* fact.[36] To take the first case, suppose that the top figure in the column is 5, that I have been adding from the bottom up, and that the total before I added the top figure is 57. Then my conclusion that the whole column adds up to 62 is based on knowledge which I had at the time, or just previously: namely, knowledge of the fact that all the figures below the top one came to 57. It would also be based on three other "facts," according to Moore: the fact that the top figure was 5, the fact that the figure 5 together with all the lower ones were all the figures in the column, and the fact that 57 plus 5 equals 62. Similarly, my knowledge of the fact that Cambridge won, which I got by reading the paper, is based on knowledge which I had at the time, or just previously, of another fact: namely, the fact that "a certain paper contains a certain report," and perhaps some other facts as well.

Moore distinguishes two main senses in which our knowledge of one fact (Q) is *based on* our knowledge of some other fact (P). (i) There is first the case where Q is immediately based on P,[37] i.e., where P and Q occur within the *same* specious present.[38] To revert to the former illustration, my knowledge that the whole column came to 62 is immediately based on my knowledge that the total exclusive of the top figure came to 57, since the two occurred within the same specious present. (ii) There is, next, the case where Q is non-immediately based on P; that is, where P is

35. *Ibid.*, p. 23.
36. *Ibid.*, pp. 23–24.
37. 'Immediately', as it occurs in 'immediately based on' must not be confused with 'immediately' in 'immediately know'; ('immediate knowledge', etc.). All actualized knowledge, except mediate knowledge which I am discussing in this section, is immediate knowledge.
38. *Ibid.*, p. 27.

past relative to Q.[39] Suppose again that the next-to-top figure was 7. Then my knowledge that the whole came to 62 is based not only on my knowledge that the figures below the top one came to 57, but also on the knowledge on which *this* is based: namely, my knowledge that the sum excluding the top two figures is 50. Perhaps all these conclusions could still be reached within the same specious present, says Moore. But if we go far enough, we reach a knowledge upon which the final conclusion was based but which did *not* fall within the same specious present as this conclusion, a knowledge which was definitely *past,* relative to the conclusion. Hence, (ii) and (i) are different, and Moore holds that (ii) must be defined in terms of (i), but he does not indicate how this is to be done.[40]

V

I NOW TURN to the matter which I left unattended at the end of section III and to which I promised to return: namely, that of finding a suitable fourth condition which, when conjoined with Moore's other three conditions, provides a set of necessary conditions constituting a criterion of our knowledge of empirical propositions. Once again the first three conditions for X's knowing a proposition p to be true are:

(1) X directly apprehends p;
(2) X believes p;
(3) p is true.

One might suggest that the needed fourth condition ought to be:

(4) X has adequate evidence for p.[41]

But (4) may be ambiguous without some explication. For the reader may remember that I have already called attention to the fact that Moore objected to a condition similar to (4), namely, the condition that p must *follow from* some other proposition, on the grounds that this would lead to an infinite regress; and that, therefore, one cannot insist that *all* propositions must be known to be true evidentially, i.e., upon the basis of other propositions from which they follow. And I admit that if, by 'X has

39. *Ibid.,* p. 29.
40. *Ibid.,* pp. 29 ff.
41. This, of course, is no new discovery of mine! See e.g., John Hospers, *An Introduction to Philosophical Analysis* (New York: Prentice-Hall, 1953; 2d ed., 1967), pp. 148 f.

adequate evidence for *p'*, I meant '*X* knows some other empirical proposition(s) *q*, from which *p* follows (as a conclusion follows from premisses)', then this objection would be an appropriate one. But the latter is precisely what one would *not* mean by (4), and Moore's objection is the main reason *why* one would not mean that by (4). What, then, would one mean by (4)?

In order to answer the question I am going to distinguish three main kinds of knowledge and three corresponding kinds of statements. (This is not an exhaustive classification, as we shall see.) The three kinds of knowledge are:

(a) Necessary knowledge, or formal knowledge;
(b) Empirical knowledge, or knowledge proper (knowledge that);
(c) Apprehension, or knowledge by acquaintance.

The corresponding kinds of statements are:

(a′) Analytic (analytic proper plus tautological);
(b′) Synthetic (empirical in the common sense);
(c′) Acquaintance (e.g., sensing statements).

Examples of each of these kinds of statements are:

(a′) *AB* is *A*
$$[(p \supset q) \cdot p] \supset q$$
(b′) That is a chair.
Minetta (a cat) is on the roof.
(c′) I see blue.
I hear a scratching sound.

Before proceeding, a couple of comments are in order. First, I have for purposes of simplification limited my examples of (b′) to perceptual statements and similarly limited my examples of (c′) to sensing statements. This means that the adequacy of my four conditions will be demonstrated only with respect to perceptual claims. I am not certain that this is an actual limitation upon the view I am defending. I think that the four conditions will equally well constitute a criterion for knowledge of other empirical statements—historical assertions, etc.—but the illustration of the adequacy of the view I am maintaining for those would be much more complicated. Second, I have spoken above of three kinds of *state-*

ments—meaning by statements, declarative, assertive sentences—rather than propositions. My reason for so doing is that since a proposition is the meaning of a sentence, meaning by 'meaning' that which one understands by direct apprehension, it is not always appropriate to speak of analytic *propositions*. 'All red roses are red' could be called an analytic proposition, but 'All *AB* are *B*' could hardly be so called since it is a formal structure or schema of a proposition, rather than a proposition. Where sentences *do* express propositions, I shall talk of propositions. Third, I make no claims that the following account is a *complete* treatment of the problem at hand. Since several epistemological problems are involved—perception, memory, induction, etc.—an exhaustive solution would require a book. I merely set forth the following as a schematic suggestion as to what would be involved in an attempt toward a solution. Since this work is a study of Moore's epistemology and not an original treatise, I believe that this approach is justifiable.

Now let us return to a consideration of what one might plausibly mean by (4). By '*X* has adequate evidence for *p*', we cannot mean merely that *X* knows some other singular propositions (like those of [b']) to be true. For obviously we could always ask *X* how he knows *those* propositions to be true. And if he cites as evidence still *other* singular empirical propositions, then we can continue to ask how he knows *those* to be true. Hence, where *p* is an empirical proposition of the kind indicated, that is, a proposition stating that so and so is the case ('Minetta is on the roof', etc.), and where we are seeking the conditions for *knowing that* so and so (knowledge proper), the evidence which is cited can never be merely more knowledge that so and so; that is, we can never cite only further empirical propositions as constituting our evidence. What then can we cite as evidence? Obviously, we cannot cite analytic statements (or propositions) as evidence. We are left then with acquaintance propositions. Will these do as evidence? That is, can we find evidence for the truth of empirical propositions which consists solely of acquaintance propositions? This looks like a tempting possibility. But will it work? Is it possible to justify the view that all knowledge that so and so is the case, all knowledge proper, *rests on* knowledge by acquaintance?

Let us try an example and see if it works. An excellent one is already provided by Professor R. Chisholm in *Perceiving*.[42] I shall arrange some

---

42. (Ithaca: Cornell Univ. Press, 1957), pp. 55 ff.

quotations from Professor Chisholm's book into a running dialogue form. Consider a conversation between Jones and Smith who are riding through New Hampshire.

JONES: I see that that is Mt. Monadnock behind the trees.

SMITH: How do you know it's Monadnock?

JONES: I've been here many times before and I can *see* that it is.

SMITH: What makes you *think* that's Monadnock that you see? What reason do you have for *taking* that to be Monadnock?

JONES: I can see that the mountain is shaped like a wave and that there is a little cabin near the top. There is no other mountain answering that description within miles of here.

SMITH: What makes you think you see a cabin near the top?

JONES: I see that it's more or less rectangular and that it's dark blue. I remember that there's such a cabin on Monadnock. It isn't probable that that thing could be anything else.

SMITH: What makes you think that the cabin is blue?

JONES: Well, it *looks* blue from here. And if a thing that far away looks blue in this light then in all probability, it is blue.

SMITH: What makes you think something appears blue?

JONES: I am appeared to in a way which is blue.

SMITH: What makes you think you are appeared to in a way which is blue?

JONES: I just am.

Let us examine this conversation with respect to our problem. (My discussion will only partially parallel Professor Chisholm's.) Jones first utters an empirical statement ('That is Mt. Monadnock')—empirical in the sense which I designated above, whereby perceptual statements, for example, are empirical, but sensing statements (and, of course, analytic statements) are not. When pressed for evidence, Jones utters another empirical perceptual statement. But he also does more. He utters an additional empirical statement which is *not* a perceptual statement, but one which supplies additional information pertinent to the question asked, one which is based on memory. And he cites *both* the second perceptual statement ('I see that it is') and the independent information statement ('I've been here many times'), both of which are empirical (though the second is not perceptual) as evidence for the first empirical (and in this case perceptual) statement. This happens several times, so that we have the following.

QUESTIONS	PERCEPTUAL STATEMENTS	STATEMENTS OF INDEPENDENT INFORMATION
	Begin here:	
	That is Monadnock.	
How do you know?	I see it is.	I've been here before.
What makes you think you see Monadnock?	It has a cabin near the top (etc.)	No other mountain near here has a cabin (etc.)
What makes you think you see a cabin?	It's dark blue.	I remember that Monadnock has a dark blue cabin.

But notice that the next question—'What makes you think that the cabin is blue?'—provides a different sort of statement in reply. Instead of a perceptual statement, Jones utters a statement which is not *obviously* perceptual—'It *looks* blue'. Similarly, Jones's new statement of independent information is different from all the others which he presented. All of the preceding were singular existential statements. The new independent information is a *generalization:* 'Anything that looks blue from that distance and this light (probably) is blue'. The evidence heretofore consisted of a perceptual statement and a singular independent information statement (there could have been more than one of each), both of which are empirical statements. This time the evidence consists of an ambiguous statement (it may be a perceptual statement or a sensing statement or both) plus, as independent information, a generalization. And when his statement, 'It looks blue', is challenged, note that Jones utters a statement which is clearly a *sensing* statement: 'I am appeared to in a way which is blue', which might be translated in Professor Chisholm's terms as 'I am appeared to bluely' or 'I sense bluely'; or in more traditional terms, 'I sense a blue appearance'. And note that he utters *no* statement of independent information this time. Finally, when Jones's sensing statement is challenged, when asked 'What makes you think you are appeared to bluely?', he answers 'I just am'. The latter is simply a repetition of what he said just previously.

I think that this illustration *suggests* an answer to the problem at hand.[43] I have been trying to find, first, a suitable fourth condition which, when conjoined with the other three (provided by Moore), constitutes a criterion for our knowledge of empirical propositions (here of the perceptual sort). I mentioned that it might be 'X has adequate evidence for p'. Hence, I have been trying to discover, second, what constitutes adequate evidence. One possibility suggested itself: in order to avoid an infinite regress, evidence for an empirical proposition must consist of acquaintance propositions (in this case, sensing statements). And I have been concerned, third, to see whether this answer is tenable. Our example shows that this answer is acceptable as a *part* of what we mean by having adequate evidence, but that acquaintance propositions cannot constitute the *whole* of evidence which we deem adequate. For, as we have seen, at one point we had to introduce a generalization as well as acquaintance propositions.[44] In this case it was a generalization about things appearing in a certain way in this light and from that distance (whatever this and that may be in the situation at hand). We might then hold: Adequate evidence for empirical propositions consists of acquaintance propositions, plus one or more generalizations (and statements of memory, etc.). If so, it is false to say simply that our knowledge that so and so is the case (knowledge of empirical propositions) rests solely upon knowledge by acquaintance. It rests, among other things, upon knowledge by acquaintance *plus* knowledge by generalization, or knowledge of certain general principles. And it is the latter factor which prevents empirical propositions from having indubitable certainty. If we could cite solely acquaintance propositions as evidence for empirical propositions, if in this case we could "reduce" statements about material objects to specific statements about sense-data, then one might hold that empirical propositions could be known to be certainly true. But it is reasonable to believe that we cannot perform this feat, as I have tried to show. We will always require (among other things) some generalization or other which introduces the factor of probability, since generalizations themselves are only probable statements. But I see no reason to be dismayed over this. Some philosophers have long noted that some statements may be known to be *certainly* true, whereas others may *not*. But to say that the latter may not be known with certainty does not mean that they cannot be known at all. Jones was quite sure that he saw Mt. Monadnock. But realizing that he has some-

43. I do not mean to assert that it is an exact account of what happens every time.
44. This involves us in the problem of Induction. Statements of memory also entered in.

times suffered from illusions, etc., he will perhaps be cautious with respect to at least some perceptual judgments and admit that it is logically possible for him to be wrong this (or any) time, even though he is quite sure that he is not—quite sure because he has all the evidence which one can reasonably expect him to have in his situation.

(N.B. I have not in this chapter gone into a discussion of Moore's account of sensing and perceptual statements, or if you will, of his views regarding our knowledge of sense-data and of the external world and of the relation between the two. These matters will be taken up in Part Three.)

VII

Consciousness and

Knowledge

MOORE'S MAIN CONTRIBUTIONS to the philosophy of mind
have been held to be: (1) the distinguishing of the act of consciousness and the object of consciousness; and (2) the emphasis upon
mental *acts* rather than *the mind*. I shall discuss each of these issues in this
chapter. Moore is quite clear on the first, but his discussion of the second
is more problematic and not always consistent.

I

THROUGHOUT MANY OF HIS MAJOR PAPERS Moore vehemently insists upon
the recognition of a distinction which, he thought, many philosophers
overlooked: namely, that of the *act* of consciousness from its *object*. His
concern to distinguish the two was apparently so great that he hammered
at the issue in three important papers, all written within a short period
(1902–3),[1] the most famous of which is "The Refutation of Idealism." But

1. "Mr. McTaggart's 'Studies in Hegelian Cosmology,'" *PAS*, II (1901–2), 177–214;
"Experience and Empiricism," *PAS*, III (1902–3), 80–95; "Refut.," pp. 433–53.

he made the same point in various later works as well.[2] Since the discussion—on this one point—follows pretty much the same pattern in all three papers (for once Moore is consistent![3]), I shall here consider only his comments in "The Refutation of Idealism." Needless to say, I am not here concerned to show whether or not Moore refuted Idealism. I am only concerned to bring out the act-object dichotomy. However, I shall keep it in its context.

Moore maintains that a premiss fundamental to *all* Idealist arguments that whatever is real is so only because of "its presence as an inseparable aspect of a *sentient experience*," is: *'Esse is percipi'*. He takes *'percipi'* in the wider sense of 'to be experienced', rather than 'to be perceived'. He holds that Idealists assert that "whatever is experienced, is necessarily so," that being and being experienced are "necessarily connected," that "whatever is is also experienced."[4] Moore maintains that the source of this thesis is the Idealists' failure to distinguish between a sensation or an idea and its object.[5] He asks us to consider the question "What is a sensation or idea?" Take a sensation of blue and one of green. What do they have in common? How do they differ? The common element is *consciousness,* "in respect of which all sensations are alike." But since a sensation of blue is obviously different from a sensation of green, there must be a second factor of any sensation, something "in respect of which one sensation differs from another."[6] This second element Moore calls the *object* of a sensation. Hence, in every sensation (or idea) we have two distinct elements: consciousness and the object of consciousness. "This must be so if the sensation of blue and the sensation of green, though different in one respect, are alike in another: blue is one object of sensation and green is another, and consciousness, which both sensations have in common, is different from either."[7]

We may perhaps see this more clearly in the following way. Sometimes, for any individual, the sensation of blue exists. Sometimes it does not. A question arises: When the sensation of blue exists, is it consciousness alone which exists, or blue alone, or both? All three alternatives are different.

2. For example, "The Character of Cognitive Acts," *PAS*, XXI (1920–21), 132–40; "The Subject Matter of Psychology," *PAS*, X (1909–10), 36–62; "Facts and Propositions," *PASS*, VII (1927), 171–206, reprinted in *PP*, pp. 60–88.

3. With one exception, to be noted later.

4. "Refut.," pp. 12, 16.

5. *Ibid.*, p. 14.

6. *Ibid.*, p. 17.

7. *Ibid.*, p. 17. Cf. "Mr. McTaggart's 'Studies in Hegelian Cosmology,'" p. 187.

Now one thing is certain. Consciousness does exist. For if I say that a sensation of blue and a sensation of green both exist, what I mean is: that which is common to both exists, i.e., consciousness, by virtue of which both are sensations. In other words a sensation is a case of knowing or being aware of something or other. Hence, if we know that a sensation of blue exists, we know that our awareness of blue exists. But this awareness must be different from blue, for blue is what the awareness is of.[8]

Hence, we have eliminated the possibility that blue alone exists. Moore holds that the plausibility of this view stems from the fact that the element of consciousness is transparent. "That which makes the sensation of blue a mental fact seems to escape us . . . we look through it and see nothing but the blue."[9] That is, while we can hold both *blue* and *green* "before our minds" and compare them, we cannot in any similar manner hold consciousness and blue before our minds in order to compare them. "The moment we try to fix our attention upon consciousness and to see *what,* distinctly, it is, it seems to vanish: it seems as if we had before us a mere emptiness. When we try to introspect the sensation of blue, all we can see is the blue: the other element is as if it were diaphanous."[10] Yet it *can* be distinguished if we "look attentatively enough."

What about the alternative that consciousness alone exists? That consciousness *does* exist, the Idealist recognizes. But he ought also to recognize that since consciousness does exist, it would be self-contradictory to say that the existence of blue is the same thing as the sensation of blue, since such a statement asserts that blue is the same thing as blue together with consciousness or that it is the same thing as consciousness alone. In short, to identify blue or any other object of a sensation with the sensation is a self-contradictory error. It is the error of identifying a part (say, blue) with the whole of which it is a part (blue and consciousness) or with the other part of that same whole (consciousness). Hence, the existence of blue is not the same as the sensation of blue; what is experienced is not identical with the experience of it; the *esse* (of anything) is *not percipi.* The existence of blue is distinct from the existence of the sensation. Blue might, therefore, exist and yet the sensation of blue not exist.[11]

Thus, says Moore, since we are justified in distinguishing an awareness

8. "Refut.," pp. 17–18, 26.
9. *Ibid.,* p. 20.
10. *Ibid.,* p. 25.
11. *Ibid.,* pp. 17–19.

from its object, knowledge of a thing from the thing known; both the awareness and the object (consciousness and blue, e.g.) exist. "In every sensation or idea we must distinguish two elements, (1) the 'object,' or that in which one differs from another; and (2) 'consciousness,' or that which all have in common—that which makes them sensations or mental facts." [12] Hence, what some, persuaded by the Idealist philosophy, have held to be a predicament is none at all.

There is . . . no question of how we are to 'get outside the circle of our own ideas and sensations.' Merely to have a sensation is already to *be* outside that circle. It is to know something which is as truly and really *not* a part of *my* experience, as anything which I can ever know.[13]

Finally, Moore holds that once we recognize the nature of being aware *of* something, and that it is involved in *every* experience, "from the merest sensation to the most developed perception or reflexion," and that the object of any awareness is independent of our awareness of it, then we have reason to believe that material objects, too, exist apart from our awareness of their existence.[14]

I mentioned above (in a footnote) that there was one exception to Moore's persistent defense of this view. It occurs—like many other changes of mind—in one of his last writings, his "Reply." In a paper entitled, "Moore's 'The Refutation of Idealism',"[15] C. J. Ducasse argues against Moore's position. Moore had maintained, as we noted above, that in no case is the *esse* of anything *percipi*, i.e., in "no case does it follow from the fact that a thing of a certain kind exists that that thing is perceived." Ducasse writes:

As against Professor Moore, I believe there is a certain class of cases concerning which it is true that *esse* is *percipi*. . . . I think it can be definitely proved that, so far as this class is concerned, Professor Moore's argument does not prove, as it claims to do—or even render more probable than not—that *esse* is *percipi* is false. I shall, however, try to show not only this but also that, for this class of cases, *esse* is *percipi* is true.[16]

---

12. *Ibid.*, p. 20. Cf. "The Subject Matter of Psychology," pp. 38 ff.
13. "Refut.," p. 27. Cf. "The Character of Cognitive Acts," *PAS*, XXI (1920–21), pp. 134, 137.
14. "Refut.," pp. 29–30. I shall not now pause to consider this last remark. See below, Chaps. IX–X.
15. *PGEM*, pp. 225–51.
16. *Ibid.*, p. 225.

Moore's reply is brief: "I may say at once that, on this point, I now agree with Mr. Ducasse and Berkeley, and hold that that early paper of mine was wrong. As an argument for my present view I should give the assertions that a toothache certainly cannot exist without being felt, but that, on the other hand, the moon certainly can exist without being perceived." [17] Hence, Moore at this point holds that there is a class of things for which it is true that *esse* is *percipi,* another class of things for which '*esse* is *percipi*' is false.

So much for the first of the two topics to be dealt with in this chapter, Moore's distinction of the act of consciousness from its object. I now turn to the second issue: Moore's inclination, at times, to emphasize mental *acts* rather than a *mind.*

II

AN INTERESTING PASSAGE occurs in the opening pages of Moore's 1910-11 lectures (*SMPP*). It may be remembered that in his discussion of "What Is Philosophy?", Moore maintained that the task of the most important branch of philosophy is to give a general description of the whole universe. Moore attempts such a description from the standpoint of common sense and lists, as the first kind of things which there are in the universe, material objects of all sorts. Then Moore writes:

But now, besides material objects, we believe also that there are in the Universe certain phenomena very different from material objects. In short, we believe that we men, besides having bodies, also have *minds;* and one of the chief things which we mean, by saying we have *minds,* is, I think, this: namely, that we perform certain mental acts or acts of consciousness. That is to say, we see and hear and feel and remember and imagine and think and believe and desire and like and dislike and will and love and are angry and afraid, etc. These things that we do are all of them mental acts—acts of mind or acts of *consciousness:* whenever we do any of them, we are conscious of something in some way or other: and it seems to me that the thing of which we are most certain when we say we are certain that we have minds, is that we do these things—that we perform these acts of consciousness.[18]

Two things are worthy of note in this passage. The *first* (second in Moore's passage) is merely touched upon here: the assertion that when-

17. "Reply," p. 653.
18. *SMPP,* p. 4.

ever we "perform" an act of consciousness, we are conscious of something in some way or other. Since I already discussed this issue in section I, I shall not say any more regarding it. But I do wish to elaborate in this section on the second thing that Moore says.

Note again that Moore's discussion proceeds from a *common-sense standpoint*. Speaking commonsensically, we all say that there are in the universe at least two kinds of things, material objects and minds, and that the two are different. But note also that Moore is not content to remain at the common-sense standpoint nor in this case to carry over the common-sensical statement into a philosophical use. He is concerned, one might say, to *explicate* what 'There are minds' or 'Minds exist' may be reasonably taken to mean if we take these statements as *philosophical* propositions. He, therefore, wishes to state "one of the chief things which we mean, by saying we have *minds*." And he holds that one of the main things we mean by saying this is: "that we perform certain mental acts or acts of consciousness." That is, Moore does not attempt to *argue* that *minds* exist. He accepts the fact as a commonsensical assertion. But, taken as a philosophical assertion, he *seems* to suggest that it needs explication. The explication is given in terms of acts of consciousness. And, in fact, throughout the remainder of the chapter Moore carefully says 'acts of consciousness' rather than 'minds'. However, in later chapters of the same book he reverts to talk about minds, and not merely in a commonsensical way.

One might be inclined to view this passage as an instance of reductional analysis. In this case Moore would be suggesting that all statements about minds must be reduced to statements about acts of consciousness. Just as other reductional analysts tried to reduce statements about physical objects to statements about sense-data, so Moore is in this view doing essentially the same thing with respect to minds. I think that to consider the passage quoted above as an instance of reductional analysis would be a rather violent distortion of Moore's remarks. Moore in no way suggests that a reduction can be performed. He is not saying that every statement containing 'mind' is translatable into some other statement containing only (descriptive) terms which refer to or involve reference to acts of consciousness. What he is suggesting, I think, is that taken philosophically (not commonsensically) the expressions, 'mind', 'There are minds', 'We have minds', etc., need explication. The explication consists of statements in *other* terms, which elucidate what might reasonably be meant by someone who insists that there are minds, statements in which 'acts of consciousness' or expressions denoting particular kinds of acts of consciousness (believing, desiring, etc.) occur. Such an explication does not consist of an actual construction of the sort which phenomenalists once tried to provide for physical objects, minds, etc. It is much more schematic. By calling Moore's approach "schematic," I simply mean that he is not concerned to provide either a strict definition or a set of reduction sentences for "mental" terms and expressions. He, rather, gives an explication of such terms by talking, often at great length, about how such terms are used. The explication uses non-mental terms in order to indicate without strict precision what mental terms can be taken to mean.[19]

Someone may suggest that even my interpretation reads too much into this passage. I admit that we do not have a full-blown development of this view in the passage. But I believe it is there, although without elaboration.

In almost every other paper and book, Moore seems to have a more substantialist view of mind. This is true even when he stresses acts of consciousness—these are the acts of *a mind*.[20] He nowhere continues the discussion which goes along the lines of the passage just quoted. In one paper, however, he is strongly inclined to believe that the mind is a doubtful entity. This is a paper written in 1909, "The Subject Matter of Psychology."[21] In the first part of the paper Moore classifies all the kinds of "entities which are undoubtedly mental." These are: (1) *acts* of consciousness, (2) certain *qualities* of acts of consciousness (by which different acts of consciousness differ from one another), and (3) collections of acts of consciousness which have any sort of unity. The second part of the paper deals with "doubtful mental entities." The first entity which he considers under this heading is "the mind itself." Moore's discussion is rather puzzling. He first says:

I do not doubt that the mind is a mental entity. I do not doubt, for instance, that I have a mind; that there is such a thing as my mind; and that it is a mental entity. But all that I mean when I say this, is that I am quite sure that

---

19. Cf. Prof. Bergmann's discussion of the sketch- and blueprint-theorists: Gustav Bergmann, *The Metaphysics of Logical Positivism* (New York: Longmans, Green & Co., 1954), pp. 87 ff. See also G. Bergmann, *Meaning and Existence* (Madison: Univ. of Wisconsin Press, 1959); and *Logic and Reality* (Madison: Univ. of Wisconsin Press, 1964). For a discussion of definitions and reduction sentences, see C. Hempel, *Fundamentals of Concept Formation in Empirical Science* (Chicago: Univ. of Chicago Press, 1952), pp. 2 ff.

20. See almost any page of *SMPP*, for example.

21. "The Subject Matter of Psychology," pp. 36–62.

when I or other people talk about 'my mind,' we are talking about *something which really is and which is mental;* that 'my mind' is the *name of some entity* or other, and that a mental one. What I do doubt about, in the case of my mind, is what sort of an entity it is: in particular whether it is an entity of one of the kinds which I have already described; or whether it is a new kind of entity different from any of these, and which is also 'mental' in a different sense from that in which any of them are 'mental' (italics added).[22]

This is not just commonsensical talk about the mind. Moore is looking for a philosophical account of the mind and is convinced that the mind really exists, although he is not sure about what its nature is.

But in the very next paragraph, Moore writes:

There is a view (and I think Hume held it, for one) that my mind merely consists in the sum of all those mental acts, which are related to one another in the way which we describe by calling them all 'mine'; including, of course, any other entities (if there are any), beside mental acts, which may be related to my mental acts in the same way in which they are related to one another. And I cannot be sure that this view is not a true one. I am, in fact, much more sure that there are such things as my mental acts, than that there is any entity distinct from these, which could be called my mind.[23]

In this case the mind would consist of a collection of acts of consciousness and, hence, be one of the mental entities referred to above. Moore continues: "In favor of this view I have to urge the difficulty that I find in discovering any entity, other than my mental acts, which could be my mind."[24] But Moore finds arguments against this view. We certainly talk, he says, as if it were my mind which hears, thinks, wills, etc., in short as if "my mind were some entity, *of* which my mental acts are acts; as if it were identical with the Ego, the 'me,' the subject, which is conscious whenever I am conscious."[25] In Hume's view whenever I say that *I,* or my mind, am seeing, thinking, etc., we would have to hold that what we mean is merely that my seeing, thinking, etc., are each among the mental acts which constitute my "mind." Moore finds that this is not what he means by such expressions. "It seems to me that, when I say that *I* am seeing this room now . . . I mean to assert quite a different relation between me and my seeing, than that the latter is *a part* of me—one

22. *Ibid.,* p. 52.
23. *Ibid.*
24. *Ibid.*
25. *Ibid.,* p. 53.

member of a collection of acts which constitutes me." [26] Furthermore, says Moore, in Hume's view, there is no way of accounting for the kind of relation which all my mental acts have to one another which constitutes them mine, which distinguishes them from the mental acts of other people. "What I seem to know, when I know that all my mental acts are mental acts of mine, is that they all have a peculiar relation to some other entity which is me." [27]

Hence, Moore concludes that "there is something to be said for the view that *I* am an entity, distinct from every one of my mental acts and from all of them put together." [28] But, he says, even if I am such an entity, it does not follow that this entity is a *mental* one. There is another view, against which Moore says he can find no conclusive arguments; namely,

that this entity which hears and sees and feels and thinks is some part of *my body*. I cannot see anything conclusive against Locke's view that matter may be capable of being conscious; and hence that it may be my body which is conscious whenever I am conscious. . . . I myself should not, then, be a mental entity: I should be my body.[29]

He finally suggests that we might combine this with Hume's view and say that my mind is the collection of my mental acts and what makes them mine is the fact that they all have a common relation to my body.[30] Which of these alternatives he finally accepts, Moore does not say. But he holds that the view that my mind is a mental entity, distinct from my mental acts, or the collection of them, is one acceptable alternative, against which he can find no conclusive arguments.

I have not, and shall not, here go into Moore's complete concept of mind. I have dealt only with certain facets of it which are relevant to the present chapter and its position in Part Two.

III

LET US IN CONCLUSION see more explicitly what Moore has to say about the relationship of consciousness to knowledge. Is every act of knowing one in which consciousness is involved, and vice versa? As we have seen, Moore holds, rightly I think, that in one sense of 'know'—the dispositional sense —a subject may be said to know something or other, even though he is

26. *Ibid.*
27. *Ibid.*, p. 54.
28. *Ibid.*
29. *Ibid.*
30. *Ibid.*

not conscious of any object, and even though he is not conscious at all. Hence, not all knowing involves consciousness.[31]

But then does all consciousness involve knowledge? In some passages Moore suggests that this is the case. But in others he distinguishes "differences in the mode of consciousness." [32] He here contrasts various mental acts: apprehending, knowing, believing, willing, etc. Hence, according to Moore, knowing is only one way of being conscious. At times Moore's thesis is that not all consciousness involves knowledge.[33]

But the issue is a little more complex than this. As we have seen, there are, for Moore, several kinds of knowledge, one of which, dispositional knowledge, is quickly dismissed by Moore. There remain: apprehension, propositional knowledge, and indirect knowledge. First, Moore must deny that all consciousness involves knowledge when 'knowledge' refers solely to propositional knowledge or indirect knowledge. For we are often conscious of something when we do not know some proposition to be true, directly or indirectly. We may, for example, believe a proposition to be true, without knowing it to be so. We still have apprehension to consider. For Moore, all consciousness involves some form of apprehension. Better: every act of consciousness is, at least, in part, an act of apprehension, although *some* acts of consciousness may involve more than mere apprehension. Let 'p' be a sentence, expressing a proposition p, which refers to a state of affairs P. Then whether I believe p, or am sure about p, or know p to be true, or desire P, or will P, or perceive P, or think about p or P, etc., I am directly or indirectly apprehending either p or P, although in some cases I may be doing something else in addition to apprehending. For example, I may be knowing that p is true, i.e., that p "corresponds" to P, or that there is some state of affairs P which constitutes a verification of p.

We may say then that, for Moore, every act of consciousness is also a noetic act in the sense that at least apprehension is involved. This is true even of an act of sensing. If I sense, say, a red datum, then I am "performing" an act of apprehension; I am being acquainted with that datum; I am knowing something in *one* sense of knowing, even though I may not be knowing in some other sense; e.g., I may not know that the red I sense is a quality of some particular physical object.

31. See Chap. VI, sec. I.
32. Cf. "The Subject Matter of Psychology," pp. 49 f.
33. See also *SMPP*, Chaps. XIII, XIV.

VIII

Truth and Falsity

I N CHAPTER VI, I discussed the various kinds of knowledge which
Moore distinguishes. Chapter VII dealt with the relationship of consciousness to knowledge and stressed what might be called the "subjective" side of knowledge. I turn now to the "objective" side of our problem,
the question: What is it that makes a belief or assertion true or false? [1]
The question has often been phrased more grandiosely: What is truth,
and what is falsehood? What are the criteria of truth?

The matter of falsehood limits the area of investigation. For it is not
appropriate to speak of falsity or error with respect to *all* of Moore's kinds
of knowledge. For example, there is no need to introduce the matter of
falsity into a discussion of apprehension or knowledge by acquaintance.
There can be no erroneous apprehension (at least when the apprehension
is of things). I either apprehend something—say, a red sense-datum—or I
do not. But if I do apprehend it, then in apprehending it I know it to be
what it is. It would be rather peculiar to wonder if I might be wrong.

1. Actually, the present discussion involves both "subjective" and "objective" aspects.

Thus there is, one might say, an indubitableness about apprehension. Similarly, a discussion of falsity is inappropriate with respect to dispositional knowledge. I either know *how* to do something, say tie a square knot, or I do not. I may not succeed in tying it every time I try. Occasionally I may come up with a granny. But if I can tie a square knot, say nine out of ten times, then most people would say that I know *how* to tie one. Or even if I can only tie one every other time, there is still a sense in which I know how to tie one, although I am not very good at it. On a particular occasion when I tied a granny, someone might say that I *did* it *wrong,* but he would hardly speak of my performing a falsehood or being in a state of error. He would just wait for me to try it again.[2] The issue of *truth and falsity,* then, does not come up with respect to apprehension or dispositional knowledge. It *does* come up, however, with respect to propositional knowledge, knowledge that so and so is the case. It does so because we may believe or say what is false as well as what is true. Hence, the question arises: What distinguishes a true belief or proposition from one which is false? By this question, however, I mean *not* 'How are we to go about finding out which beliefs or propositions are true and which are false? How do we verify our assertions?', but 'What is it that makes any proposition true or false? What is meant by saying of a proposition that it is true or that it is false? What is the nature of truth?'

In one of his earlier works Russell once stated that there are three conditions which any theory of truth must fulfill. (1) It must allow truth to have an opposite, namely, error. (2) It must make truth, and falsehood, a property of beliefs. (3) It must make truth and falsehood dependent upon the relation of beliefs to things outside of the beliefs.[3] I think that these conditions make up an adequate criterion for a theory of truth, and later I shall judge Moore's theory partly on the basis of how well it fulfills these conditions.

I shall begin my discussion with the following question. In Moore's words: "What . . . is the difference between true and false belief?"[4] Moore holds that by starting with an investigation of beliefs, we may perhaps be led to some criterion which distinguishes those which are true

---

2. I believe that the illustration comes from Professor Gilbert Ryle in *The Concept of Mind* (London: Hutchison & Co., 1949).

3. *The Problems of Philosophy* (Oxford: Oxford Univ. Press, 1912; 2d ed., 1946), pp. 120–21.

4. *SMPP,* p. 249.

from those which are false and that, by so doing, we can come to know "what truth is" or "what is the difference between truth and falsehood."

I

LIKE MOORE, I shall begin with a consideration of *false* beliefs. Moore finds that the case of false beliefs, like that of imaginings, presents a very puzzling state of affairs. Suppose first, he says, that a man believes that God exists, and suppose that his belief is true. If his belief is true, then it is a fact that God exists—God's existence has reality. If God does not exist, his belief is false. Similarly, with respect to any belief. Hence, one might be inclined to say that the difference between true and false beliefs, generally, is: Where a belief is true, *what* is believed *is,* or is a fact, or is the case, etc.; where a belief is false, what is believed is not, or is not a fact. But now suppose that the man believes that God exists and that the belief is actually false. Here, as before, it is natural to say that what he believes is *that God exists,* or in other words, *God's existence.* In believing that God exists he believes *something,* that there *is* such a thing as what he believes in, i.e., God's existence.[5] Hence, it seems that whether his belief is true or false, there *is* such a thing as God's existence. If he believes *truly* that God exists, then God does exist and there is such a thing as God's existence, which is what he believes. But if he believes *falsely* that God exists, then God does *not* exist; yet there still *is* such a thing as God's existence, for this is still what he believes. We were inclined to say that where a belief is true, what is believed *is,* or is a fact. But now we seem to be required to say that even where a belief is false, what is believed *is,* or is a fact.[6] And yet, in another sense, it *is not,* or is not a fact—which is a contradiction. Of course, this troubling circumstance does not affect our ordinary ability to distinguish between true and false beliefs. Hence, even if there *is* such a thing as *what* is believed, when a belief is *false,* what is believed, we would say, *is not* in the *same* sense as it would be if the belief were true. Are there then two senses of *is,* or of *being,* so that when a belief is true, what is believed is in only one sense? Or must we distinguish, say, existence and being, so that when X believes truly that God exists, God exists and has being; whereas in the other case, God merely has being?

5. 'Thing' perhaps sounds peculiar. One might better say 'state of affairs', 'actuality', etc.
6. The reader will recognize that this is another instance of the Pegasus controversy, except that Moore's discussion is in terms of sentences rather than names.

"How do you answer the argument which seems to prove that what is believed, whether truly or falsely, in any case certainly must be?"[7]

Let us take an instance (the illustration is Moore's) of a clearly *false* belief. Smith believes right now that we at the present hour have gone out to hear a brass band, whereas we actually did *not* go out to hear the band and are *not* now, in fact, hearing any brass band at all. Smith then falsely believes that we are hearing the noise of a brass band. His mistake seems to lie in this: Whereas he believes that we are hearing the noise of a brass band, the fact is that we are not hearing it. All that is necessary to make the belief true is that we should be hearing it. This states correctly the difference between truth and falsity in the case of this particular belief. "What I want to ask is: Supposing that it is a correct statement of the difference, what exactly is the difference that has been stated?"[8] Two things seem clear, says Moore. First, since the belief is false, there simply *is not* in the universe one thing which would be in it if it were true. Second, this thing which is not in the universe is the fact which would be if we were now hearing the noise of a brass band, the fact which would consist in our actually now hearing it.[9] These two points, says Moore, suggest a "definition" of truth and falsity. It is this:

To say of this belief that it is true would be to say of it that the fact to which it refers *is*—that there is such a fact in the Universe as the fact to which it refers; while to say of it that it is false is to say of it that *the fact to which it refers simply is not*—that there is no such fact in the Universe.[10]

Applying this to all beliefs, we might say generally: "To say that a belief is true is to say always that *the fact to which it refers is* or has being, while to say of a belief that it is false is to say always, that the fact to which it refers, is not or has *no* being."[11]

But, says Moore, this definition is not adequate because it leaves one point obscure: What is meant by 'the fact to which a belief refers'? Moore says: Every true belief is so related to one fact, and one fact only, that we have to use the name of the fact in naming the belief. Hence, we might say: the fact to which a belief refers is always the fact which has the

7. *SMPP*, p. 251.
8. *Ibid.*, p. 254.
9. *Ibid.*, p. 255. 'Belief' throughout the present discussion, of course, means 'that which is believed'.
10. *Ibid.*, p. 255.
11. *Ibid.*, p. 256. Cf. Aristotle *Metaphysics*, IV, 7.

same name as the *name* we have to use in naming the belief.[12] For example, suppose Jones believes that lions exist. Then we "name" his belief by expressions like 'that lions exist', or 'the existence of lions', etc. But if we want to name the fact to which the belief refers, we have to do so by using the same expressions. Jones's belief is the belief *that lions exist,* and the fact to which it refers is the fact *that lions exist.* Now one might be inclined to say that this provides a new definition of a true belief: a true belief is one such that there is in the universe a fact which has the same name. But, Moore notes, this will not do, for then no belief could be true until it had a name. Hence, we must stay with our first definition of truth and find some other relation which obtains between a true belief and a fact, other than having the same name, a relation which is meant when we say of a fact that it is *the* fact to which a belief refers.[13]

Before continuing I cannot help but mention that the notion of naming facts is, as Russell has suggested, an odd one. Russell maintained that propositions are not names for facts because there are two propositions "corresponding" to each fact. Suppose that the fact is: Socrates is dead. Then two propositions are possible, depending upon the knowledge possessed by various subjects. These are: 'Socrates is dead' and 'Socrates is not dead'. In a different sense of 'corresponds' from that of Moore's, Russell holds that these two propositions correspond to the same fact: i.e., there is only *one* fact in the world which both makes the first proposition true and the second one false. Thus the relation of a proposition to a fact is different from the relation of a name to a thing. A proposition may have either of two relations to a fact: "being true" to the fact or "being false" to the fact. But a name can have only one relation to what it names. A name can just name a particular thing. If it does not, it is only a noise, not a name. It cannot be a name without that *one* relation. But a proposition is still a proposition, even if it is false.[14]

To return to Moore's discussion: What then is the *relation* which holds between a true belief and the fact to which it refers? Take our case of the brass band. Here we know very well what the fact would be like, that fact which would *be* if Smith's belief were true. To know how this fact, if there were such a fact, would be *related* to the particular belief in question

---

12. *SMPP*, p. 256.
13. *Ibid.*, p. 258.
14. "The Philosophy of Logical Atomism," *Logic and Knowledge,* ed. R. Marsh (New York: Macmillan, 1956), Lecture I.

we have only, it seems, to discover what the *belief itself* is like. Very well, if some person were believing now that we are hearing the noise of a brass band, in what would this belief consist? What is the correct analysis of this belief? One alternative which has been suggested is this. It has been held that in the case of every belief, whether true or false, we must distinguish two constituents: the *act* of belief and the *object* of belief, or *what* is believed. The act of belief is the same in all cases. What distinguishes cases is that the objects are different. The object of belief is, in all cases, *a proposition*. A proposition is what is expressed by certain forms of words, namely, sentences. It is what we hold before our minds when we do not merely read or hear a sentence, but understand it. It is the *meaning* of a sentence. According to this view, the object of belief, the proposition, is something which *is,* something which really is in the universe, in *all* cases, whether the belief be true or false. Suppose that Mortimer believes *both* (a) that lions exist and (b) that griffins exist. Then there is such a thing as *that lions exist* and there is such a thing as *that griffins exist,* for both are objects of belief. But, of course, lions (spatio-temporal objects of flesh and blood, etc.) exist, whereas griffins do not. Hence, we have to say in this view that when the belief is true, there are in the universe both the proposition that lions exist and the fact that lions exist; and when a belief is false, there is in the universe only the first of these.

Now what theory of truth does this analysis of belief suggest? According to Moore, it is this: Where a belief is true, the proposition believed not only is, or has being; it also has another "simple unanalyzable property" which may be called 'truth'.

'Truth,' therefore, would, on this view, be a simply unanalyzable property which is possessed by some propositions and not by others. The propositions which don't possess it, and which therefore we call false *are* or 'have being' just as much as those which *do;* only they just have *not* got this additional property of being 'true.' [15]

Moore then raises an objection to this view, an objection which strikes me as rather odd upon the basis of his prevailing views. It is an objection to "the supposition that there are such things as propositions at all, and that belief consists merely in an attitude of mind towards these supposed entities." [16] Moore asks us to consider what happens when a man enter-

15. *SMPP*, p. 261.
16. *Ibid.*, p. 263.

tains a false belief. "It doesn't seem as if his belief consisted merely in his having a relation to some object which certainly *is*. It seems rather as if the thing he was believing, the object of his belief, were just *the* fact which certainly is *not*—which certainly is not, because his belief is false." [17] But, as Moore notes, a difficulty now arises. For if the object of belief *is not,* if there is no such thing, then it is impossible for him to have any relation to it. For a relation to hold between two things, both of them must be. How then is it possible for anyone to believe in a thing which has no being? This is the difficulty which arises if you say that a false belief does *not* consist in a relation between the believer and something which is, a proposition. Moore confesses that he does not see a clear solution of the difficulty, but he is, nevertheless, now inclined to hold that this is what we must say. The relation of belief holds even though one of the terms has no being. And he thinks that certain things can be mentioned which make his view plausible. What are they?

First, Moore now talks about *sentences* (forms of words) and warns that whenever we have before us a sentence which *seems* to express a relation between two objects, we must not always assume that the names which seem to be names of objects between which some relation holds are really names of any objects at all. Let us go back to the brass band. We can certainly conceive the "hypothesis" that we are not now hearing the brass band, or that we *are* hearing it for that matter (though, in fact, we are not). In merely conceiving it without believing it, the very same difficulty arises as in the case of false belief. Take the *sentence* 'We are now conceiving the hypothesis of our being now actually hearing a brass band'. This sentence *seems* to state that there is a relation, that of conceiving, which obtains between us and the object named 'our now hearing the noise of a brass band'. But in this case, there is nothing which that "name" names—we are not now hearing that noise. Hence, we must conclude (1) that when we now say 'We are now conceiving the hypothesis of our being now hearing the noise of a brass band', the sentence does *not* express a relation between us and an object named 'our being now hearing the noise of a brass band'; and (2) that the form of words 'our being now hearing the noise of a brass band' is in this case *not* a name for anything at all. The situation is precisely the same in cases of *believing* as in those of (imaginary) conceiving. In some cases, namely, in the cases of

17. *Ibid.*

127

false beliefs, when we believe a thing, there really is no such thing as that which we are *said* to believe. In those cases the words which *seem* to denote the thing believed really are not a name of anything at all. In cases of false belief the whole sentence 'I believe so and so' expresses some fact, but 'so and so' by itself does not. Nor does the whole sentence express any relation between me and some other object named by 'so and so', for there is no such object. Furthermore, "since there seems plainly no difference, in mere analysis, between false belief and true belief, we should have to say of all belief and supposition generally that they *never* consist in a relation between the believer and something else which *is* what is believed." [18] Suppose I believe truly that lions exist. There is in this case a fact named 'that lions exist'. But my *belief itself* does not consist in a relation between me and the fact. Since my belief is true, this implies that there *is* such a relation between me and the fact. "But it is the *truth* of my belief which consists in that relation; the belief itself does *not* consist in it." [19] Hence, if we say 'I believe in the existence of lions', the words 'the existence of lions' do not in this sentence stand for any fact. They are not the name of anything. The whole sentence 'I believe in the existence of lions' is the name for a fact. But we cannot analyze this fact into two components, me and the proposition *the existence of lions,* related together.

According to this view of Moore's then, there are no propositions. But Moore immediately goes on to say: "Of course, we can, and must, still continue to talk *as* if there were such things as propositions." [20] We must, says Moore, still use expressions like 'The proposition that lions exist' or 'the proposition that 2 plus 2 equals 4'. For example, we will still use the sentence 'The proposition that 2 plus 2 equals 4 is true' to express a "fact."

All that our theory compels us to say is that one part of this expression, namely, the words 'The proposition that 2 plus 2 equals 4,' though it seems to be the name of something, is not really a name for anything at all, whereas the whole expression 'The proposition that 2 plus 2 equals 4 is true' is a name for a fact and a most important fact; and all that our theory says is that we must not suppose that this fact can be analysed into a fact called 'the proposition that twice two are four' and a relation between this fact on the one hand and truth

18. *Ibid.*, p. 265; cf. 289–90.
19. *Ibid.*, p. 265.
20. *Ibid.*

on the other. This is all that the theory requires. It does not require that we should discontinue the use of these expressions, which are not names for anything; or that we should suppose that sentences in which they occur can't be true.[21]

Moore next notes that this theory which he has now suggested still does not provide an analysis of beliefs. It merely says that beliefs cannot be analyzed in a certain way. It does not say how they *are* to be analyzed. He then says that he knows of no satisfactory analysis and hence proposes to give up the attempt.

We were led into the discussion of the nature of beliefs because we had hoped to determine thereby "what truth is." Does failure to analyze beliefs mean that the attempt to define truth must fail too? No, says Moore, the former is irrelevant to the question of the nature of truth. He then refers to his earlier "definition": "To say that a belief is true is to say that *the fact to which it refers is* or has being; while to say that a belief is false is to say that the fact to which it refers is not—that there is no such fact." He now states this in another way, which he proposes to submit as "the fundamental definition of truth": "Every belief has the property of *referring to* some particular fact, every different belief to a different fact; and *the* property which we name when we call it true, is the property which can be expressed by saying that *the* fact to which it refers *is*." [22] But we are again faced with the difficulty of defining 'referring to'. Moore says that he admits he cannot define this expression in the sense of analyzing it. But, he says, from the fact that we cannot analyze it, it does not follow that we may not know what its referent is. We may be perfectly well acquainted with it. And he maintains that we all are "perfectly familiar" with it, and hence we understand this definition of truth, even though we cannot "analyze it down to its simplest terms." Take any belief whatsoever. It is "quite plain" that there is only one fact which would have being if it were true and which would have no being if it were false. Hence, if Smith believes that we are now hearing the noise of a brass band, his belief is false. It is false because it shares a property with other false beliefs, the property which consists in the fact that *the fact* to which it refers has no being, that it *is not,* that there is *no* such fact.

---

21. *Ibid.,* p. 266.
22. *Ibid.,* p. 268.

II

THE ABOVE DISCUSSION is based on one of Moore's 1910–11 lectures.[23] In the next lecture Moore makes another attempt to get his meaning across and introduces a new term, 'correspondence', which was frequently used in early twentieth-century philosophy.

Suppose that my friend, Jake, believes that I have gone away for the holidays. We would hold first, says Moore, that if his belief is *true,* then I must have gone away for the holidays; his belief cannot be true unless I have actually gone away. Conversely, we would say that if I have gone away, then his belief is true; it cannot be other than true. In other words, my having actually gone away is both a necessary and a sufficient condition for the truth of Jake's belief. At least, so it seems. Similarly, we would say that if his belief is *false,* then I cannot have gone away for the holidays; and conversely, if I have not gone away, then his belief that I have gone is false. Hence, my *not* having gone away is both a necessary and sufficient condition for the falsity of Jake's belief. Here then is a condition which is both necessary and sufficient for the truth of this belief and a condition which is both necessary and sufficient for its falsity.[24]

However, Moore continues, that these conditions are both necessary and sufficient does not constitute a definition of truth or of falsity. We might be tempted to hold that to say that (a) the belief that I have gone away is true is the *same* thing as to say that (b) I have gone away. Perhaps in ordinary situations, the one amounts to the same as the other. For if Jake's belief exists, then neither (a) nor (b) can be true unless the other is. But strictly speaking, the two are not the same fact. If we say 'The belief that I have gone away is true', we mean to assert "that this belief has some property, which it shares with other true beliefs: the possession by it of this property is the fact asserted." But if we say 'I have gone away', "we are not attributing any property at all to this belief. . . . We are merely asserting a fact, which might quite well be a fact, even if no one believed it at all." [25] That is, I might have gone away without Jake's believing that I had. In that case his belief would not be true—simply because it does not exist! Hence, to say that his belief that I have gone away is true is *not* the same thing as to say that I have gone away.

23. *SMPP*, Chap. XIV.
24. *Ibid.*, pp. 274–75.
25. *Ibid.*, p. 276.

Moore has said that this belief, if true, "shares a property" with other true beliefs. What then is this property? I think I had better quote Moore's answer at some length:

Well, it seems to me we can see quite plainly that this belief, if true, has to the fact that I have gone away a certain relation, which that particular belief has to no other fact. This relation, as I admitted . . . , is difficult to define, in the sense of analysing it: I didn't profess to be able to analyse it. But we do, I think, see this relation; we are all perfectly familiar with it; and we can, therefore, define it in the sense of pointing out what relation it is, by simply pointing out that it is *the relation* which does hold between this belief, if true, and this fact, and does not hold between this belief and any other fact. Surely you are aware of a relation which would hold between the belief that I had gone away, if true, and the fact that I had gone away—a relation which would hold, between that belief, if true, and that particular fact, and would not hold between that belief and any other fact—a relation which is expressed . . . by the partial identity of name between the belief and the fact in question. . . . We may take different views as to what the exact nature of this relation is—as to how it is to be analysed, and as to how it resembles or differs from other relations; but in merely attempting to answer these questions, we do, I think, presuppose that we are already acquainted with it—that we have it before our minds; for you cannot try to determine the nature of, or to compare with other things, a thing which you have not got before your mind.[26]

Now the difficulty which we have in defining truth and falsity, according to Moore, stems largely from the fact that this relation with which we are acquainted has no unambiguous name. Once we give it a name "it becomes, I think quite easy to define truth and falsehood." Hence, Moore gives it a name. He proposes to call it the relation of *correspondence.* Hence, we may now say: "To say that this belief is true is to say that there is in the Universe *a* fact to which it corresponds; and to say that it is false is to say that there is *not* in the Universe any fact to which it corresponds."[27] This statement, Moore holds, fulfills the requirements of a definition. "For the properties which we have now identified with truth and falsehood respectively *are* properties which this belief may *share* with other true and false beliefs. We have said that to say it is true is merely to say that it does correspond to a fact; and obviously this *is* a property which may be common to it and other beliefs."[28] And the same is true of

26. *Ibid.,* pp. 276–77.
27. *Ibid.,* p. 277.
28. *Ibid.*

the property "identified" with falsehood. Moreover, it now follows from these definitions that the conditions which we thought to be necessary and sufficient for the truth (or falsity) of a belief *are* necessary and sufficient for its truth (or its falsity). If Jake's belief corresponds to a fact, then I must have gone away. And if I have gone away, then his belief does correspond to a fact.[29]

Moore qualifies his remarks by adding that the definitions are correct for at least *one* of the senses of truth, or falsity. And all that he wishes to maintain is that *very often* when we say that a belief is true, the belief is true if and only if it corresponds to a fact. This theory is in accord with "millions of instances," all occasions when a particular belief corresponds to some other fact. The chief defect with other theories of truth is that they conflict with these "millions of obvious facts."[30]

What are some of these other theories? I shall briefly mention them and then turn to a discussion of Moore's view.

III

THE TWO THEORIES which Moore selects for criticism are Pragmatism and Bradley's Idealism.

According to Pragmatism, true beliefs are distinguished from false ones by the fact that true beliefs "work." What is meant by saying that true beliefs work is left rather vague, says Moore. But sometimes Pragmatists say that to work is the same thing as to be useful. Sometimes they hold that to work means to lead, perhaps in the long run, to some kind of satisfaction. Roughly then, by saying that a belief works, they mean that it leads to some kind of satisfactory effect. Hence, according to the Pragmatists, a belief is true if, and only if, it leads up to the right kind of satisfactory effect (whatever it may be). But, as Moore points out, this implies such things as the following. It implies, for example, that Jake's belief that I had gone away for the holidays might be true, even if I had *not* gone away; that it would be true provided only that it led to certain satisfactory results. And, similarly, in "millions of other instances." In short, the Pragmatists' view implies that it is unnecessary for a belief to

29. *Ibid.*, p. 278. Cf. "Facts and Propositions," *PASS*, VII (1927), pp. 199–200, reprinted in *PP*, pp. 82–84.
30. *SMPP*, pp. 280–81.

correspond to a fact in order for it to be true.[31] However, sometimes the Pragmatists seem to say that the "property" of leading to some sort of satisfactory result is only a *criterion* of truth. In this case the above objection would not apply. For merely to hold this would not imply that a belief could be true, even if it corresponded to no fact. It would only imply that every belief which led to satisfactory results also corresponded to a fact. Whereas the former view said that a belief is true whenever it leads to a satisfactory result, even if it does not correspond to a fact, this view says only that leading to a satisfactory result always goes along with corresponding to a fact: wherever you have the one, you have the other.[32]

Bradley's theory, Moore says, is neither a definition of truth (and falsity) nor a criterion. It is a theory *about* truth and falsity. It lays down a universal proposition about beliefs: "Absolutely every belief, without exception, is *both* partially true, and *also* partially false; *no* belief is *wholly* true, and none is *wholly* false; but absolutely all are *partially* both." [33] One might be inclined to say: Take Jake's belief that I have gone away for the holidays, and suppose that I have gone away. Well then, is this belief only partially true? Is it partially false? Is it not obvious that it is wholly true? If I have gone away, and Jake believes just that, then it seems obvious that his belief is wholly true. So this refutes Bradley's thesis. However, Moore points out, this argument probably would not convince Bradley. Therefore, he wants to try to give another argument. He wants to show that if 'false' is used in its ordinary sense, and if Bradley's view that every belief is partially false were true, then it would follow that *every* belief is false in the same sense. And in that case, there could never be such a thing as my having gone away for the holidays, or my being here now, etc.[34]

What Moore is trying to get at is as follows. Take a belief of the form '*p*'. To say that this is partly false is to say nothing, since it has no parts. Hence, if it is false in any way, then it is simply and wholly false. Now take a belief of the form '*p* and *q*'. Suppose that the first conjunct corresponds to a fact, but the second does not. Then the whole belief, *taken as a whole,* is false. It is not *wholly false,* however, since the first part is *true.* Hence, if a belief is a complex one, consisting of two or more

31. *Ibid.,* pp. 281–82.
32. *Ibid.,* p. 283. Cf. "Professor James' 'Pragmatism,'" *PAS,* VIII (1907–8), 33–77, reprinted in *PS* as "William James' 'Pragmatism,'" pp. 97–146.
33. *SMPP,* p. 284.
34. *Ibid.,* p. 285.

components, we can talk about it being partly false. We said the *q* did not correspond to a fact; hence, it is false. But if *p* is also false (because every belief is "partly false"), then '*p* and *q*' is not only false as a whole, but *wholly false*. And similarly with any combination. Thus, it would follow, by this view, that every belief is wholly false. There are no true beliefs at all.

IV

IN THE INTRODUCTION to this chapter I mentioned three conditions which, according to Russell, any theory of (empirical) truth must fulfill. Let me briefly mention why I agree with Russell.

The first condition was: a theory of truth must admit of its opposite, falsity. Surely this needs little explication. It is clear that we often make errors and that we often know that we do. No theory of truth can be adequate if it allows every belief or proposition to be true or if it fails to account for false cases as well as true ones.

Second, an adequate theory of truth must make truth (and falsity) a property of beliefs. As Russell says, it seems evident that if there were no beliefs there could be neither truth nor falsehood. If there were a world of matter alone, there would be no place for truths or falsehoods. It would contain merely facts or states of affairs. Only when judgments about those states of affairs occur do truth and falsity enter in.

Third, an adequate theory of truth must make truth and falsity dependent upon the relation of beliefs to things outside of the beliefs. If I believe truly that Wittgenstein died in England, my belief is *true,* not because of something intrinsic to the belief, but because of an event or state of affairs which took place in England several years ago. Hence, although truth and falsity are predicable of beliefs, they are dependent not upon the "internal quality" of the beliefs themselves but upon the relation of the beliefs to other things "outside" the beliefs.[35]

I submit that Moore's theory, when sharpened, clarified, and slightly amended, *does:* admit and account for falsity as well as truth; make truth and falsity predicable of beliefs; and make truth and falsity dependent upon things outside of the beliefs. By the relation of correspondence, truth and falsity are dependent upon objective states of affairs, external to the

35. Cf. Russell, "The Philosophy of Logical Atomism," p. 121.

subjective beliefs of the observer. By admitting beliefs, we have something of which truth and falsity are predicable, and we account for error. By 'belief', here is meant: the *object* of belief, that which is believed, not the act of believing. Hence, a belief is a proposition, and in spite of Moore's attempt to eliminate propositions, they remain in his theory. For he still has to talk about beliefs as being true or false. And belief must mean the object of believing, not the act. One could hardly say that an act of believing is true or false. That a certain act of belief took place may be true or false, but now 'that a certain act of belief took place' refers to an object of belief, not an act of believing. Hence, propositions *do* remain in Moore's theory, and properly so. For even a syntactically correct sentence is a mere string of words until words have meanings. A proposition is a complex meaning, consisting of parts, and is an indispensable part of Moore's theory.

Let us now consider an example and apply Moore's theory with some slight amendments. I take the example from Russell.[36] Othello believes (falsely) that Desdemona loves Cassio. Since Desdemona does not love Cassio, there is no such state of affairs in the world (supposing now that Othello, Desdemona, and Cassio are actual persons) as: that Desdemona loves Cassio or Desdemona's loving Cassio. Hence, Othello cannot be related, by believing, to any such state of affairs as Desdemona's loving Cassio. Since Desdemona does not love Cassio, the object of his belief cannot be the actual state of affairs in the world which consists of Desdemona's loving Cassio. Yet surely Othello does believe something. Suppose that you had seen Othello looking very troubled and had gone up to him and asked, "What's the matter, old boy?" and that he had answered, "I believe that Desdemona loves Cassio." Would it not be the height of effrontery to ask him, "Do you really think you are believing anything when you believe that?" Othello did not have a blank mind when he believed that Desdemona loved Cassio. He believed that Desdemona loved Cassio, that the proposition that Desdemona loves Cassio is true. He did not believe the state of affairs which consists of Desdemona loving Cassio, for there was no such state of affairs—which is to say that his belief did not refer to or correspond to any complex of objects, his belief did not correspond to any fact. This situation may be conveyed by the following diagram. We might call it a paradigm for false belief.

36. *Ibid.*, p. 124.

I. FALSE BELIEF

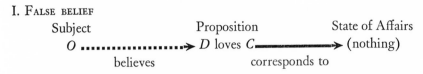

Subject   Proposition   State of Affairs

O ....➤ D loves C ━━━━━━➤ (nothing)

believes   corresponds to

Let us now structure the situation for a true belief. Suppose that Othello believes that Cassio loves Desdemona and that Cassio *does* love Desdemona. Then we have:

II. TRUE BELIEF

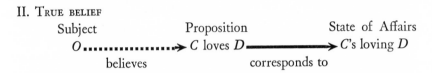

Subject   Proposition   State of Affairs

O ....➤ C loves D ━━━━━━➤ C's loving D

believes   corresponds to

In (I) Othello believes that Desdemona loves Cassio, but this belief (the proposition) is *false* because it does not correspond to any fact. In (II) Othello believes that Cassio loves Desdemona, and this belief is *true* because it does correspond to a fact, i.e., to some event, situation, or state of affairs (again, supposing that Othello, Desdemona, and Cassio are actual persons). By saying of a belief that it *corresponds* to some state of affairs, I do not mean that it must necessarily "picture" it in any literal sense, word for word. I merely mean that there is some state of affairs with which a proposition is compatible. For example, if I say 'I believe that there is a tire jack in my trunk', then my belief that there is a tire jack in my trunk corresponds to a fact if, upon opening the trunk, I were to find a tire jack there.

Here then we have a fairly simple "theory of truth," which provides not only a *definition* of truth and falsity, but a *criterion* which we can apply to various propositions in order to determine their truth or falsity—that is, a criterion not only for *true belief,* but for *knowledge.*

"But why are you distinguishing true belief from knowledge?", someone might ask. "Aren't they the same?"

Of course not. Othello might very well believe, truly, that Cassio loves Desdemona, and Cassio might actually love Desdemona, without Othello *knowing* that Cassio loves Desdemona. Othello might, for example, believe that Cassio and Desdemona are madly in love with each other, perhaps because of the way Desdemona smiled at Cassio on a certain occasion. He comes to believe that Desdemona loves Cassio and he later infers that Cassio loves Desdemona. But even if he *believes truly,* and even if Cassio does love Desdemona, he could not be said to *know* that Cassio loves Desdemona. To know this something else is required. And this gets us back to the discussion of knowledge in Chapter VI. There I discussed a view which maintained that in order for X to *know* p the following must hold:

(1) X directly apprehends p;
(2) X believes p;
(3) p is true; and
(4) X has adequate evidence for p.

For Othello to know and not merely truly believe that Cassio loves Desdemona, he must then have adequate evidence for his belief that Cassio loves Desdemona. Well, suppose that one day he sees Cassio approaching the palace with a bouquet of roses and hears him say to a servant, "Bring these to Desdemona." And suppose that at another time Othello peeks through Desdemona's keyhole and sees Cassio trying to kiss Desdemona. And so on. He then can say, "I almost have all the evidence I need for my thesis that Cassio loves Desdemona." Well, to make it obvious, suppose that Othello is hidden in the bushes in the garden and sees Cassio falling on his knees before Desdemona saying, "I love you!" Now we may safely say that Othello has adequate evidence for his belief that Cassio loves Desdemona—that is, he knows that the proposition that Cassio loves Desdemona is true.[37] Hence, we may set up a paradigm for knowledge as follows.

III. KNOWLEDGE

SUBJECT	PROPOSITION	STATE OF AFFAIRS

37. For brevity I have simplified the account of having adequate evidence.

I have here omitted the factors of additional information, generalization, memory, etc., but in a complete schema they would have to be brought into consideration, as they were in Chapter VI.

Here then is a brief consideration of a theory of truth which is, at least, implicit in Moore's remarks. I do not pretend that it occurs in Moore's writings in anything like the form in which I stated in this section. But as we have seen in sections I and II, the basic content is there. I have tried to sharpen it somewhat and have amended it slightly. I have also attempted to show that it fits with a tenable theory of knowledge. I do not claim that it is the only possible theory, but I think it is one alternative and one which is worthy of consideration.[38]

38. Cf. A. Tarsky, "The Semantic Conception of Truth," *Philosophy and Phenomenological Research*, IV (1944), 341–75; reprinted in L. Linsky, *Semantics and the Philosophy of Language* (Urbana: The Univ. of Illinois Press, 1952), 13–47.

PART THREE
The Problem of Perception

IX

Perception and the External World

T HE PROBLEM OF PERCEPTION has been variously phrased: What is the relation of sense experience to reality, or to a reality external to us? Or how can "the human mind" (or consciousness, etc.) have any knowledge of a physical world which exists and which, we believe, continues to exist whether or not minds exist (or whether or not we are conscious of that world)? We have all assumed and very likely do now assume—perhaps some would say 'know'—that such a physical, external world does exist. Of course, we do not customarily talk about an *external world,* but we do talk about *physical objects* of one sort or another. And many of us also commonly assume—or perhaps know—that we know of the existence of such objects by *perceiving* them, by seeing, touching, or smelling them. If I were to ask you how you know that there are trees on the boulevard, you would probably answer, "Because I *see* them, of course." But philosophers have questioned these assumptions or these assertions which we claim to know. They have gone on to ask, "How do we know that our senses give us information about a world which exists whether we do or not? Indeed, how can we be sure that there is such a world at all?" [1]

I

LIKE MANY PHILOSOPHERS, Moore is greatly concerned with the problem of perception. He devotes as many pages to it as he does to problems of ethics. And in a sense, it is rather strange that he does so, for as early as 1910 Moore maintained that he had absolutely no doubt about the truth of certain perceptual statements. In *Some Main Problems of Philosophy* we constantly encounter statements which Moore claims to know, assertions like "This pencil exists," and "I *do* know that this pencil exists." [2] How does Moore know these things? "I do know *both* of them immediately." [3] (We saw in Chapter VI what problem this utterance led to.) Similarly, in his "Defence of Common Sense," Moore maintains that he knows with certainty various perceptual propositions to be true. He claims to know, without any doubt, that "My body is at a greater distance from the bookcase than it is from the mantelpiece," "There are other living bodies on the earth," "This is a human hand," "That is the sun," etc. [4] If we were to ask Moore, "But how do you know that that is a hand, or a dog, etc.?", he would very likely answer, "Because I see it, and I wouldn't see it if it weren't there to be seen, would I?"

One of the most vivid passages in which Moore maintains this same position occurs in "Certainty." [5] This passage is rather long, but worth quoting, I think.

I am at present, as you can all see, in a room and not in the open air; I am standing up, and not either sitting or lying down; I have clothes on, and am not absolutely naked; . . . there are a good many other people in the same room which I am; and there are windows in that wall and a door in this one.

Now I have here made a number of different assertions; and I have made these assertions quite positively, as if there were no doubt whatever that they were true. . . . I *implied,* though I did not say, that they were in fact certain—implied, that is, that I myself knew for certain, in each case, that what

1. John Hospers, *An Introduction to Philosophical Analysis* (New York: Prentice-Hall, 1953), p. 379.
2. *SMPP*, pp. 119 ff.
3. *Ibid.,* p. 125.
4. "Def.," sec. I.
5. "Certainty," *PP*, pp. 227–51.

I asserted to be the case was, at the time when I asserted it, in fact the case. And I do not think that I can be justly accused of dogmatism or over-confidence for having asserted these things positively. . . . In the case of assertions such as I made . . . the charge would be absurd. On the contrary, I should have been guilty of absurdity if, under the circumstances, I had *not* spoken positively. . . . Suppose that now, instead of saying . . . 'I have got some clothes on,' I were to say 'I think I've got some clothes on, but it's just possible that I haven't.' Would it not sound rather ridiculous for me now, under these circumstances, to say 'I *think* I've got some clothes on' or even to say 'I not only think I have, I know that it is very likely indeed that I have, but I can't be quite sure'? [6]

Moore then has no doubt about the truth of various common-sense perceptual propositions like those mentioned. About them he often says that they are known immediately or that they are self-evident.[7]

But Moore does not claim to know only these commonsensical propositions to be true. He also claims to know the philosophical doctrine that *the external world exists* (or that there is a reality external to my mind) to be true. And his proof of this *philosophical* doctrine is sometimes based not on some other philosophical investigation, not (here) on introducing entities such as sense-data, but rather on these commonsensical perceptual statements. About perceptual statements like those which occur at the beginning of the long passage which I just quoted, Moore writes: "All of them were propositions which implied the existence *of an external world* —that is to say, of a world *external to my mind*." [8] From propositions like 'Here is a hand, and here is another', Moore "proves" that there is an external world. But let us consider one of his proofs at some length. The most detailed one occurs in his Hertz lecture, "Proof of an External World." [9]

II

Moore begins his lecture with a quotation from Kant: "It still remains a scandal to philosophy . . . that the existence of things outside of us . . . must be accepted merely on *faith,* and that, if anyone thinks good to

6. *Ibid.,* pp. 227–28.
7. See above, Chap. II.
8. "Certainty," p. 242.
9. "Prf.," *PP,* pp. 127–50. Cf. "Certainty," pp. 226 ff; "Some Judgments of Perception," *PAS,* XIX (1918–19), 1–29, reprinted in *PS,* pp. 221 ff.

doubt their existence, we are unable to counter his doubts by any satisfactory proof." [10] It is a matter of some importance, says Moore, to discuss the question of what sort of proof, if any, can be given of the existence of "things outside of us." But 'things outside of us' is an "odd" expression, the meaning of which is not clear. Perhaps 'external things' would do better. But even this must be made clearer still. The things we are talking of are things external to our minds. But even 'things external to our minds' is far from clear. 'Things' in that expression may mean things in themselves, *or* appearances, to use Kant's terms. The former are things which are external in a transcendental sense. The latter are things which are external in an empirical sense—we might call them "things which are *to be met with in space.*" [11]

The last expression, says Moore, does indicate the kind of things with regard to which he wants to inquire as to what sort of proof might be given of their existence. Included in the class of things that are to be met with in space are: my body, the bodies of other men, the bodies of animals, plants, stones, the sun, chairs, etc.—in short, the things we commonly call physical objects. However, 'things that are to be met with in space' also refers to things which are *not* physical objects—e.g., shadows. Moore will understand the expression in its wider meaning. He will not, however, widen it so as to include things like negative afterimages, for, although these are "presented in space," it would be misleading to say that they are "to met with in space." An important difference between the two characters is: 'To be met with in space' suggests that there are some conditions such that *anyone* who fulfilled them could perceive the object in question. But in the case of things presented in space, this is not true. In the case of the negative afterimages which I just now saw, it is not conceivable that anyone else could have seen any of them, although others might have seen some very like those which I saw. [12] Finally, some things are neither to be met with in space nor presented in space: e.g., the afterimages which you see by looking at an electric light and closing your eyes. Since your eyes are shut, you are not seeing any part of space at all. Hence, in one sense, 'presented in space' is a wider

---

10. *Critique of Pure Reason*, trans. Norman Kemp Smith (London: Macmillan, 1933), p. 34 (B xxxix n.); "Prf.," *PP*, p. 127.

11. "Prf.," pp. 127–30.

12. *Ibid.*, pp. 130–31. An example of a negative afterimage is the grey star-shape which one might see after looking first at a white star on a black ground and then at a white sheet of paper. See p. 131.

notion than 'to be met with in space'. From the fact that a thing is presented in space, it does not follow that it is to be met with in space. But in another sense, 'to be met with in space' is a wider notion than 'presented in space'. For there are many things which are to be met with in space but which are not (now) presented in space. And there is no absurdity in supposing that many things which were once to be met with in space were never presented and that many things are now to be met with in space which are not now presented and never were and never will be.[13]

Moore, then, is so using the phrase 'things that are to be met with in space' that from the proposition that there are certain kinds of things—bodies, tables, etc.—it follows that there are things to be met with in space. Hence, if he can prove that two chairs exist, or a chair and a dog, etc., he will (he says) have proved that there are things to be met with in space.

But, Moore continues, someone might object that, if you prove that there are two dogs, etc., then, although you will have proved that there are things to be met with in space, you will not necessarily have proved that there are things *external to our minds*. A dog, though it is to be met with in space, might not be external to our minds. But, as we have seen, 'external' is ambiguous. If we mean by 'external' 'existing as a thing in itself', then from the proposition 'Two dogs exist', it does *not* follow that there are external things. But if we use 'external' to mean 'empirically (not transcendentally) external', then from propositions like 'Two dogs exist', it will follow that there are things external to our minds. Take any kind of thing that is to be met with in space, e.g., a stone. There is no contradiction in asserting that it existed before I perceived it nor in saying that it will continue to exist after I stop perceiving it. It would not be a stone, as opposed to, say, an image, unless its existence at any time were logically independent of my perception of it at that time. Hence, from the proposition that a thing that I am perceiving is a stone, it follows that it is external to my mind and to all other minds. It is not the sort of thing that can exist only when someone is perceiving it (like a pain or after-image). The same is true for other *kinds* of things besides stones: i.e., hands, dogs, chairs, etc.[14]

Hence, Moore continues, in the cases of all such kinds of things, if there is either a pair of things both of which are of one kind, or a pair of things

13. *Ibid.,* p. 133–35.
14. *Ibid.,* pp. 137–45.

one of which is of one kind and one of them of another kind, then it follows that there are some things outside of us. Thus, says Moore, if I can prove that there exist now, say, two shoes or two socks or one shoe and one sock, etc., I shall have proved that there are now things outside of us.

> Cannot I prove any of these things? It seems to me that . . . I can now give a large number of different proofs, each of which is a perfectly rigorous proof. . . . I can prove now, for instance, that two human hands exist. How? By holding up my two hands, and saying, as I make a certain gesture with the right hand, 'Here is one hand,' and adding, as I make a certain gesture with the left, 'And here is another.' . . . But did I prove just now that two human hands were then in existence? I do want to insist that I did; that the proof I gave was a perfectly rigorous one; and that it is perhaps impossible to give a better or more rigorous proof of anything whatever.[15]

Such is Moore's "proof." What determines whether or not a purported proof is a genuine one? Three conditions, according to Moore: (1) The premiss by which the conclusion is proved must be different from the conclusion. (2) The premiss must be one which I *know* to be true. (3) The conclusion must really follow from the premisses. Moore insists that these three conditions were satisfied by his proof. (1) The premiss 'here is one hand, and here is another' differs from the conclusion 'Two human hands exist at this moment'. That these are different may be seen from the fact that the conclusion might have been true even if the premiss had been false. (2) Moore insists that he did at the moment *know* that the premiss was true.

> I *knew* that there was one hand in the place indicated by combining a certain gesture with my first utterance of 'here' and that there was another in the different place indicated by combining a certain gesture with my second utterance of 'here.' How absurd it would be to suggest that I did not know it, but only believed it, and that it perhaps was not the case![16]

(3) The conclusion did follow from the premiss, Moore merely asserts.

Similarly, a "rigorous" proof can be given that external objects have existed in the *past*. "Here is one proof. I can say: 'I held up my two hands above this desk not very long ago; therefore, two hands existed not very long ago; therefore at least two external objects have existed at some time in the past, Q.E.D.' "[17]

15. *Ibid.,* pp. 145–46.
16. *Ibid.,* p. 146.
17. *Ibid.,* p. 148.

These then are Moore's two "conclusive proofs" of the existence of external objects.[18] There are, he says, thousands of similar ones which he could have given. But Moore anticipates that many philosophers will still feel that he has not given a satisfactory proof. Why? One reason might be that Moore has not proved the propositions which he used as premises in his two proofs. These philosophers want a proof of these premises or a general statement as to how *any* propositions of the kind used in his premises may be proved.

This, of course, I haven't given, and I do not believe that it can be given: if this is what is meant by a proof of the existence of external things, I do not believe that any proof of the existence of external things is possible. . . . How am I to prove now that 'Here is one hand, and here's another'? I do not believe I can do it. In order to do it, I should need to prove for one thing, as Descartes pointed out, that I am not now dreaming. But how can I prove that I am not? I have, no doubt, conclusive reasons for asserting that I am not now dreaming; I have conclusive evidence that I am awake; but that is a very different thing from being able to prove it.[19]

Moore concludes:

I can know things which I cannot prove; and among things which I certainly did know, even if . . . I could not prove them, were the premises of my two proofs. I should say, therefore, that those, if any, who are dissatisfied with these proofs merely on the grounds that I did not know their premises, have no good reason for their dissatisfaction.[20]

III

ONE IS TEMPTED TO ASK: (1) But why did Moore not stop here? He seems, in his own mind at least, to find no *problem* of perception. Why then did he write so many pages about that problem? Why did he not hold that the problem of perception was solved or that there was no such problem? Why did he write forty- to sixty-page essays on objects of perception, judgments of perception, etc., in which all sorts of qualifications, refinements, etc., occur? (2) Why did he introduce sense-data into the discussion? Why did he hold (in works which we have not yet considered) that

18. I must emphasize that, in each case, what Moore calls the proof is only one stage in a larger complex proof developed throughout the essay.
19. *Ibid.,* p. 149.
20. *Ibid.,* p. 150.

a consideration of sense-data—of their existence, nature, and relation to other things—was such an important and absolutely essential task?

(1) Moore undoubtedly realized that what we perceive is at least partially dependent upon our sensory organs. We may reasonably believe that if those organs were different, what we see, hear, etc., would be different. There *are* cases in which we do not perceive things as they are. We discover that we sometimes experience illusions. A straight stick, half-immersed in water, looks bent, etc. We seem to require a distinction between how things appear and how they are. Sometimes we even perceive "things that aren't there"—pink rats, etc. And so on. For these reasons, Moore (along with many other philosophers) came to believe that there is more to the problem of perception than he indicated in writings like the "Proof of an External World."

(2) Because of the sorts of experiences mentioned in (1), Moore came to believe that there are "appearances" as well as "realities," or rather that there *are* such things as sense-data, as well as material objects. At least, he construed such experiences to mean that sense-data are things and that there is a genuine problem about sense-data. That is why he discussed the sense-data issue at such length. Furthermore, in spite of what he said in various works, like those quoted earlier, Moore held that the introduction of sense-data is integral to the solution of the problem of perception, that it cannot be solved without considering sense-data—what they are, how they are related to physical objects, etc. Indeed, at times he held the view that physical objects are not given to me independently of sense-data; that seeing a physical object necessarily involves seeing sense-data; that a sense-datum always mediates my perception of a physical object.[21] This issue will be dealt with at some length. But before we can turn to it, we must discuss some other related topics: whether there are sense-data, what they are, etc. After that we may finally consider how, for Moore, the introduction of sense-data is integral to the solution of the problem of perception. As we shall see, their introduction also presents some problems.

21. "Some Judgments of Perception," *PS,* pp. 229 ff.; "Reply," p. 644.

X

The Introduction

of Sense-Data

THAT THERE ARE SENSE-DATA, Moore never doubted. In fact, that they exist and that we are acquainted with different sense-data at different times are perhaps the only (non-ethical) philosophical doctrines which Moore *clearly* maintained throughout his entire philosophical career, after his revolt against Idealism. His certainty regarding these two theses is seen in every work devoted to perception or to various aspects of it. So certain was he of these two views that he failed to see how anyone else could doubt them. He says, first, that sense-data are things "the existence of which no one disputes or ever has disputed." [1] And second: "I quite certainly am at this moment acquainted with many different sense-data; and in saying this, I am merely using language to express a fact of such a kind that nobody has ever thought of disputing the existence of facts of that kind." [2] Moore's certainty that there are sense-data may be seen in his earlier, middle, and later writings. His earlier writings:

1. "Is There Knowledge by Acquaintance?", *PASS*, II (1919), 181.
2. *Ibid.*, p. 180.

"There is, of course, no question whether there *are* such entities, the entities meant certainly *are,* whether or not they be rightly described as 'sensations,' 'sense-presentations,' 'sense-data,' etc." [3] His middle writings: "Some philosophers have, I think, doubted whether there are any such things as other philosophers have meant by 'sense-data' or 'sensa.' . . . But there is no doubt at all that there are sense-data, in the sense in which I am using that term." [4] And his last writings: "If he [O. K. Bouwsma] had understood how I was proposing to use the term 'sense-data,' he would have said that there certainly *are* sense-data." [5]

But if there are such things as sense-data, or if one even argues *that* there are sense-data, several questions immediately arise. Some of these are:

1. *What are* sense-data (from an observational, not an ontological, standpoint)? (A) What sorts of things are included in the class of sense-data? (B) Can a definition of 'sense-data' be given?
2. What *grounds* are there for maintaining that there are such *things* as sense-data?
3. If one grants that there are or might be sense-data, then what is their *ontological* status? (physical? mental? etc.)
4. What is the *relation* of sense-data to physical objects? (This question would only be asked if the answer to [3] is not 'physical'.)

1. *What are sense-data?*

A. Detailed lists of the kinds of things which he held to be included in the class of sense-data are given in several of Moore's works; for example:

By sense-data, I understand a class of entities of which we are very often directly conscious, and with many of which we are extremely familiar. They include the colours, of all sorts of different shades, which I actually see when I look about me; the sounds which I actually hear; the peculiar sort of entity of which I am directly conscious when I feel the pain of a toothache, and which I call 'the pain'; and many others. . . . But I wish also to include among them those entities called 'images,' of which I am directly conscious when I dream and often also when awake; which resemble the former in respect of the fact

3. "The Subject Matter of Psychology," *PAS*, X (1909–10), 58.
4. "Def.," pp. 54; cf. "The Status of Sense-Data," *PAS*, XIV (1913–14), 355–80, reprinted in *PS*, pp. 168 ff.
5. "Reply," p. 647; cf. pp. 627–28, 644. Cf. "Visual Sense-Data," *British Philosophy in the Mid-Century*, ed. C. A. Mace (Cambridge: Cambridge Univ. Press, 1957), *passim.*

that they *are* colours, sounds, etc.; but which seem as a rule, like rather faint copies of the colours, sounds, etc., actually seen or heard, and which . . . differ from them in respect of the fact that we should not say we actually saw or heard them, and the fact that they are not, in the strictest sense of the words 'given by the senses.' All these entities I propose to call sense-data.[6]

It should be noted that Moore here mentions several kinds of sense-data. The first class includes those "entities" which are given by some particular sense or senses: e.g., the colors, sounds, and shapes which we associate with physical objects. In some discussions of 'What are sense data?', Moore dealt only with this first class. For example, in *Some Main Problems of Philosophy* he writes: "I propose to call these things, the colour, size, and shape, *sense-data,* things *given* or presented by the senses —given, in this case, by my sense of sight."[7] The second class includes things which are perhaps given by the senses but are not given by any particular one of them, e.g., a pain.[8] The third class includes entities "which are not given by the senses at all," e.g., waking and dream images, afterimages, double images, hallucinatory "entities," etc.[9] Besides these three main classes, Moore, in at least one passage, also includes as sense-data the spatial relations which color patches, etc., have to one another.[10]

But a curious later view of Moore's negates all that has been said and drastically reduces the membership of the class of sense-data. In a paragraph from which I quoted above[11] Moore writes: "But now, what happened to each of us, when we saw that envelope? I will begin by describing *part* of what happened to me. I saw a patch of a particular whitish colour, having a certain size, and a certain shape. . . . These things: this patch of a whitish colour, and its size and shape I did actually see." These words are followed by a statement in which the color, size, and shape, but *not* the *patch,* are called sense-data. At this point a footnote which was written in 1952 appears. It reads: "I should now make, and have for many years made, a sharp distinction between what I called the 'patch,' on the one hand, and the colour, size, and shape, *of* which it is, on the other; and should call, and have called, *only* the patch, *not* its colour,

6. "The Subject Matter of Psychology," pp. 57–58.
7. *SMPP*, p. 30.
8. "Prf.," *passim.*
9. "The Status of Sense-Data," *PS*, p. 170. Cf. the long passage quoted above.
10. "The Nature and Reality of Objects of Perception," *PAS*, VI (1905–6), reprinted in *PS*, p. 71.
11. *SMPP*, p. 30.

size, or shape, a 'sense-datum.' " [12] This is a rather severe change of mind, but since the bulk of Moore's writings do *not* maintain this position, and since, in the two late works, "Addendum to My 'Reply' " and "Visual Sense-Data," Moore apparently forgot about this revised doctrine and returned to his earlier views, I shall not give it much weight and shall continue the discussion in terms of the views which Moore rather consistently held with the exception of this one footnote.[13]

B. We have now seen some examples of what sorts of things are (or are taken to be) sense-data. But someone might ask for a rigorous *definition* of the term 'sense-data'. Moore has such a definition.

According to Moore's definition, a sense-datum is that which is directly apprehended. The clearest statement of this is in his "Reply": "The sense in which I used, and intended to use, 'sense-datum' was such that anything whatever which is *directly apprehended . . . must* be a sense-datum.' " [14] About this assertion, two things must be said. First, the statement as a whole is simply false. Moore did not always use 'sense-datum' in such a way that *anything* whatever that is directly apprehended must be a sense-datum. In *Some Main Problems of Philosophy* he also held that propositions and direct apprehensions themselves [15] are objects of direct apprehension. Second, with respect to the definition itself, 'sense-datum' is defined in terms of 'direct apprehension'. But what is direct apprehension? If we turn to *Some Main Problems of Philosophy*, we find that direct apprehension is a "way of perceiving." "It is . . . that which happens when you actually see any colour, when you actually hear any sound . . . etc., etc. In all these cases you directly apprehend the sense-datum in question—the particular colour, or sound, or smell." [16] Similarly, elsewhere Moore states that direct apprehension is "the relation which I have to a sensible" (another term for 'sense-datum' for Moore) "when I am actually seeing or hearing it." [17] But at least two things are wrong with this definition of 'direct apprehension'. First, the definition leads to circularity: it makes use of the term 'sense-datum' (or a term synonymous

---

12. *SMPP*, p. 30, n. 2. (It should be remembered that these lectures were given in 1910–11.)

13. "Addendum to my 'Reply,' " *PGEM*, pp. 677–87; and "Visual Sense-Data" (see above, n. 5).

14. "Reply," p. 643.

15. *SMPP*, pp. 67 ff.; pp. 49 f.

16. *Ibid.*, p. 46.

17. "The Status of Sense-Data," *PS*, p. 173. Cf. *SMPP*, p. 67. Again it must be pointed out that consideration of propositions and direct apprehension has been omitted.

to it) which is the expression that we originally sought to define. Second, a new and equally problematic term, or set of terms, is introduced: 'actually see', 'actually hear', etc. If by 'actually see' Moore merely meant 'see', and if by 'actually hear' he merely meant 'hear', there would be no new problems at this point. But that he does *not* mean these things is clear from numerous passages. Hence, it behooves us to discover what Moore does mean by such expressions as 'actually see', etc. I shall limit the discussion to this one expression, but similar remarks can be and are made by Moore about 'actually hear', etc.

What then does Moore mean by 'actually see'? In some passages Moore defines 'actually see' in terms of 'direct apprehension', which obviously will not do.[18] In others he says that seeing is the relation which one has to material objects, while actually seeing is the relation which one has to sense-data, and (again) that the latter is direct apprehension. This will not do either, both for the reason just mentioned and also because what we have been trying to define is 'sense-datum'; hence, we cannot use this term in our definition of a term by which we hope to define 'sense-datum'. Elsewhere, Moore attempts an *explication* rather than a definition of 'actually see'. Suppose that a coin which is lying on the ground is situated obliquely to my line of sight. What I *see* from this position is elliptical and not circular. From another position, it is less elliptical. From a third, it is no longer elliptical. Similarly, while I am seeing it as elliptical, someone else may be seeing it as something else—circular, or less elliptical. For these reasons, Moore holds, while we may in one sense be said to *see* the coin from any of our vantage points, still, in another sense, what we *see* is not the coin but something else. Call the first sense 'see$_1$', and the second, 'see$_2$'. What I see$_1$ is something which I know (for Moore) to be round, but from many positions I see$_2$ it as an elliptical, not a round, thing. Seeing$_2$ is identical with actually seeing. And we may now know that a sense-datum is that which we actually see or see$_2$.[19]

Of course, the explication of 'actually see' also makes use of the notion as to what sense-data are, but it does so in terms of examples of what sense-data are (elliptical shapes, etc.), examples with which Moore has already provided us. Hence, I cannot see that the explication is a faulty one, *if* one agrees that it is sensible to say that there *are* such things

18. Cf. *SMPP*, pp. 51, 82 f.

19. "The Status of Sense-Data," *PS*, pp. 185 ff. Moore does not use the expressions 'see$_1$' or 'see$_2$'. Cf. "Reply," pp. 641 f., for 'actually hear'.

as sense-data as well as physical objects, instead of maintaining that there are only physical objects, and that these sometimes look one way (e.g., circular) to an observer and at other times look otherwise (elliptical) to that observer.[20]

2. *What grounds are there for maintaining that there are such things as sense-data?*

In Chapter IX, section III I briefly discussed some of the grounds for maintaining that there are such things as sense-data, but let us see what Moore has to say on the matter. Since these arguments are by now familiar, I shall be brief.

A. The argument from hallucinations

Hallucinations must be distinguished from illusions, which will be discussed shortly. Hallucination is one form of sensing sense-data for which one has no reason to believe that there is existent a "corresponding" material object, although one may not know that there is no such reason at the time of any given sensing. The drunkard's pink rats are the standard example. But a stimulant is not required: it is possible (and has happened) that one might be under the effect of no such external influence and yet experience an hallucinatory object. One might, for example, take something to be a red apple on the table and find out later that there was none. A case might be made for the views that one did see a red object, though not a material object, to be sure. What one saw—the object of sensing—is, Moore says, a sense-datum.[21]

B. The argument from afterimages

Somewhat similar to hallucinations are such things as afterimages (both negative and regular), the spots one senses when one "sees spots," etc. Moore's favorite illustration is that of someone looking at an electric light, closing his eyes, and getting an afterimage of the light while his eyes are still *closed*. If one does this, says Moore, he "can be said to 'see' this after-image," and he does see an object, though not a physical object.[22]

C. The argument from illusion

Sometimes one senses an object for which there is also a "corresponding" material object, but the two differ in some way. The straight stick which looks bent when half-submerged in water is the favorite example.

20. This is the view of some Oxford philosophers. See G. A. Paul, "Is There a Problem About Sense-Data?", *PASS*, XV, 88–101.
21. "Reply," pp. 629 ff.
22. "Visual Sense-Data," pp. 208 f.; "Prf.," pp. 131–41; "Reply," pp. 629 ff., 644, 647.

Or suppose that I see what I take to be a red apple on the table and later find that there *is* an apple there, but that it is of a different color. In these cases I sensed objects which were not physical, but also not hallucinatory, since there were a stick and an apple there. However, I did not perceive them veridically. Such experiences, Moore holds, also give evidence for the existence of sense-data.[23]

D. The argument from perspectives

Moore once held up a white envelope and asked his audience to look at it. Moore and each member of the audience saw a whitish patch of color, of a particular size and shape. The color, size, and shape which were sensed may have been very similar, but they did vary considerably for different individuals. Probably no two people saw the very same shade of color. Some shades were different from others, depending upon how the light fell on the paper, the different positions in which the viewers sat, the strength of their eyesight, and their distance from the paper. Similarly with regard to the size of the patch they saw. And similarly with respect to the shape. Some saw a more nearly rectangular shape, others a more rhomboidal figure. Because of these various perspectives, Moore holds, all the viewers saw the same *envelope,* but they did not all see the same shade of color or the same sized or shaped patch—i.e., they did not see the same *sense-data.* Indeed, probably even no *two* of them saw exactly the same sense-data, says Moore. And certainly "we should not *know* that any two did; whereas we should say we did *know* that we all saw the same envelope." [24] Now if all the viewers saw the same envelope, the envelope which they saw cannot be identical with the sense-data they saw, for these were all slightly different from one another. Hence, one has further grounds for believing that there are such things as sense-data.[25]

The same argument might be put forth with respect to any *one* person and an object viewed from several perspectives. Suppose that I look at my table from my present position. It has a certain shape, color, etc. Or at least, I sense a color, shape, etc. Now I move to another position. The shape is slightly different, as is the color (due to the reflection of light), etc. As I move around the table, I sense still (slightly) different colors, shapes, etc. I do sense *something* different from each stance, but I have no

23. "Reply," p. 647.
24. *SMPP,* p. 33.
25. Cf. "The Nature and Reality of Objects of Perception," *PS,* pp. 67–68. An excellent example in terms of hearing occurs in "Reply," p. 641. See also "Visual Sense-Data," p. 208.

reason to believe that the *table* changes shape and size that rapidly. Hence, I do have reason to hold that there really *are* such things as sense-data.[26]

These, then, are the various arguments which Moore gives for the *existence* of sense-data. Similar arguments occur in the writings of Russell and are rehearsed by Broad and Price.[27] Had I been writing for those unfamiliar with such discussions, I should have elaborated them in more detail, but I fear that my readers are too painfully familiar with them; hence, I have spared them the anguish of a long exposition.

Does Moore ever consider arguments which might be put forth *against* the existence of sense-data? Yes, he does, but these arguments, for Moore, are of the sort which arise when one attempts to determine the relation of sense-data to physical objects. Hence, I shall defer treatment of them until I deal with that topic.

3. *What is the ontological status of sense-data?*

Let us suppose or grant that there are or may be such things as sense-data, the objects of sensing, etc. Another question immediately arises: What is their ontological status? We may have reason to suppose (in spite of Professor Ryle) that certain entities in the universe are "mental" and that others are "physical." And perhaps there are other "realms of being," as some would say. What about sense-data? Are they mental, or physical, or neither?

A. Are sense-data mental?

According to Moore, the first fundamental sense in which anything is mental is if it is an act of consciousness of some sort. Moore thinks that many philosophers have held sense-data to be mental in this fundamental sense because they have failed to distinguish between sense-data and our acts of consciousness *of* them. They have, for example, failed to distinguish a blue *color* which I see and the direct *consciousness* which I have of it when I see it. As an instance, we may cite Hume who "often confused an act of consciousness with that of which we are conscious. . . . He thought sense-data to be mental partly because he mistook them for acts of consciousness. But it is, I think, clear that they are not acts of consciousness, whatever they are. They are not, therefore, 'mental' in my first and

26. Cf. Bertrand Russell, *The Problems of Philosophy* (Oxford: Oxford Univ. Press, 1912), Chap. I.
27. C. D. Broad, *Scientific Thought* (New York: Harcourt Brace, 1923), Chap. IV; H. H. Price, *Perception* (London: Methuen, 1932; 2d ed., 1950).

fundamental sense." [28] Part of the confusion has stemmed from the use of the term 'sensation'. Some philosophers have held that sense-data—colors, etc.—are *sensations*. But, says Moore, this is misleading. We could certainly say that we *had* a sensation when we saw the color. But what we mean by 'a sensation' here is our *seeing* of the color and *not* the *color* which we saw. The color is not what we mean to say we *had* when we had a sensation. What we did have is an experience which consisted in our seeing the color. Hence, sensations are the acts of apprehending sense-data, and not the sense-data themselves.[29]

A second sense in which things might be called mental is if they are what Moore refers to as "the 'qualities' of conscious acts." What he means by this is somewhat obscure, but I think he means the following (I use his example). We may distinguish different kinds of acts of consciousness, e.g., mere apprehensions, beliefs, volitions. I can, for example, merely apprehend (understand) the proposition that Hitler is dead. But I can also believe it, rather than merely apprehend it. Hence, these are two different kinds of acts of consciousness, and they have different qualities —whatever they are—which distinguish one from the other. Similarly, if I will that Hitler is dead, my act of consciousness is qualitatively different from my merely believing or understanding the proposition that he is. Now when I sense—and, for Moore, am conscious of—a blue color, my act of consciousness is *of* the color. The color is *what* I apprehend; it is not a quality of my apprehension. Hence, sense-data are not mental in this second sense either.[30]

Moore then would not, for example, as Professor Chisholm does,[31] say 'I sense bluely'. He would, rather, say 'I sense a blue object' or 'I sense a blue datum', etc.

A third view by which one might hold that sense-data are mental is to say that "they have to my mental acts and to one another exactly that relation which my mental acts have to one another, and which I describe by calling them all 'mine'." [32] Moore says that he "cannot persuade" himself that a blue color he sees is related to him in exactly the same way in which his seeing is related to him. In fact, it seems to be related to him in no way at all except by the fact that he is conscious *of* it.

---

28. "The Subject Matter of Psychology," p. 58.
29. *SMPP*, pp. 30–31. Cf. "Refut.," *passim*.
30. "The Subject Matter of Psychology," pp. 58–59.
31. *Perceiving* (Ithaca: Cornell Univ. Press, 1957), Chap. X.
32. "The Subject Matter of Psychology," p. 59.

But his consciousness of it is related to him in a different way. "Its relation to me is simply that it is my consciousness, an act of consciousness of mine: and the blue which I see certainly does not seem to be 'mine' in this sense."[33] Hence, Moore cannot accept the view that sense-data are related to his mind in the way in which his conscious acts are so related and are related to each other, the relation which we indicate by calling them 'mine'. And he denies that sense-data are mental in this third sense.

But some philosophers have, nevertheless, insisted that sense-data are mental. Let us consider the argument by which they have come to that conclusion.

They have held, *first,* that no sense-datum or "part of one" exists except at the moment when I am apprehending it. According to this view then, the *esse* of sense-data is *percipi.* If I, say, look at a white envelope and turn away my eyes, then while I saw that patch of color, there *was* that patch of color in the universe, but now that I no longer see it, it has ceased to exist (in this view). Both the color and my seeing it are things which were but are no longer. According to this view, there may still be in the universe a patch of color just like the one I saw, one which someone else is seeing now or one which I would see if I now turned and looked at the envelope again. But this new color-patch, though exactly like the old one, is not the same. The same thing holds true for all sense-data. These philosophers have held, *second,* that no two of us ever apprehend exactly the same sense-data. We apprehend sense-data which may be exactly alike but which can never be numerically the same. This follows from the first view. If this patch of color which I see at time$_1$ has at time$_2$, when I turn away my head, ceased to be, then it follows that no one can be seeing it at time$_2$. Even if someone came and stood in exactly the same spot, and under the same perceptual conditions, he would not, according to this view, be able to see the same sense-data which I saw. The *third* view held by these philosophers is: None of the sense-data apprehended by one person can ever be *in the same space* with any sense-data apprehended by any other person. The patch of color you see and the one I see have no spatial relations *to one another.* All my sense-data are within a private space of my own. Hence, no point in this space can be at any distance from, or be above or below, any point in your private space.[34]

From these three views some philosophers have argued that sense-data

33. *Ibid.*
34. *SMPP*, pp. 40–42.

are mental, that they exist *in the mind* of the person who apprehends them. Or they have held that these three things are what is meant by saying that sense-data exist only in our minds. Moore has two main criticisms of this argument.

(i) He says, first, that even if these three things were true about all the sense-data which I ever apprehend, it would not follow that sense-data exist only in my mind, or that they are *in* my mind in any sense. They are not in my mind in the sense in which my apprehension of them is in my mind. "This whitish colour, even if it does exist only while I see it, and cannot be seen by anyone else, does not seem to be in my mind in the sense in which my seeing of it is *in my mind*. My seeing of it is, it seems to me, related to my mind in a way in which this which I see is not related to it." [35] This, of course, is merely an assertion or an expression of an opinion on Moore's part and not an argument.

(ii) But Moore (in some writings) questions the truth of one of the three views which make up this argument that sense-data are mental: namely, the first, which says that every sense-datum which any person ever directly apprehends exists only as long as he apprehends it—i.e., the view that sense-data do not exist at times when they are not being experienced at all. Actually he expresses five different views on the subject, some of which differ only slightly from others.

(a) In at least one passage Moore finds that he cannot determine whether or not this assertion is true. "I confess I cannot make up my mind. . . . I have never seen any arguments in its favour which seem absolutely conclusive. . . . I can perfectly well conceive that the very same sense-data, which I see at one time, should exist even when I am not seeing them; and I cannot by merely considering the possibility, determine whether it is true or not." [36]

(b) Elsewhere Moore is *inclined* to think that the assertion that no sense-data exist when they are not being experienced is *false*. In "The Status of Sense-Data," he holds that a negative answer to the question 'Can sense-data exist when they are not being experienced?' is based upon two different a priori reasons. The first is the dictum that the *esse* of sense-data is *percipi*. This should mean that to suppose a sense-datum to exist and yet not be experienced is self-contradictory. "This at least seems to me to be clearly false . . . to suppose that there are patches of colour

35. *Ibid.,* p. 43.
36. *Ibid.,* p. 44.

which are not being experienced is clearly not self-contradictory, however false it may be." [37] The second a priori reason which some have put forth for a negative answer is that we can clearly see that nothing can have the one property without having the other. "I do not see my way to deny that we may be able to know a priori that such a connection does hold," Moore says. "In the present case, however, I cannot see that it does hold." [38] Moore concludes by saying that he has, in Hume's phrase, "a strong propensity to believe" that the sense-data which I sense, say, in looking at this paper, still exist unchanged when I am no longer sensing them and that there may be a vast number of sense-data which exist at any moment when they are not being experienced at all. [39]

(c) In other passages Moore definitely denies that all sense-data exist only when they are being directly apprehended. In *Some Main Problems of Philosophy* his conception of a sense-datum is such that "anything which was a coloured patch, of the sort which we directly apprehend instances, would be a sense-datum, even if it had never been seen; . . . and similarly with regard to all other classes of sense-data." [40]

(d) In still other passages Moore maintains that the assertion that sense-data exist only when they are being perceived is true with respect to some sense-data and is false with respect to others. In "The Subject Matter of Psychology," he says that the assertion may very likely be true about images, but not about sense-data which are given by the senses. [41] Elsewhere, he holds that pains, for example, do not exist when they are not perceived but that other kinds of things—colors, etc.—do exist when they are not perceived. [42]

(e) Finally, as a result of Ducasse' criticism, Moore radically revised his views and in his "Reply" maintains that it is *impossible* that sense-data should exist *un*perceived. But Moore fails to give any reason for this view. He justifies a particular case by an appeal to the general statement, but he nowhere justifies the general statement. Moore writes:

In that early paper I really was asserting that the sensible quality 'blue' . . . *could* exist without being perceived; that there was no contradiction in suppos-

37. "The Status of Sense-Data," *PS*, p. 180.
38. *Ibid.*, p. 181.
39. *Ibid.*, p. 182. Cf. "The Nature and Reality of Objects of Perception," *PS*, pp. 72 ff.
40. *SMPP*, p. 129. Cf. "Are the Materials of Sense Affections of the Mind?", *PAS*, XVII (1916–17), 426.
41. "The Subject Matter of Psychology," pp. 60–61.
42. "The Nature and Reality of Objects of Perception," *PS*, pp. 91–92. Cf. "Reply," p. 653.

ing it to do so. Mr. Ducasse's view is that it *cannot:* that there *is* a contradiction in supposing it to do so. And on *this* issue I am now very much inclined to think that Mr. Ducasse is right and that I in that paper was wrong; my reason being that I am inclined to think that it is as impossible that anything which has the sensible quality 'blue,' and, more generally, *anything whatever which is directly apprehended, any sense-datum,* that is, should exist unperceived, as it is that a headache should exist unfelt.[43]

One might think that it is because of Ducasse' criticism that Moore changed his mind. Yet throughout this section of his "Reply" he maintains that Ducasse' criticism is *wrong*. Moore concludes the section: "I cannot see that he has given any good reason at all for supposing that the *esse* of sensible qualities is *percipi,* though I believe that there *must* be some good reason." [44]

We have seen that Moore *denies* that sense-data are mental in any of the three senses which he distinguishes, the senses in which acts of consciousness, the "qualities" of conscious acts, or the relation by which my conscious acts are related to me (which we express by 'mine') are mental. We have also seen that he at first denies that the three assertions that no sense-datum can exist except when I am apprehending it, that no two of us can apprehend the same sense-data, and that the sense-data of one person can never be in the same space with those of any other imply that sense-data are mental or in the mind. One would suspect that, since he changed his mind on the first of these assertions, Moore would now have to agree that sense-data *are* mental. However, as we saw above, he holds that even if any or all of these three assertions were true, it does not follow that all sense-data are mental or that they exist only in the mind of the person apprehending them. However, Moore does go on to say that all sense-data that I apprehend are, if these three assertions are true, *dependent* upon my mind, even if they are not in my mind. "If it is really true of all of them that they exist only while I am conscious of them, that nobody else is ever conscious of them, and that they are situated only in a private space of my own . . . —then certainly nothing could be more thoroughly dependent on my mind than they are." [45] We saw that Moore changed his mind and held the first of the assertions to be true. Or rather, he found reasons for thinking that it might be true. But he also found reasons for

43. "Reply," p. 658.
44. *Ibid.,* p. 660.
45. *SMPP,* p. 43.

thinking that it might be false. We may then, with the single exception just mentioned, say that Moore's rather consistently held (and perhaps final) view with regard to the ontological status of sense-data (with respect to whether or not they are mental) is that although sense-data are mind-dependent, they nevertheless are not mental.

B. Are sense-data physical? [46]

If sense-data are not mental, though they are mind-dependent, then are they physical? But the question 'Are sense-data physical?' is, as Moore would say, ambiguous. It may mean one of two things. It may mean either (i) 'Is any given sense-datum physical, in the sense that it is a *whole* physical object?' or it may mean (ii) 'Is a sense-datum physical, in the sense that it is some *part* of a physical object (e.g., its surface)?' Moore rules out the first of these alternatives with one class of exceptions—certain non-opaque objects such as soap bubbles. In the "Defence" Moore says that what he knows regarding the sense-data he senses when he knows, say, 'This is a human hand' is *not* that the sense-datum *itself* is a human hand. For he knows that his *hand* has many parts—the other side which is not now seen, the bones inside it, etc. These are not parts of the present sense-datum; hence, a sense-datum cannot be physical in the sense of being a *whole* physical object (with the one class of possible exceptions).[47] With an affirmative answer to (i) ruled out (for nearly all cases), the only sense in which sense-data might be physical, for Moore, is in sense (ii). Thus, we may ask, next, are sense-data physical in the sense of being *parts* of physical objects? Again Moore has varied and contradictory opinions on this subject.

Before turning to them, one should note that the question 'Are sense-data physical?' as asked by Moore makes sense primarily with respect to *visual* and perhaps tactile sense-data. One would hardly even ask if a sound, a smell, or a taste, as an object of direct acquaintance, was a physical object or a part of one. As I mentioned before, Moore limited his discussions almost entirely to visual sense-data, and I shall do the same. He often thought that whatever applied to these applied *mutatis mutandis* to others. As O. K. Bouwsma has pointed out, this is not always the case. In his "Reply," "Addendum," and "Visual Sense-Data," Moore began to realize that there are important differences.

46. In the following I shall have to assume, in the manner in which Moore himself does, that we know that there are physical objects and what they are like. Otherwise one could hardly ask if sense-data are physical.

47. "Def.," pp. 54–55. Cf. *PS*, pp. 229–30, 236; *SMPP*, p. 33.

I turn now to Moore's varied answers to the question 'Are sense-data, at least visual sense-data, physical (in sense [ii])?'

(a) In some passages Moore holds that it is *quite possible* that sense-data *are* (in sense [ii]) physical. "In cases of visual perception of the kind to which I am confining myself, (1) it is quite certain that we are always directly aware of a sense-datum and (2) it is quite possible that the sense-datum in question may be a part of the surface of the physical object we are seeing." [48] Similarly, in the "Defence," he wonders if it is true that (visual) sense-data are parts of the surfaces of physical objects and answers, "I think it may just possibly be." [49]

(b) Elsewhere he was more sure and said that sense-data are, or very *certainly seem to be,* parts of the surfaces of physical objects. *"On philosophical inspection,* it does seem to be true that this sense-datum is a part of the surface of my thumb, and that, *therefore,* I am directly apprehending a part of its surface." [50] In "Some Judgments of Perception" he concludes a long discussion by saying that he is "inclined to favour the view that what I am judging of this presented object is that it is itself a part of the surface of an inkstand—that, therefore, it really is identical with this part of the surface of this inkstand." [51]

(c) In still other passages Moore is quite sure that (visual) sense-data are *not* physical (in sense [ii]). With respect to a view which Moore attributes to Russell, the view that "the sense-datum is always, in a certain sense, 'physical'," Moore holds "that it is very doubtful." [52] He sums up a discussion in *Some Main Problems of Philosophy* by: "This seems to be the state of things with regard to these sense-data—the colour, the size, and the shape. They seem, in a sense, to have had very little to do with the real envelope. . . . It seems very probable that *none* of the colours seen was really a part of the envelope; and that none of the sizes and shapes seen were the size or the shape of the real envelope." [53] And later: "No sense-datum, or part of a sense-datum, or collection of sense-data, can possibly be a material object." [54] His "Reply" is somewhat ambiguous on the subject, but he devotes a long passage to one of his earlier views that

48. "The Nature of Sensible Appearances," *PASS*, VI (1926), p. 184.
49. "Def.," p. 56.
50. "The Nature of Sensible Appearances," p. 187.
51. *PS*, p. 251. Cf. *PS*, pp. 236 f., 247–48; "Def.," p. 56.
52. "The Implications of Recognition," *PAS*, XVI (1915–16), 205.
53. *SMPP*, p. 38.
54. *Ibid.*, p. 130.

sense-data are *not* physical and seems to affirm that view.[55] In a later passage he sums up his position:

I am inclined to think that it is as impossible that . . . *anything whatever which is directly apprehended,* any *sense-datum,* that is, should exist unperceived as it is that a headache should exist unfelt. If this is so, it would follow at once, that *no* sense-datum can be identical with any physical surface, which is to say that no physical surface can be directly apprehended: that it is a contradiction to say that any is. Now at the end of the last section, I said I was strongly inclined to agree . . . that physical surfaces are directly apprehended. I am, therefore, now saying that I am strongly inclined to take a veiw incompatible with that which I then said I was strongly inclined to take. And this is the truth. I am strongly inclined to take both of these views. I am completely puzzled about the matter, and only wish I could see any way of settling it.[56]

Finally, in the last essay Moore wrote he says that in the case of seeing an opaque object a sense-datum "cannot possibly be identical" with part of the surface of a physical object.[57]

Why did Moore have such great difficulty in deciding whether or not a sense-datum is identical with the surface of a material object? Let us suppose that we were present at the lecture at which Moore held up an envelope. As was mentioned earlier, depending upon our position, etc., each of us saw different sets of sense-data—slightly different shades of color, etc. Hence (the argument from perspectives), we were led to believe that a sense-datum must be different from the physical object, for each of the sets of sense-data was slightly different from the rest; therefore, they cannot *all* be exactly the same as the envelope (the physical object).

Moore anticipates that someone might object: When we say we saw an envelope, we do not mean the *whole* of it, but only some *part* of it. Can we not suggest then that our reason for saying we saw the envelope is that each of the sets of sense-data is a *part* of the envelope or a *part* of the surface of the envelope? [58]

Moore next considers this possibility. Could we plausibly maintain that

55. "Reply," pp. 644 ff.
56. *Ibid.,* pp. 658–59.
57. "Visual Sense-Data," pp. 210–11.
58. *SMPP,* p. 33.

any of the sense-data or sets of sense-data which we saw are parts of the material object or parts of its surface? I here paraphrase Moore's discussion. First, take the color. Can the colors we saw be parts of the surface of the envelope? Probably each of us saw a slightly different color. If we are to suppose that all those colors are parts of the surface of the envelope, then we will have to hold that they are *all* in the same place—that all of them occupy the very same surface or part of it at the same time. "I myself find it difficult to believe that this is so," says Moore.[59] Someone might suggest that the color which *one* of us saw was on the surface of the envelope, whereas the colors which the rest of us saw are not there. "This also, I think, is difficult to believe." [60] Next, take the size. Each of the sense-data which we saw was probably of a different size, depending upon how far back we sat, etc. Or, at least, there were many different sizes. "And if this be so, then certainly it seems to be absolutely impossible that they should *all* of them be the size of this side of the envelope; it cannot have several different sizes." [61] Again, one might maintain that some one size which one of us saw is the real size. "But it seems also possible that none of them are." [62] And, similarly, with the shape. For these reasons Moore concludes that it is very probable that none of the colors, sizes, or shapes which we saw were the color, size, or shape of the real envelope—the physical object.[63]

We may reach the same conclusion by considering a case in which each of us senses a different sense-datum, say two different shapes, both of which, we may reasonably believe, are associated with the same physical object, an object which has not perceptibly changed its shape. Suppose that at 4:30:00 I look at a round penny and see a round sense-datum and, moving to the side, at 4:30:10 I look at the same coin and see an elliptical sense-datum. I have no reason to believe that the coin changed its shape that rapidly, although, of course, under the "molecular hypothesis" the penny may have changed very slightly, but not enough to be noticed. If sense-data are identical with the surfaces of physical objects, we shall have to hold not only that I saw two different sense-data (which is true) but that the material object changed its shape extremely rapidly; and this too

59. *Ibid.*, p. 35.
60. *Ibid.*
61. *Ibid.*
62. *Ibid.*, p. 36.
63. *Ibid.*, p. 38. Cf. "The Status of Sense-Data," *PS*, p. 194; "Def.," p. 56.

seems an implausible view.[64] For reasons such as these, Moore was "inclined to believe" that sense-data are *not* parts of (the surfaces of) material objects. Yet, largely because of his dissatisfaction with other views as to how sense-data are related to physical objects (views which I shall discuss shortly), Moore was also inclined to believe that sense-data *are* parts of the surfaces of material objects. Hence, he was prompted to introduce what is undoubtedly the most monstrous philosophical doctrine that appears anywhere in his works.

Suppose again that I see the penny from in front and then from the side —or that I see a tree from a few yards away and then from a distance of a half-mile, etc. Moore writes:

> What now seems to me possible is . . . that the sense-datum which corresponds to a penny, which I am seeing obliquely, is not really perceived to *be* different in shape from that which corresponded to the penny when I was straight in front of it, but is only perceived to *seem* different—that all that is perceived is that the one seems elliptical and the other circular.[65]

Similarly, the second tree-datum, from a half-mile away, is only perceived to *seem* smaller than the first from close by! Moore goes on: "Possibly in making this suggestion that sense-data, in cases where most philosophers have assumed unhesitatingly that they are perceived to be different, are only really perceived to *seem* different, I am . . . talking sheer nonsense." [66] Possibly, indeed! In "Visual Sense-Data" Moore admits that this sort of view does seem to be nonsense and, as we saw, finally *rejected* the view that sense-data are parts of the surfaces of physical objects and, hence, that they are physical at all.[67]

We have seen then that, for Moore, sense-data are *not* mental (though they are mind-dependent) and that, in his final view, they are *not* physical. But what are they? What is their ontological status? Moore nowhere discusses what it might be. Hence, we must assume that there is some third ontological category for Moore, in addition to the mental and the physical and that the class of all sense-data belongs to or is coincident with that ontological category. But if sense-data are not physical, how are they *related to* physical objects? This must be our next topic.

64. "Some Judgments of Perception," *PAS*, XIX (1918–19), reprinted in *PS*, pp. 243–44.
65. *Ibid.*, p. 245. Cf. *SMPP*, pp. 39 f.
66. "Some Judgments of Perception," *PS*, pp. 246–47.
67. "Visual Sense-Data," p. 211.

4. *What is the relation of sense-data to physical objects?* [68]

A. One possible view regarding the relation of sense-data to physical objects is that the relation is one of *identity,* either that sense-data are physical objects or that sense-data are the surfaces (or parts of the surfaces) of physical objects. But, as we have just seen, Moore finally found this view untenable, or at least was strongly inclined to think that it was so. Hence, we must turn to a consideration of what other alternatives might be found. Moore discusses several.

B. A second alternative: In talking of 'an inkstand' we say 'This is an inkstand', when what we really mean is 'The inkstand of which this is part of the surface'; that is, the inkstand is only known to us by description (as the inkstand of which *this material surface* is part of *the surface*). Similarly, when we talk of 'this material surface', what we really mean is the material surface of which *this* (sense-datum) has a certain *relation*. Again, this surface is also only known to me by description (as the surface—or part of one—which has that certain relation to the sense-datum). And in this view, what I am judging if I say of the sense-datum I see in 'This is part of the surface of an inkstand' is not that the sense-datum itself is that part, but that the thing which stands to the sense-datum in *a certain relation* is part of the surface. Thus, what I am judging with regard to that thing is 'There is one thing and one only which stands to this sense-datum in this certain relation, and the thing which does so is part of the surface of the inkstand (physical object)'.[69] But, asks Moore, if we accept this view, a question immediately arises: What "on earth" *is* that relation?

Some philosophers, according to Moore, hold that the relation is a causal one. They hold that this part of the surface of the inkstand is the cause of the sense-datum which I sense. They hold that what I am judging above is 'This sense-datum has one and only one cause, and that cause is part of the surface of the inkstand'. Moore thinks it is obvious that this view is untenable. He does not believe, and doubts whether anyone does, that the sense-datum has only one cause. He believes that it has a series of different causes. This part of the surface of the inkstand may be and very likely is *one* of the causes of *my perception of* the sense-datum. And perhaps it is

68. Assuming again that the latter exist, or taking a commonsensical stand regarding their existence.
69. "Some Judgments of Perception," *PS*, pp. 247–48. Cf. "Def.," pp. 220–21.

also one of the causes of the *sense-datum* itself, but Moore cannot find any reasons for thinking that it may be.[70]

Another suggestion which Moore makes is that there may be some "ultimate, not further definable relation" which we might call the relation of "being a manifestation of." And when we judge that there is only one thing which stands to this sense-datum in a certain relation and that that thing is part of the surface of the inkstand, what we are judging, is: 'There is one and only one thing of which this sense-datum is a manifestation, and that thing is part of the surface of the inkstand'. Moore says that this may be a true account, but he cannot find "the slightest sign" of being aware of any such relation.[71]

A third alternative suggested by Moore regarding the relation of sense-data to physical objects is what he calls the "Mill-Russell" type of view. According to Moore this seems to be the position Mill had in mind when he said that material objects are "permanent possibilities of sensation." According to this view, when I know, for example, that 'This is part of the surface of an inkstand', what I am knowing about the sense-datum is not that the sense-datum is itself a part of the surface, nor that there is a thing which has to the sense-datum a certain relation and which is part of the surface, but a set of hypothetical facts: " 'If *these* conditions had been fulfilled, I should have been perceiving a sense-datum intrinsically related to *this* sense-datum in *this* way', 'If *these* (other) conditions had been fulfilled, I should have been perceiving a sense-datum intrinsically related to *this* sense-datum in *this* (other) way', etc., etc." [72] For example, suppose (again) that some coins are on the ground, oblique to my line of sight. In the Mill-Russell view all that can be meant by saying (i) *that I see the coins* is some such thing as: If I were to move my body in certain ways, I would apprehend other sense-data, say, tactile ones, which I would not have apprehended if my present visual experiences were hallucinatory, etc. Similarly, all that can be meant by saying (ii) *that the coins have another side* (which I do not at present see) is: If I were to turn the coins over, I would have other sensations of such and such a sort. But if this view is to

70. "Some Judgments of Perception," *PS*, pp. 248–49. Cf. "The Status of Sense-Data," *PS*, p. 192.
71. "Some Judgments of Perception," *PS*, pp. 249–50. Cf. "Def.," p. 57; "The Status of Sense-Data," *PS*, pp. 192–93.
72. "Def.," pp. 57–58.

be successful, the interpretations which were just given of (i) and (ii) cannot be correct ones. Why? The conditions under which we would experience other sense-data are, in these interpretations, expressed in terms of *physical objects* and not merely in terms of sense-data and our experience of them. The conditions are expressed in such terms as 'If I were to move my body', 'If I were to turn the coins over', etc. Hence, all of these propositions would have to be again interpreted, in terms of sense-data, if our original propositions (i) and (ii) have to be so interpreted. Thus, any *"ultimate* interpretation" of propositions like (i) and (ii) would be very complicated. Moore finds himself unable to come anywhere near to stating what they would be.[73]

In one paper Moore found this fact that the procedure would be so complicated a "grave" objection to the view.[74] Elsewhere he held that some form of the Mill-Russell alternative may be the only true view. In "Some Judgments of Perception" he writes: "Indeed, this paper may be regarded . . . as an argument in favour of the proposition that some such view must be true." [75] Nevertheless, he found other objections which prevented him from consistently accepting it. For example, in the Mill-Russell view, though we could say that the *coins* existed before we saw them and that *they* are *circular,* etc., these expressions, in order to be true, would have to be understood in a Pickwickian sense. When, for example, I know that the coins existed before I saw them, what I know is not that anything existed at that time in the sense that these sense-data which I now see in looking at them exist. All I know is that since I see elliptical, colored patches which exist now, if certain conditions *had been* realized, I would have had other "sensations" that I did not have; or, if certain conditions *were to be* realized in the future, I would have certain other sensations. This fact that my assertions that the coins exist, are round, etc., will be true only in a Pickwickian sense is a great objection to it, for Moore. For, as he says at one point, he has a "strong propensity to believe" that when he knows that the coins existed before he saw them, what he knows is that something existed at that time in the very same sense in which the elliptical sense-data which he now senses in looking at them exist. But he says,

73. "The Status of Sense-Data," *PS,* pp. 188–90. Cf. "Def.," *PP.* pp. 57–58; "Some Judgments of Perception," *PS,* pp. 250–52.
74. "Def.," p. 58.
75. *PS,* p. 251. Cf. "The Status of Sense-Data," *PS,* p. 190.

This belief may be mere prejudice. It *may* be that when I believe that I *now* have, in my body, blood and nerves and brain, *what* I believe is only true, if it does not assert . . . the *present* existence of anything whatever, other than sensibles which I directly apprehend, but only makes assertions as to the kind of experiences a doctor would have if he dissected me.[76]

I cannot find that, on this problem of the relation of sense-data to physical objects, as on so many others, Moore ever resolved the problem or ever came to any definite conclusion as to what the relation is. Almost every alternative involves him in paradoxes or is fraught with objections.

76. "The Status of Sense-Data," *PS*, p. 192. Cf. "Def.," p. 58.

X I

The Problem of

Perception and

Its Solution

I T MAY BE REMEMBERED that in Chapter IX I referred to a view
of Moore's which needed to be considered in some detail. It is his
view that the introduction of sense-data in some sense solves the problem
of perception. Indeed, Moore holds that the problem cannot be solved
unless we introduce sense-data. But, as we have seen and shall see again,
the introduction of sense-data also complicates the problem. For if there
are sense-data, and if they are anything like what we found them to be in
Chapter X, then we have a right to ask: How do we know that there are
material objects or anything beside our own acts of consciousness and our
private sense-data? And since we are now on a philosophical level of
argumentation (by virtue of introducing technical terms like 'sense-data'),
we cannot return to our commonsensical beliefs. Our next two problems,
then, to be dealt with in this chapter, are: Why does Moore maintain
that the problem of perception cannot be solved without the introduction
of sense-data? If there are sense-data, and if they are what Moore takes
them to be, how do we ever know of the existence of an *external world*?

I

IF WE ACCEPT MOORE'S FORMULATION of the problem of perception, i.e., 'How can I know of the existence of material objects or of an external world?', then why does Moore hold that the introduction of sense-data is essential for the solution of the problem? I must again emphasize that in many or most of his writings Moore does *not* hold that the introduction of sense-data is at all required for the solution. For example, with respect to Hume's view that we do not have any *knowledge* of any external facts (knowledge that there are physical objects, etc.) Moore says: "It is, in fact, absurd to suggest that I do not know any external facts whatsoever." [1] But what argument is there for the view that we *do* know external facts? "The only proof that we do know external facts lies in the simple fact that we do know them." [2] Here Moore takes a commonsensical stand on the issue. As I suggested in Chapter II, he often attacks a philosophical position (and, in his mind, refutes it) simply because it conflicts with common sense, or he defends some assertion as being true because it agrees with common sense. He does so because of his fairly prevalent belief that "we should . . . make our philosophical opinions agree with what we necessarily believe at other times." [3]

But in many writings Moore does tackle a philosophical problem in a philosophical way, i.e., in such a manner that an appeal to common sense is not the ultimate touchstone for determining the truth or falsity of a philosophical view. It is in one of these works that he holds that the introduction of sense-data is essential for the solution of the problem of perception. Let us follow his argument.[4] Moore sets out to answer two questions: (1) "How do we know that anything exists except our own perceptions and what we directly perceive?" [5] (2) "How do we know that there are any other people, who have perceptions in some respects similar to our own?" [6] Moore takes up (2) first.

The second question gets progressively refined and qualified. By (2)

1. "Hume's Philosophy," *The New Quarterly* (Nov., 1909), reprinted in *PS*, p. 157.
2. *Ibid.*, p. 160. Cf. "Prf.," pp. 146–50; "Def.," *passim.*
3. "Hume's Philosophy," *PS*, p. 163.
4. "The Nature and Reality of Objects of Perception," *PAS*, VI (1905–6), 68–127, reprinted in *PS*, pp. 31–96.
5. It must be remembered that what we directly perceive are sense-data.
6. "The Nature and Reality of Objects of Perception," *PS*, p. 32. By (1) and (2) Moore says that he is asking: "What reasons do we have for believing in an external world?" (p. 40).

Moore says that he means (2a): "Does *each single one* of us know any proposition which is a reason for believing that *others* exist?"[7] But another restriction is necessary. If we were to ask someone 'How do you know that you saw that statement in the *Times?*' and he were to answer 'Because I *did* see it in the *Times*', we would not think that he had given us a *reason* for his belief that he saw it in the *Times*, for his answer asserts the very thing for which we are requesting a reason. Hence, we must reformulate our question as (2b):

Which among the true propositions which (as we commonly assume) each of us believes, and which do not themselves assert the existence of anything other than that person himself, his own perceptions, or what he directly perceives, are such that they would probably not be true unless some other person existed, who had perceptions in some respects similar to his own?[8]

Often, says Moore, I have certain perceptions which it is unlikely that I would have unless someone else were having certain perceptions. If I am at a lecture, it is unlikely that I would be having certain auditory perceptions unless someone else, the lecturer, were having other perceptions—marks on paper, hearing his voice in a louder than usual way, etc. Our question now becomes (2c): "What reason has *each* of us for believing . . . that he would not have certain perceptions that he does have, unless some other person had certain particular perceptions?"[9] But what good reason *can* be given for believing that proposition? We have no good reason for believing it, says Moore, unless we have good reason for believing some *generalization,* a generalization that things of a particular kind are more often than not preceded, accompanied, or followed by things of another kind: e.g., a generalization that when some man has a particular kind of perception, some other man generally has had some other perception. Well, what reasons have we for believing such generalizations? Only one answer can be given, says Moore. If we have any reason for believing such generalizations, it must be based on *observation.* Thus, our question may again be revised (2d): "What reason can be found in observation for . . . a proposition which asserts that when one man has one kind of perception, another man generally has or has had another?"[10] But by 'observation' we may mean the ordinary sense in

7. *Ibid.,* p. 42. Moore emphasizes that he means a *good* reason.
8. *Ibid.,* p. 45.
9. *Ibid.,* p. 49.
10. *Ibid.,* p. 53.

which we are said to observe the perceptions of others, or the stricter sense in which we only observe our own. The first is the very thing about which we are asking. Hence, we must mean the second. Our question must, accordingly, be revised (2e): "What reasons do my own observations give me, for supposing that any perception whatever, which I have, would probably not occur, unless some other person had a certain kind of perception?" or for supposing that some of my own observations "are generally preceded or accompanied by observations of other people?" [11] Now someone might maintain that my observations give me *no* reason for any propositions of this kind. Moore's chief argument against this view is that it would have paradoxical consequences. But, says Moore, (2e) is a question to which no answer that he has ever seen appears to be correct. In order to answer it, we must first consider two other questions: (i) "Of what nature must observations be, if they are to give a reason for any generalization asserting that the existence of one kind of thing is generally connected with that of another?" (ii) "What kinds of things do we observe?" [12]

(i) To answer the first question, Moore says that he will point out only the kinds of observations which are *necessary* to justify a generalization (not those which are sufficient). Suppose the generalization is that the existence of one kind of object, *A,* is generally preceded, accompanied, or followed by the existence of another kind, *B.* Then to justify the generalization that the existence of *A* is generally *preceded* by the existence of *B,* I must, *first,* have observed an object, *a,* which is in some respects like *A,* and another, *b,* which is in some respects like *B. Second,* the *a* and *b* which I observed must have existed or been real. *Third,* the most that we reasonably can believe about *A* and *B* is that the relation of *A* and *B* is the same relation in which we observed *a* and *b* to stand. For example, suppose that our generalization is 'Hens' eggs (*A*) are generally laid by hens (*B*)'. We must, first then, have observed a hen and a hen's egg. Second, the hen and the hen's egg must have been real. By 'real' here Moore explicitly states that he means the sense in which percepts are real. He is not here speaking of physical objects. Third, the relation of laying which we observed must be that which occurs in the generalization. [13]

(ii) What kinds of things do we observe? In this essay, by observation

11. *Ibid.,* pp. 54, 55.
12. *Ibid.,* p. 61.
13. *Ibid.,* pp. 61–67.

Moore means direct perception. And, as we saw, what we directly perceive (actually see, etc.) are primarily sense-data but are also direct
perceptions themselves. Moore here holds that the *esse* of sense-data is not
necessarily *percipi*.[14]

Moore now returns to the main question, (2e), and asks: What that we
observe can give us reason to believe that *any one else* has various
perceptions, thoughts, or feelings? Some have held that 'The observation
of my own perceptions, thoughts, and feelings can give me such a reason'.
Moore hopes to show that this view is false, and that 'The observation of
my own perceptions, thoughts, feelings, *and sense-data,* can give me such
a reason' is true.[15]

Assume, as the first view suggests, that only my own perceptions,
thoughts, and feelings exist, but *no sense-data.* Where among them am I
to look for any which might give me reason for supposing that other
perceptions (similar to my own) exist? I have perceptions which I *call*
perceptions of other people's bodies and which are similar to other perceptions "of my own body." And I observe that some perceptions "of
my body" are preceded by other perceptions, etc. For example, I may
observe (what I call) my hand grab my foot. This perception was
preceded by a certain feeling of pain. I may observe this kind of happening often enough to justify a generalization. But I may also have the
perception I call the perception of another person grabbing his foot in a
way similar to that in which I perceived my hand grab my foot. But I *do
not* observe *my* feeling of pain preceding this second perception. Will my
generalization allow me to infer that this second perception is preceded by
a similar feeling of pain in the *other* person? Not at all. First, the
perceptions I call perceptions of another's body are different from those I
call perceptions of my own. Second, this inference violates the third
necessary condition mentioned above. If a feeling of pain may be supposed to precede the second perception (someone else's), it must stand in
the *same* relation to *my* perception of *his* hand grabbing *his* foot as the
one in which *my* perception of *my* hand grabbing *my* foot does. That is,
the only kind of feeling of pain that my observation (of him) would
justify me in inferring is a feeling of pain of *my own.* I have no more
reason to believe that the feeling of pain which precedes my perception of
foot-grabbing in another's body is the feeling of *another* person than I

14. *Ibid.,* pp. 67–78.
15. *Ibid.,* pp. 78–79.

have to believe that the hen whose existence preceded the egg can be a hen which had never been within a thousand miles of the egg. Hence, where I do perceive the second perception but not the pain, I can only infer an *unperceived* pain of *my own.* Moore concludes that no observations of *only* perceptions, thoughts, and feelings (but no sense-data) can give me any reason for supposing that there are any such *in another.*[16]

"But," says Moore,

how different is the case if we adopt the hypothesis which I wish to recommend—if we assume the existence of that other class of data which I have called 'sense-contents!' On this hypothesis, that which I perceive, when I perceive a movement of my own body, is *real;* that which I perceive when I perceive a movement of another's body is *real* also. I can now observe not merely the relation between my *perception* of a movement of my body and my own feelings, but also a relation between a *real* movement of my body and my own feelings. And there is no reason why I should not be justified in inferring that another person's feelings stand *in the same relation* to the real movements of his body, in which I observe my own feelings to stand to similar real movements of mine.[17]

This is a rather puzzling passage. First, what is it that is being perceived and held to be real in the second sentence? Since Moore has been, throughout this essay, using 'perceive' to mean 'directly perceive',[18] and since the preceding sentence stresses the introduction of sense-data, it must be the case that that which I perceive when I "perceive a movement of my own body" is *not* necessarily the *body* but *sense-data.* And hence, in the second and third sentences, what Moore is claiming to be real are sense-data. This is so because he here rejects the view that sense-data are parts of physical objects. Similarly, in the fourth sentence, 'a real movement of my body' refers not to the physical object but to the sense-data perceived. Hence, we still have not got to physical objects; that part of the problem is not yet solved. Nor have we shown that there *are* other persons. All we are entitled to do is to *infer* that the sense-data we see when we "see another body" are existent objects for another person, just as those which we see when we see our own body are existent for each of us. But if we have to settle for an *inference,* then someone might reasonably maintain that the inference that I actually am acquainted with

16. *Ibid.,* pp. 79–83.
17. *Ibid.,* p. 83.
18. See "The Nature and Reality of Objects of Perception," *PS,* pp. 68–69.

other persons and that I actually see their bodies is just as good an inference and is more economical in that it does not involve adding entities to the universe. Furthermore, in the passage quoted Moore refers secondly to another person, another body, his body, etc. This seems to be circular argumentation. The only way by which Moore could avoid this charge is to insist that he is starting with our commonsensical notion of 'other persons' and 'other bodies' and is giving a philosophical explication of what such terms mean, thereby demonstrating that their *referents,* which we commonsensically assume to exist, *do* in fact exist; that we now have good grounds for maintaining our commonsensical beliefs about other persons or other bodies. It is not at all clear that this is what Moore *is* trying to do, but he would have to maintain that he is attempting something of this sort in order to escape the circularity charge.

Moore turns finally to a consideration of the other question with which he planned to deal: "How do we know that *any* particular kind of thing exists, other than our perceptions, thoughts, and feelings, and what we directly perceive?" [19] In answer to this question Moore merely says that all the arguments by which he tried to show that observation of one's own perceptions, thoughts, and feelings, but no sense-data, can give no reason to believe in the existence of any such in another *person,* apply equally to show that it can give me no reason to believe in the existence of any *material objects*. He concludes:

It would seem, therefore, that if my own observations do give me any reason whatever for believing in the existence either of any perception in any other person or of any material object, it must be true that not only my own perceptions, thoughts, and feelings, but also *some* of the other kinds of things which I directly perceive—colours, sounds, smells, etc.—do really exist: it must be true that some objects of this kind *exist* or are *real* in precisely the same simple sense in which my perceptions of them exist or are real. [20]

Thus, in order to obtain satisfactory solutions to questions (1) and (2), which constitute "the problem of perception," sense-data must be introduced. I should say again that in a very real sense the problem has *not* been solved by Moore. The most that we are entitled to assert upon the basis of Moore's "solution" is that the problem has been solved on the level of sense-data and percepts. We still have not been shown that there

19. *Ibid.*, p. 89.
20. *Ibid.*, p. 90.

are physical objects. We can *infer* only that there probably are material objects which are causes of sense-data, or some such thing. Of course, Moore might have maintained that certain groupings of sense-data are what we *mean* by physical objects. But he does not maintain this, and it would be inconsistent with nearly all he said in this area for him to make that sort of assertion. For he has nearly always maintained that the two are radically different. This was the point of his distinguishing 'actually see' from 'see', etc. But, then, perhaps a philosophical proof of the existence of physical objects is impossible. Perhaps we can only start with our commonsensical beliefs (such as those of the "Defence" or "Proof") and try to square our philosophical theories with those beliefs. Sometimes Moore was content with such a procedure. At other times he was not and hoped to provide some philosophical argument for the existence of physical objects. It is to such an argument that we may now turn.

II

WE HAVE SEEN IN CHAPTER VI that there are, for Moore, four main kinds of immediate (as opposed to derivative) knowledge: knowing how, direct apprehension (or acquaintance), indirect apprehension, and knowledge that (or knowledge proper). Which of these, if any, could be the way by which we have knowledge of the *existence of material objects?* What is the cognitive relation between us and some material object which we claim to perceive?

In answering this question, Moore merely asserts that the relation is *not* the first of the four ways of knowing, knowing how. He also holds that the cognitive relation is *not* that of direct apprehension. The objects of direct apprehension can be only such things as sense-data, images, propositions, etc. He also (at times) holds that the relation cannot be that of knowledge proper. Why? "Knowledge proper is a relation which you can only have to a proposition; and a material object is certainly not a proposition." [21] Finally, Moore holds that the cognitive relation involved in perceiving material objects cannot be indirect apprehension either. Someone might hold, for example, that when I say that I saw a tree, I mean that when I saw it I only apprehended sense-data, but *later,* when I somehow (Moore does not say how) *know* that I saw it, I indirectly apprehend the tree with which the sense-data were "connected." Moore

21. *SMPP*, p. 83.

replies that if this were the only sense in which we perceived a material object, we could never have any *knowledge of the existence* of material objects at all. If I look at a tree, I might, in addition to apprehending sense-data, be *believing* in the existence of something else other than sense-data (the tree). Insofar as I am believing in the existence of this something else, I am, of course, indirectly apprehending it. If this something else really is the tree, then I am indirectly apprehending a material object. But even if I directly apprehend sense-data and also indirectly apprehend (by belief, say) something else, it does not follow that I *know* through my perception of the existence of a material object. First, even if I do indirectly apprehend something beside the sense-data, that only means that I am *thinking* of something else beside them. And from the fact that I am thinking of a thing, it does not follow that such a thing *exists*. It might be that only the sense-data exist and that my belief in a material object is mistaken. Second, even if there really is something besides the sense-data and my belief is therefore correct, it does not follow that I *know* that the something else exists. Third, even if there *is* something else, and even if I *know* that there is, it does not follow that this something else is a *material object*: i.e., something which is situated in space and which is not a mind or act of consciousness.[22] Thus, to know of the existence of a material object, I must do more than merely apprehend sense-data and believe in the existence of something else (even if the something else does exist). But this sounds very much as if Moore were maintaining after all that we can know of the existence of material objects only through knowledge proper. And this is, in fact, true. Moore writes: "We are now talking of *knowledge* in the sense which I called knowledge *proper:* we are now talking of *knowledge* in the sense in which mere direct apprehension is *not* knowledge, nor mere indirect apprehension either. We are talking of knowledge in the sense in which you cannot *know* anything but a fact." [23] Hence, Moore must have slipped when he earlier maintained that you cannot know the existence of material objects through knowledge proper (on the grounds that all you can know in this way are propositions). It *is* through knowledge proper that we know of the existence of material objects if we know of their existence at all.[24]

22. *Ibid.,* pp. 82–86.
23. *Ibid.,* p. 86.
24. It ought to be noted that in his discussion of knowledge proper (see Chap. VI) Moore maintains throughout that we use knowledge proper to know of the existence of material objects.

Moore then turns to a consideration of some classes to which propositions must belong if (according to some philosophers) anyone is to *know* them to be true. He does this by discussing some of Hume's views on the subject. According to Moore's interpretation (on this occasion) of Hume, all propositions fall into two classes: those which assert that a particular thing does exist, has existed, or will exist, and those which do not assert the existence of anything. The latter are known to be true by intuition or demonstration. The former—the ones we are now interested in—cannot be so known. They can be known only if one or the other of three conditions is fulfilled: (1) X may know that a thing exists if at that moment he directly apprehends it. (2) X may know that a thing *did* exist if he directly apprehended it in the past and now remembers it. (3) X may know of the existence of a thing, A, which he is not directly apprehending or which he has not directly apprehended, only if he knows that some other thing, B, which he has directly apprehended or is directly apprehending, would not have existed unless A had existed, or were existing, or was about to exist. For example, I believe now that my brain, which I am not directly apprehending, exists at this moment. I cannot know this unless I know that something which I am directly apprehending now (e.g., some sounds of my voice) would not exist unless my brain were existing too; or unless I know that something which I directly apprehended a moment ago would not have existed unless my brain had been *going to* exist at this present moment. No matter whether I *do* know either of these things. *If* I did, then I could know that my brain is existing now. And so on, for other cases of knowledge of the past or future existence of a material object.[25]

Moore calls the above view Hume's first principle. He mentions a second. Hume asks: Under what conditions can I know that A would not have existed unless B had existed, did exist, or were about to exist? He answers: Only through *my* experience. Take a case in which I suppose myself to know that B must have been preceded by A. To know absolutely that B must have been preceded by A, I must have observed in the past that things like B were constantly preceded by things like A; and to know that B was probably preceded by A, I must have observed that things like B were generally preceded by things like A. This means that each of us can learn things of the above sort only by his *own* experience.

25. *SMPP*, pp. 90–96.

Since we do learn by the experience of others, says Moore, a modification is necessary. We may say: *I* can never know that *B* was, say, probably preceded by *A,* unless either: *I* have *observed* that things like *B* were generally preceded by things like *A;* or *I* have *observed* that statements which assert that someone else has observed a general connection between things like *B* and *A* are generally true.

But, asks Moore, what does Hume mean by 'observed' or 'observation'? Does he mean direct apprehension *or* the relation we have to material objects? He should not mean the latter, since the purpose of his principles is to state under what conditions we can know of the existence of objects which we do not directly apprehend. They state that we cannot know of the existence of such an object unless we have earlier observed a similar object. But even if we have previously observed a similar object, this would not suffice if 'observation' does not mean direct apprehension. For even if we have earlier observed a similar object, we should not have directly apprehended it. But then, by this rule, we would not know of *its* existence unless we had observed previously to it *another* object similar to it, and so on *ad infinitum.* Thus, Hume meant by 'observation' direct apprehension. According to Moore, this makes his principles less plausible. They now state that I can never know of the existence of any object which I have not directly apprehended, unless I have previously apprehended an object similar to it, or unless I know that someone else has done so. Why is this an implausible view? Because "so much of our knowledge does seem to be based on previous *observation*—observation, in the sense in which we *do* observe material objects, and in which observation does *not* mean direct apprehension." [26]

This remark, of course, is a mere assertion. It does not prove that we *do* have knowledge of the sort specified. Moore does not attempt to argue the point but asks us to consider the consequences of Hume's view. For example, I believe that there are, now, *bones* in my hand (Moore's example). I am not directly apprehending any of them. How then can I, following Hume's principles, know that they even probably exist? Suppose I say that I do so by means of sense-data which I now directly apprehend—the appearances of the skin of my hand; and by means of my knowledge that in the past visible appearances similar to these were connected to certain other sense-data which I should see if I dissected my

26. *Ibid.,* p. 102.

hand and saw the skeleton appearances. But this means that the only things whose existence I can infer are more *sense-data*—bone appearances, etc. "And what applies to the present existence of the skeleton of my hand, applies equally to the existence, past, present or future, of any material object whatever. I can never know that any *material object* even probably exists" (italics added).[27]

Hume's two rules or principles then are: (1) "Nobody can ever know of the existence of anything which he has not directly apprehended, unless he knows that something which he has directly apprehended is *a sign* of its existence." (2) "Nobody can ever know that the existence of any one thing A is *a sign* of the *existence* of another thing B, unless he himself (or, under certain conditions, somebody else) has experienced a general conjunction between *things like* A and *things like* B. And the important thing about this second rule is that nobody can be said to have *experienced a conjunction* between any two things, unless he has *directly apprehended* both the things."[28]

According to Moore, many philosophers, from the assumption that Hume's rules are true, have concluded that we can never know of the existence of physical objects. They have argued that if the rules are true, then no one ever knows of the existence of a material object. And they have concluded that since the rules are true, no one ever *does* know that any material object exists. There are two ways to answer this argument, says Moore: first, to show that even if Hume's rules were true, we could know of the existence of material objects; second, to show that Hume's rules are false.[29]

Before turning to either of these ways by which to answer the argument, Moore considers two views (of other philosophers) which have been based on the assumption that Hume's rules are true. Both start by agreeing with Hume that anyone can know only of the existence of things which he is now directly apprehending or has directly apprehended and remembers. And both hold that the only existing things that anyone ever directly apprehends are his own acts of consciousness, and sense-data and images. The first of these two views is that our knowledge of what exists *beyond* what we are directly apprehending or have directly apprehended is confined to: first, what acts of consciousness we may have in the

27. *Ibid.*, p. 106.
28. *Ibid.*, pp. 109–10.
29. *Ibid.*, p. 110.

future and what sense-data and images we are likely to apprehend directly, and also to the awareness that we have performed acts of consciousness and directly apprehended sense-data in the past (Moore calls all these the contents of one's own mind); and second, the contents of other people's minds. The second of these two views holds that we can know that *something else* exists which is (or are) the cause(s) of sense-data. But, according to it, we can never know if this something else is like anything which we have directly apprehended. Both of these views then deny that we can ever know of the existence of *material objects*.[30]

Moore points out that these two views are quite different from what we normally believe. If we look at a pencil, we believe that the sense-data we see are signs of the existence of a material object which has a cylindrical shape and an inside. This statement is undeniable. We do *believe* such things. But Moore goes on to add:

I . . . claim to know that there does exist now, or did a moment ago, not only these sense-data which I am directly apprehending . . . but *also* something else which I am not directly apprehending. And I claim to know not merely that this something else is the *cause* of the sense-data which I am seeing or feeling: I claim to know that this cause is situated here . . . *in space.* . . . And . . . I claim to know . . . roughly *what* its shape is. I claim to know that the cause of the sense-data I am now directly apprehending is part of the surface of something which is really roughly cylindrical; and that what is enclosed within this cylindrical surface is something different from what is here just outside it.[31]

How does Moore *know* all this? Not a word in answer to this question is to be found. And a few pages later, he admits that all of his beliefs would *not* permit him to *know* of the existence of a material object. It would only allow him to know of the existence of further sense-data, certain colors, shapes, etc., which he might see if he were to "cut the pencil" at various points. And he admits that all these patches of colors, etc., do not constitute the *whole* of the material object in which he *believes*. (We note that Moore has shifted again to *believing* in the existence of the material object.) For he believes that besides all the sense-data, there is in that place where "the pencil is" something *else*. He concludes that if Hume's rules were true, he could not know of the existence of this something else.

Thus Moore agrees that *if* Hume's principles are true, then we cannot

30. *Ibid.*, pp. 110–15.
31. *Ibid.*, p. 116.

know of the existence of material objects. In order to prove that he knows that material objects exist, he must prove that Hume's principles (one or both) are false. Can he prove this? "It seems to me that . . . there really is no stronger and better argument than the following. I *do* know that this pencil exists; but I could not know this, if Hume's principles were true; *therefore,* Hume's principles, one or both of them, are false." [32] He adds: "I really think this argument is as strong and good a one as any that could be used. . . . I think that the fact that, if Hume's principles were true, I could not know of the existence of this pencil, is a *reductio ad absurdum* of those principles." [33]

But now Moore has again switched to *knowing* that the pencil exists! Once more, how does he know this? It is at this point that Moore introduces his notion of immediate knowledge, which I discussed in Chapter VI. And he claims to know that the pencil exists in this way—immediately.[34] He says no more than this. Is there, perhaps, no more to be said?

III

BUT MOORE MAKES ONE MORE EFFORT to tackle the problem, this time to convince us that even if we do *not* know of the existence of physical objects, still we do not *know* that we do not know it. He does so by discussing first the question: What is meant by a material object? He "defines a material object" by means of three properties. A material object is something which occupies space, is not a sense-datum of any kind, and is not a mind or an act of consciousness. From the last two (negative) properties, it follows, says Moore, that material objects cannot be directly apprehended and also that they are the sort of thing which might exist even when no one is conscious of them. Moore has been maintaining that we *do* know that objects with these properties exist.[35]

He then discusses four alternatives to his view first by introducing an illustration and second by viewing each alternative with respect to it. First, the illustration. Consider, says Moore, what happens when you ride in a railway train. You may be directly apprehending many sense-data,

32. *Ibid.,* p. 120.
33. *Ibid.*
34. *Ibid.,* p. 125. It should be remembered that immediate knowledge is not the same as direct apprehension.
35. *Ibid.,* pp. 127–32.

colors, sounds, shakings, etc. And you may know that other people are apprehending similar sense-data. And you may also know that *other* sense-data, which no one is now apprehending, *would be* directly apprehended under certain circumstances. You may know, for example, that the sense-data which you now apprehend are signs that, if the train stopped and you got out, you would directly apprehend *still other* sense-data, which we call appearances of the wheels and of the couplings, etc. The "hypothesis" that you could, while you ride in the train, know all this is held by all five views, Moore's and the four alternatives which he holds to be mistaken. Let us now turn to these four. (1) The first says that the sorts of things mentioned above are *all* you can know about the existence of the train in which you are riding and that when you believe that the train exists, this is *all* that you believe. The existence of the train consists merely in all these kinds of sense-data. You cannot know (and do not believe) that the train is really running on *wheels*. All you know is that it is running on and is supported by the possibility that certain sense-data will exist in the future. (2) According to the second alternative, your car really does run on wheels, etc., even though no one is seeing them, and you can know that the wheels exist. But all you can know is that they are "something or other," unknown causes of your sense-data or something of this sort. You cannot, for example, know that they are round. (3) The third alternative is the view that the sense-data or some of them which you would see, feel, etc., if you got out of the train, exist now, even though no one is apprehending them, and that these sense-data are what you mean by the wheels. The car is running on and is supported by these sense-data. (4) According to the fourth alternative, the wheels, etc., really exist when you think that they do, but they consist not of sense-data, but of *minds*. Since minds have no position in space, it follows that the car is not really *upon* the wheels, and so forth. Moore's objections to each of the four alternatives are nearly the same: (a) These views are "quite different from what we commonly believe." (b) It is "difficult to believe" that we do not know "a great deal more" than each alternative allows that we know. (c) Each of the alternatives may seem plausible if you consider it "in abstract terms," but each becomes implausible if you realize what it means "in particular instances" (translate it to concrete terms).[36]

36. *Ibid.,* pp. 134–39.

Moore compares the view that we may know the existence of material objects with another view that some maintain: namely, that, contrary to Hume's view, you do *know* that when two things have been conjoined in the past, they are likely to be conjoined again in the future; and that, hence, experience is a sound basis for inference. Moore writes: "But if you are going to assert this, why should you not assert also that you do know of the existence of material objects? Is the one proposition, in fact, any more certain than the other?" [37]

With respect to those who maintain that the proposition that we cannot know of the existence of material objects follows from certain principles such as Hume's, Moore writes: "If . . . any principle, from which it would follow that I cannot know of the existence of any material object, is to be known with certainty, it must first be known, with a greater certainty, that I do not, in fact, in any particular instance know of one. And is this, in fact, known with any certainty? It seems to me it certainly is not." [38]

Finally, Moore concludes his discussion:

All this, I am aware, is only strictly an argument in favour of the position that we do not know that we do not know of the existence of material objects. But there is, I think, a real and important difference between this position and the dogmatic position that we *certainly do not* know of their existence. And, in practice, if not in logic, it is, I think, an important step towards the conviction that we *do* know of their existence.[39]

37. *Ibid.*, p. 141.
38. *Ibid.*, p. 143.
39. *Ibid.*, p. 144.

Conclusion

IN THE PRECEDING CHAPTERS I have attempted an evaluation and criticism (both positive and negative) of Moore's epistemological writings. But perhaps it is advisable to briefly review the points I have made in order to establish the main thesis at which I have arrived as a result of my study of Moore's works: the thesis, namely, that on almost every major issue Moore leaves as many unsolved problems at the end of his reflections as there were before he began them.

(1) Let us consider, first, the problems having to do with philosophical method. I have pointed out some of the difficulties which some might find connected with the common-sense aspect of Moore's philosophy. Just what are common-sense statements? And how do we *know* them to be true? The first question is not as troublesome as the second. As we have seen, Moore, in answer to the second question, frequently merely appeals to self-evidence. Or he simply asserts, "I have nothing better to say than that it seems to me that I *do* know them to be true." Now, in certain cases, we may have to grant that there seems to be no more to say. If

Moore is lecturing to an audience, it would be absurd for him to wonder if he really has clothes on, although a skeptic might suggest that the possibility that Moore is dreaming needs to be considered. On the other hand, many common-sense statements are of a different nature. Several of Moore's common-sense truisms—'The earth has existed for many years past', etc.—seem to require evidence, since they are not directly perceptual. And where evidence is required, one might reasonably suggest that the certainty of a statement lessens. But even some of Moore's *directly* perceptual common-sense statements are not free from difficulties with respect to ascertaining their truth or falsity. As I have mentioned, we have at times been wrong about any given statement of this kind. And Moore knows that we have been wrong. Yet he ignores this factor when he maintains that all propositions of the kinds which he has specified are known by all of us to be certainly true. Many would maintain that if we can be wrong, we do not possess absolute certainty, even though our belief that a proposition is true may seem reasonable at the time of the belief, reasonable because *generally* we have found similar propositions, on other occasions, to be true.

I have also suggested that Moore's appeal to common-sense statements, "which we all know to be true," in order to refute philosophical propositions ('Time is not real', etc.) seems to be inappropriate. Metaphysical discourse is no more on the same plane as ordinary language than scientific discourse is. (I do not say that the first and the last are the same either.) We do not refute a physicist's statement—'A table is a whirling mass of electrons, etc.'—by pointing to the ordinary view of the solidity of objects like tables. Similarly, we cannot rightfully refute a metaphysical statement by showing that it disagrees with common sense. McTaggart knew that he got out of bed before he left his bedroom. But such facts have nothing to do with his view that time is unreal. Moore's approach on these issues is quite shocking. His own metaphysical utterances, in works such as *Some Main Problems of Philosophy* and *Principia Ethica,* ought to have made him dubious about the propriety of his common-sense refutations of other philosophers. (I have suggested, however, that Moore might recognize all this and still maintain his emphasis on common sense because his main point is simply this: In philosophy we must begin with common sense because there is no other place from which to begin. It is thus the common-sense view of the world that Moore wishes to stress.)

My criticisms of Moore's views about meaning and analysis have been of a different sort. I have tried to show that Moore has several views regarding the meaning of meaning and of analysis and that he is usually unaware that he has had these different views. The fact of finding several meanings of a term or concept is not in itself a bad thing. As some have said, philosophy is the art of making distinctions. But if distinctions are made, one ought to be aware of the fact that one has made them. And if one tries to indicate features which are supposed to be crucial to a certain notion, one ought to see if this is so about *all* of the several meanings involved. I have indicated that Moore points out several different meanings of meaning and that he has several different views as to what analysis is. In the case of meaning, Moore, after making the distinctions, often blurs them over again. We see this especially in his failure to consistently distinguish the concept and object theories of meaning. We have also seen that, in Professor Langford's words, Moore has failed to give an analysis of analysis. When Moore finally turned to providing such an explication in his "Reply," he forgot about most forms of analysis and limited his discussion of criteria for a correct analysis, etc., to one form, doing so with a rather trivial illustration. In this work he has nothing to say about the form of analysis which he generally considered to be one of the most important, his variant of "reductional analysis."

Thus, on almost every topic which I have included under the heading of "philosophical method," Moore's discussion is fraught with unsolved problems. I believe that he is consistent only at the point which concerns the relation of common sense to ordinary language. I tried to show in Chapter III that he takes these to be different notions and that the latter is subsidiary to the former.

(2) The issues which I discussed under the heading "Knowing About Knowing" are not free from difficulties either. Moore's categorization of the various kinds of knowledge is fairly straightforward and, in general, quite adequate, although the characterization of some kinds is not as detailed as one might wish. Furthermore, as I indicated in Chapter VI, his statement of the conditions for knowledge proper involves him in circularity. He includes, as one of the conditions for X's immediately (non-derivatively) knowing a proposition p to be true: 'X must immediately know p to be true'. However, I suggested that with a suitable replacement Moore's four-condition schema might be saved, and I tried to show how we might thereby come closer to a more adequate handling of the problem of propositional knowledge.

Moore's views on the status of "mind" and its relationship to knowledge are left rather vague and unsettled. I have not dealt with all of the problems in this area, but I have tried to show that Moore never seems to have been able to decide what the ontological status of mind is. Is there a mind or are there only mental acts? What is the relation of the "mental" to the "physical"? Or is this a spurious problem? If so, why? And how are consciousness and knowing related? All these questions are unanswered by Moore, either because he failed to consider them or because he found too many possible alternatives and could never make up his mind regarding the superiority of any one of them. Perhaps some feel that the latter does not merit condemnation.

I have indicated that Moore's "theory of truth," when clarified and amended, has possibilities. Moore's own statement of it, however, involves him in difficulties. He wants to deny that there are propositions, yet requires them if his theory is to work. He also thinks of propositions as being names, which they surely are not. Furthermore, while I did not mention this earlier, I am aware that this whole matter of deciding on a theory of truth might be considered an unnecessary pursuit. I am not sure that it is; but I think that the topic is not as important as some others.

(3) Moore's views on perception, although occupying more pages than any other single epistemological topic, contain the greatest number of unresolved problems of all. Taking the "problem of sense-data" first, on only one point is Moore consistent: there *are* sense-data. Why so? Because they are objects of certain sorts of awarenesses, and one cannot (Moore thinks) have an awareness without an object. But would not physical objects fill the bill? Moore thinks not, for then we could not satisfactorily account for the phenomena of illusion, hallucination, afterimages, and perspectival visual sensings. Moore overlooks the view that we could say that certain things (e.g., coins) look certain ways (e.g., elliptical, etc.) without requiring that there be sense-data as entities. I believe that he never considered this to be an alternative because of his act-object distinction, which I just mentioned, and because of his attachment to the reference-theory of meaning. Suppose that I "see double." Then at most one of the objects, say a book, which I see can be a physical object. The other—the double—must, however, *be* too, in order for my report of this event to have meaning. The terms I use by which to report it must refer to some objects for their meaning. Hence, there must be such objects.

But suppose we grant to Moore that there are, or may be, such entities as sense-data. What then is their ontological status? As we have seen, Moore has five slightly different opinions regarding whether they are mental—ranging from no to yes, with many less definite stands in between. He has similar doubts with regard to the question as to whether sense-data are physical. And he ends up suggesting that they must be neither mental nor physical. But if they are not physical, then how are they (or certain ones among them) related to physical objects? Here, too, Moore could never decide on an answer. With such a multiplicity of views, such indefiniteness, hesitations, if's, and's, and but's, one can see how some philosophers have asked, "Is there a problem about sense-data?" or have called the issue a pseudo-problem. (I do not necessarily agree that it is.)

And what about the other, and perhaps main, part of the problem of perception, that of establishing the existence of an external world? I have tried to show that, in a sense, Moore fails at any philosophical attempt to accomplish this. In the last resort, we have to appeal to our common-sense views. Now it is one thing to say that we must rely on common sense and let it go at that; but it is another to say that a philosophical proof can also be given. We are then entitled to say, "Show me." Moore tried to show us but ultimately ends up by basing the whole effort on commonsensical assumptions.

II

IN ONE SENSE THEN, a close study of Moore produces disappointment. Too much is left unresolved, vague, and problematic. The reader might object: Throughout this work, you have been excessively critical of Moore. What about the positive side? If Moore is rightly held to be one of the foremost philosophers of the first half of the twentieth century, then what are his chief contributions? What significance does the work of Moore have, not only with regard to his own era, but perhaps for those of us who are doing philosophy today? I shall attempt now to suggest an answer to these questions.

First, there are several "methodological" aspects of Moore's work which are not only striking features of his philosophical activities but are, I believe, worthy of emulation. Among these are the following: a painstaking search for clarity of expression not only in his own works but in the utterances of others; a remarkable ability in making distinctions; a genius for seeing and articulating just what a given philosophical problem is and distinguishing it from others, with which it might tend to be confused; an honest effort to delineate and to examine all possible solutions to philosophical problems and to weigh their merits; a skill in argumentation and emphasis upon the importance of good reasons for one's philosophical views. I have given examples of all of these above; hence I shall not take space to restate them. I especially believe that the posing and formulation of philosophical problems and the careful consideration of alternative answers to them is itself an enormous accomplishment and deserves commendation. In Moore we see a philosopher whose critical mind enabled him to see and distinguish many facets of a problem which, to others, might seem less complex. Perhaps some of his alternative solutions are on given occasions bad, e.g., the idea of seeming to perceive sense-data. But there are, I believe, others which are more perspicuous and more fruitful and which could be (and were) developed and extended by other philosophers. Thus even if no conclusions of Moore reached the status of being totally adequate—if that is possible for *anyone*—there is still much in Moore to appreciate and be grateful for: his reminding us of what we all do know, his insistence upon making distinctions, his intense striving for clarity and precision, and all the other attributes to which I have referred.

But, second, beyond these matters, there are, I believe several substantial philosophical achievements in Moore's work which merit emphasis. Among these are the following: (1) Moore's refutation of Idealism, (2) his recognition of the role of common sense, and (3) his establishment of the role and importance of analysis in philosophy. These points all require further comments and qualifications.

The first thing that needs to be said with regard to all three is this: that Moore never clearly and completely accomplished any of them. Why then do I attribute these to Moore as his achievements? Because I believe that, with regard to all three, Moore pressed a long way and came very close to the completion of the task or suggested the route to the goal, even if he did not always adequately reach the desired end. Thus, (1) Moore did not successfully refute Idealism. Of course, one might wonder whether anyone could ever refute Idealism or anything else, for that matter, in philosophy. Some have maintained that philosophical positions are never refuted, but rather, like old soldiers, just fade away. I believe that one can argue that Moore did come very close to a refutation of Idealism, in the limited sense in which he specified what is to be understood by such a refutation. Furthermore, (2) Moore did not successfully characterize the role of common sense in philosophy, but he provided enough cues so that others could feel a great sense of debt to Moore on this matter. One of the more recent philosophers who has constantly paid tribute to Moore in this regard is Gustav Bergmann who, I believe, has more adequately delineated the role of common sense in philosophical endeavors. Finally (3) although Moore emphasized the importance of analysis, he did not always clearly describe what role analysis played in philosophical pursuits, nor did he have any consistent view as to exactly what analysis is, what is to be analyzed, and to what end. But again, he, here and there, provided suggestive hints which later philosophers, in a variety of ways, were to find fruitful.

I have, of course, said nothing about Moore's contributions to ethics or his achievements as an ontologist of the first rank. Again, since this work has emphasized Moore's epistemology, I shall not elaborate in these areas. Finally, in any appraisal of Moore's significance and role in contemporary philosophy, one must not neglect his stature as a teacher and his influence upon his students and his colleagues and fellow philosophers. Many of these have paid tribute to Moore in numerous articles, notes, etc. One of the most moving statements has come from John Wisdom:[1]

Things as they are are often hard to face. We are often driven to distort them and this may lead to a distrust of what is said and an inability to see what is there, like that which overcomes a child when he finds those about him saying what is not true, and then, perhaps, begins himself to join in the conspiracy. There are those who attack our illusions; but often we feel that they in bitterness again distort reality. In spite of the forces which make for falsehood, we are still able to recognize one who can and will speak the truth, not blind to what we must regret, but still able to see things—some great, some small— which may bring happiness and can be shared. Moore was like this not only as a philosopher but as a man.

1. John Wisdom, "G. E. Moore," in *Paradox and Discovery* (Oxford: Blackwell, 1965), p. 86.

Bibliography

I. Works by G. E. Moore

Books

Principia Ethica. Cambridge: Cambridge University Press, 1903.

Ethics. London: Williams & Norgate, 1912. 2d ed., London: Oxford University Press, 1947.

Philosophical Studies. London: Routledge & Kegan Paul, 1922. Reprinted, Totowa, N. J.: Littlefield, Adams & Co., 1965. Includes two previously unpublished papers: "The Conception of Intrinsic Value," and "The Nature of Moral Philosophy."

Some Main Problems of Philosophy. London: Allen & Unwin, 1953. (Lectures given in 1910–11.)

Philosophical Papers. London: Allen & Unwin, 1959. Includes two previously unpublished papers: "Four Forms of Scepticism," and "Certainty."

Commonplace Book, 1919–1935, ed. C. Lewy. London: Allen & Unwin, 1963.

Lectures on Philosophy, ed. C. Lewy. London: Allen & Unwin, 1967.

This bibliography was compiled with the assistance of G. Moor.

Articles

"In What Sense, If Any, Do Past and Future Time Exist?", *Mind*, VI (1897), 235–40.

"Freedom," *Mind*, VII (1898), 179–204.

"The Nature of Judgment," *Mind*, VIII (1899), 176–93.

"Necessity," *Mind*, IX (1900), 289–304.

"Identity," *PAS*, VI (1900–1901), 103–27.

"The Value of Religion," *International Journal of Ethics*, XII (1901), 81–98.

"Mr. McTaggart's 'Studies in Hegelian Cosmology,'" *PAS*, II (1901–2), 177–214.

Articles in Baldwin's *Dictionary of Philosophy* (1902). Vol. I: "Cause and Effect," "Change"; Vol. II: "Nativism," "Quality," "Real," "Reason," "Relation," "Relativity of Knowledge," "Substance," "Spirit," "Teleology," "Truth."

"Experience and Empiricism," *PAS*, III (1902–3), 80–95.

"Mr. McTaggart's Ethics," *International Journal of Ethics*, XIII (1903), 341–70.

"The Refutation of Idealism," *Mind*, XII (1903), 433–53. (Reprinted in *PS*, pp. 1–30.)

"Kant's Idealism," *PAS*, IV (1903–4), 127–40.

"Jahresbericht über 'Philosophy in the United Kingdom for 1902,'" *Archiv für Systematiche Philosophie*, X (1904), 242–64.

"The Nature and Reality of Objects of Perception," *PAS*, VI (1905–6), 68–127. (Reprinted in *PS*, pp. 31–96.)

"Mr. Joachim's 'The Nature of Truth,'" *Mind*, XVI (1907), 229–35.

"Professor James' 'Pragmatism,'" *PAS*, VIII (1907–8), 33–77. (Reprinted in *PS* as "William James' 'Pragmatism,'" pp. 97–146.)

"Hume's Philosophy," *The New Quarterly*, Nov., 1909. (Reprinted in *PS*, pp. 147–67.)

"The Subject Matter of Psychology," *PAS*, X (1909–10), 36–62.

"The Status of Sense-Data," *PAS*, XIV (1913–14), 355–80. (Reprinted in *PS*, pp. 168–96).

"The Implications of Recognition," *PAS*, XVI (1915–16), 201–23.

"Are the Materials of Sense Affections of the Mind?", *PAS*, XVII (1916–17), 418–29.

"The Conception of Reality," *PAS*, XVIII (1917–18), 101–20. (Reprinted in *PS*, pp. 197–219.)

"Some Judgments of Perception," *PAS*, XIX (1918–19), 1–29. (Reprinted in *PS*, pp. 220–52.)

"Is There Knowledge by Acquaintance?", *PASS*, II (1919), 179–93.

"External and Internal Relations," *PAS*, XX (1919–20), 40–62. (Reprinted in *PS*, pp. 276–309.)

"Is the 'Concrete Universal' the True Type of Universality?", *PAS*, XX (1919–20), 132–40.

"The Character of Cognitive Acts," *PAS*, XXI (1920–21), 132–40.

"Are the Characteristics of Particular Things Universal or Particular?", *PASS*, III (1923), 95–113. (Reprinted in *PP*, pp. 17–31.)

"A Defence of Common Sense," *Contemporary British Philosophy: Second Series*, ed. J. H. MUIRHEAD. New York: Macmillan, 1925. II, 193–223. (Reprinted in *PP*, pp. 32–59.)

"The Nature of Sensible Appearance," *PASS*, VI (1926), 179–89.

"Facts and Propositions," *PASS*, VII (1927), 171–206. (Reprinted in *PP*, pp. 60–88.)

"Indirect Knowledge," *PASS*, IX (1929), 19–50.

"Is Goodness a Quality?", *PASS*, XI (1932), 116–31. (Reprinted in *PP*, pp. 89–101.)

"Imaginary Objects," *PASS*, XII (1933), 55–70. (Reprinted in *PP*, pp. 102–14.)

"The Justification of Analysis," *Analysis*, I (1933–34), 28–30. (Lecture notes transcribed by M. McDONALD.)

"Is Existence a Predicate?", *PASS*, XV (1936), 175–88. (Reprinted in *PP*, pp. 115–26.)

"Proof of an External World," *British Academy, Proceedings*, XXV (1939), 273–300. (Reprinted in *PP*, pp. 127–50.)

"An Autobiography," *PGEM*, pp. 3–39.

"A Reply to My Critics," *PGEM*, pp. 535–677.

"Russell's 'Theory of Descriptions,'" *The Philosophy of Bertrand Russell*, ed. P. A. SCHILPP. Evanston: Northwestern University Press, 1944. Pp. 175–225. (Reprinted in *PP*, pp. 151–95.)

"Addendum to My 'Reply,'" *PGEM*, 1952 ed., pp. 677–87.

"Wittgenstein's Lectures in 1930–33," *Mind*, LXIII (1954), 1–15, 289–316; LXIV (1955), 1–27. (Reprinted in *PP*, pp. 252–324.)

"Visual Sense-Data," *British Philosophy in the Mid-Century*, ed. C. A. MACE. Cambridge: Cambridge University Press, 1957. Pp. 205–11.

II. WORKS ON G. E. MOORE

AMBROSE, A. "Moore's 'Proof of an External World,'" *PGEM*, pp. 397–417. (Reprinted in *Essays in Analysis*. London: Allen & Unwin, 1966. Pp. 214–32.)

———. "Three Aspects of Moore's Philosophy," *The Journal of Philosophy*,

LVII (1960), 816–24. (Reprinted in *Essays in Analysis*. London: Allen & Unwin, 1966. Pp. 205–13.)

AYER, A. J. "The Terminology of Sense-Data," *Mind*, LIV (1945), 289–312. (Reprinted in *Philosophical Essays*. New York: St. Martin's Press, 1964. Pp. 66–104.)

BAR-HILLEL, Y. "Analysis of Correct Language," *Mind*, LV (1946), 328–40.

BARNES, W. H. F. *The Philosophical Predicament*. London: A. C. Black, 1950. Chaps. 2–5.

BENTLEY, A. F. "Logicians' Underlying Postulations," *Philosophy of Science*, XIII (1946), 3–19.

BERGMANN, GUSTAV. "Inclusion, Exemplification, and Inherence in G. E. Moore," *Logic and Reality*. Madison: University of Wisconsin Press, 1964. Pp. 158–70.

BLACK, MAX. "The 'Paradox of Analysis,'" *Mind*, LIII (1944), 263–67.

———. "The 'Paradox of Analysis' Again: A Reply," *Mind*, LIV (1945), 272–73.

———. "On Speaking with the Vulgar," *The Philosophical Review*, LVIII (1949), 616–21.

BLANSHARD, BRAND. *Reason and Goodness*. London: Allen & Unwin, 1961. Pp. 266–74.

———. *Reason and Analysis*. London: Allen & Unwin, 1962, 310–16.

BOUWSMA, O. K. "Moore's Theory of Sense-Data," *PGEM*, pp. 203–21.

BROAD, C. D. "Certain Features in Moore's Ethical Doctrines," *PGEM*, pp. 43–67.

CHAPPELL, V. C. "Malcolm on Moore," *Mind*, LXX (1961), 417–25.

DUCASSE, C. J. "Moore's 'The Refutation of Idealism,'" *PGEM*, pp. 225–51.

DUMMETT, MICHAEL. "A Defence of McTaggart's Proof of the Unreality of Time," *The Philosophical Reveiw*, LXIX (1960), 497–504.

EDEL, ABRAHAM. "The Logical Structure of G. E. Moore's Ethical Theory," *PGEM*, pp. 137–76.

EWING, A. C. "Knowledge of Physical Objects," *Mind*, LII (1943), 97–121.

FIELD, G. C. "The Place of Definition in Ethics," *Studies in Philosophy*. University of Bristol Studies #3, 1935. (Reprinted in *Readings in Ethical Theory*, ed. WILFRID SELLARS and JOHN HOSPERS. New York: Appleton-Century-Crofts, 1952.)

FRANKENA, WILLIAM K. "The Naturalistic Fallacy," *Mind*, XLVIII (1939). (Reprinted in *Readings in Ethical Theory*, ed. WILFRID SELLARS and JOHN HOSPERS. New York: Appleton-Century-Crofts, 1952.)

———. "Obligation and Value in the Ethics of G. E. Moore," *PGEM*, pp. 93–110.

GARNETT, A. CAMPBELL. "Moore's Theory of Moral Freedom and Responsibility," *PGEM*, pp. 179–99.

HAEZRAHI, P. "Some Arguments Against G. E. Moore's View of the Function of 'Good' in Ethics," *Mind*, LVII (1948), 322–40.

HALL, E. W. "Proof of Utility in Bentham and Mill: Critique of G. E. Moore's Analysis," *Ethics*, LX (1949), 1–18.

———. "Review of Schilpp's *The Philosophy of G. E. Moore*," *The Philosophical Review*, LIII (1944), 62–68.

HANCOCK, R. "The Refutation of Naturalism in Moore and Hare," *The Journal of Philosophy*, LVII (1960), 326–34.

HICKS, G. DAWES. "Mr. G. E. Moore on 'The Subject Matter of Psychology,' " *PAS*, X (1909–10), 232–88.

HOCHBERG, HERBERT. "Moore's Ontology and Non-Natural Properties," *The Review of Metaphysics*, XV (1962), 365–95. (Reprinted in EDWIN B. ALLAIRE *et al.*, *Essays in Ontology*. Iowa City: University of Iowa Press, 1963. Pp. 121–47.)

HOLMES, A. F. "Moore's Appeal to Common Sense," *The Journal of Philosophy*, LVIII (1961), 197–207.

JONES, E. E. C. "Mr. Moore on Hedonism," *International Journal of Ethics*, XVI (1906), 429–64.

JONES, J. R. "Dr. Moore's Revised Directions for Picking Out Visual Sense-Data," *The Philosophical Quarterly*, I (1951), 433–38.

KLEMKE, E. D. "Mr. Warnock on Moore's Conception of Philosophy," *Philosophical Studies*, XIII (1962), 81–84.

LAIRD, J. "Review of *Philosophical Studies*," *Mind*, XXXII (1923), 86–92.

LANGFORD, C. H. "The Notion of Analysis in Moore's Philosophy," *PGEM*, pp. 321–42.

LAZEROWITZ, M. "Moore's Paradox," *PGEM*, pp. 371–93.

———. "Moore and Philosophical Analysis," *Philosophy*, XXXIII (1958), 193–220.

LEWIS, E. "Moore's Realism," in LAIRD ADDIS and DOUGLAS LEWIS, *Moore and Ryle: Two Ontologists*. Iowa City: University of Iowa Press, 1965; The Hague, Martinus Nijhoff, 1965.

MACE, C. A. "On How We Know that Material Things Exist," *PGEM*, pp. 283–98.

McGILL, V. J. "Some Queries Concerning Moore's Method," *PGEM*, pp. 483–514.

McKEON, RICHARD. "Propositions and Perceptions in the World of G. E. Moore," *PGEM*, pp. 453–80.

MALCOLM, NORMAN. "Certainty and Empirical Statements," *Mind*, LI (1942), 18–46.

———. "Moore and Ordinary Language," *PGEM*, pp. 345–68.

———. "Defending Common Sense," *The Philosophical Review*, LVIII (1949), 201–20.

———. "Philosophy for Philosophers," *The Philosophical Review*, LX (1951), 329–40.

———. "Moore's Use of 'Know'," *Mind*, LXII (1953), 241–47.

MARHENKE, PAUL. "Moore's Analysis of Sense-Perception," *PGEM*, pp. 255–80.

METTRICK, E. F. "G. E. Moore and Intrinsic Goodness," *International Journal of Ethics*, XXXVIII (1928), 389–400.

METZ, R. *A Hundred Years of British Philosophy*. London: Allen & Unwin, 1938.

MURPHY, A. E. "Moore's 'Defence of Common Sense,' " *PGEM*, pp. 301–17.

NAGEL, E. "Impressions and Appraisals of Analytic Philosophy in Europe," *The Journal of Philosophy*, XXXIII (1936), 10–16.

———. "Review of Schilpp's *The Philosophy of G. E. Moore*," *Mind*, LIII (1944), 60–75.

———. "The Debt We Owe to G. E. Moore," *The Journal of Philosophy*, LVII (1960), 810–16.

NAKHNIKIAN, GEORGE. "On the Naturalistic Fallacy," in *Morality and the Language of Conduct*, ed. H. N. CASTEÑADA and G. NAKHNIKIAN. Detroit: Wayne State University Press, 1963. Pp. 145–58.

NELSON, J. O. "Mr. Hochberg on Moore: Some Corrections," *The Review of Metaphysics*, XVI (1962), 119–32.

———. "Moore, George Edward," *Encyclopedia of Philosophy*, ed. P. EDWARDS. New York: Macmillan, 1967. Pp. 372–81.

PASSMORE, JOHN. "Moore and Russell," *A Hundred Years of Philosophy*. London: Duckworth, 1957. Pp. 203–41.

PATON, H. J. "The Alleged Independence of Goodness," *PGEM*, pp. 113–34.

PAUL, G. A. "G. E. Moore: Analysis, Common Usage, and Common Sense," in A. J. AYER *et. al., The Revolution in Philosophy*. New York: St. Martin's, 1957. Pp. 56–69.

PRATT, J. B. "Mr. Moore's Realism," *The Journal of Philosophy*, XX (1923), 378–84.

PRESSON, V. "G. E. Moore's Theory of Sense-Data," *The Journal of Philosophy*, XLVIII (1951), 34–42.

PRIOR, A. N. *Logic and the Basis of Ethics*. Oxford: Oxford University Press, 1949. Pp. 1–12.

RIDDELL, J. G. "New Intuitionism of Dr. Rashdall and Dr. Moore," *The Philosophical Review*, XXX (1921), 545–65.

ROBERTS, H. W. "Some Queries Suggested by G. E. Moore's Beautiful and Ugly Worlds," *The Journal of Philosophy*, XXXVIII (1941), 623–27.

ROGERS, A. K. "Mr. Moore's Refutation of Idealism," *The Philosophical Review*, XXVIII (1919), 77–84.

RYLE, G. "G. E. Moore's Commonplace Book," *New Statesman*, LXV (1963), 85.

SCHILPP, P. A. (Ed.) *The Philosophy of G. E. Moore*. Evanston: Northwestern University Press, 1942; 2d ed., New York: Tudor, 1952. Available through Open Court Publishing Co., La Salle, Ill.

STACE, W. T. "The Refutation of Realism," *Mind*, XLIII (1934), 145–55.

STEBBING, L. S. "Moore's Influence," *PGEM*, pp. 517–32.

STEVENSON, Charles L. "Moore's Arguments against Certain Forms of Ethical Naturalism," *PGEM*, pp. 71–90.

STRONG, C. A. "Has Mr. Moore Refuted Idealism?", *Mind*, XIV (1905), 174–89.

SWABEY, M. C. "Mr. G. E. Moore's Discussion of Sense-Data," *The Monist*, XXXIV (1924), 466–73.

TREDWELL, R. F. "On Moore's Analysis of Goodness," *The Journal of Philosophy*, LIX (1962), 793–802.

VEATCH, HENRY B. *Rational Man*. Bloomington: Indiana University Press, 1964. Pp. 188–203.

WARNOCK, G. J. "G. E. Moore," in *English Philosophy Since 1900*. London: Oxford University Press, 1958. Pp. 12–29.

WARNOCK, M. *Ethics Since 1900*. London: Oxford University Press, 1960. Pp. 11–55.

WHITE, A. R. "Moore's Appeal to Common Sense," *Philosophy*, XXXIII (1958), 221–39.

———. *G. E. Moore: A Critical Exposition*. Oxford: Blackwell, 1958.

WHITE, M. G. "A Note on 'The Paradox of Analysis,'" *Mind*, LIV (1945), 71–72.

———. "Analysis and Identity; A Rejoinder," *Mind*, LIV (1945), 357–61.

———. "Memories of G. E. Moore," *The Journal of Philosophy*, LVII (1960), 805–10.

WISDOM, JOHN. "Philosophy, Anxiety and Novelty," *Mind*, LIII (1944), 170–76.

———. "Moore's Technique," *PGEM*, pp. 421–50.

———. "G. E. Moore," in *Paradox and Discovery*. Oxford: Blackwell, 1965. Pp. 82–86.

———. "Mace, Moore, and Wittgenstein," in *Paradox and Discovery*, Oxford: Blackwell, 1965. Pp. 148–66.

WRIGHT, H. W. "The Objectivity of Moral Values," *The Philosophical Review*, XXXII (1923), 385–400.

III. Other Works

ADAMS, E. M. "The Nature of the Sense-Datum Theory," *Mind*, LXVII (1958), 216–26.

AUSTIN, J. L. *Sense and Sensibilia*. New York: Oxford University Press, 1964.

AYER, A. J. *The Foundations of Empirical Knowledge*. London: Macmillan, 1953.

————. *The Problem of Knowledge*. Harmondsworth, Middlesex: Penguin, 1956. Chap. III, "Perception."

————. "Perception," *British Philosophy in the Mid-Century*, ed. C. A. MACE. London: Allen & Unwin, 1957. Pp. 215–36.

———— et al. *The Revolution in Philosophy*. New York: St. Martin's Press, 1957.

BARNES, W. H. F. "The Myth of Sense-Data," *PAS*, XLV (1944–45), 89–117.

BERGMANN, GUSTAV. *The Metaphysics of Logical Positivism*. New York: Longmans, Green & Co., 1954. Reprinted, Madison: University of Wisconsin Press, 1967.

————. *Meaning and Existence*. Madison: University of Wisconsin Press, 1959.

————. *Logic and Reality*. Madison: University of Wisconsin Press, 1964.

————. *Realism*. Madison: University of Wisconsin Press, 1967.

BROAD, C. D. *Scientific Thought*. New York: Harcourt Brace, 1923. Chap. VIII.

————. *The Mind and Its Place in Nature*. New York: Harcourt Brace, 1929. Chap. IV.

————. "The Local Historical Background of Contemporary Cambridge Philosophy," *British Philosophy in the Mid-Century*, ed. C. A. MACE. London: Allen & Unwin, 1957. Pp. 13–61.

CHISHOLM, R. M. *Perceiving*. Ithaca: Cornell University Press, 1957.

FIRTH, R. "Sense-Data and the Percept Theory," *Mind*, LVIII (1949), 434–65; LIX (1950), 35–56.

GÖTLIND, E. "Some Comments on Mistakes in Statements Concerning Sense-Data," *Mind*, LXI (1952), 297–306.

HAMPSHIRE, STUART. "The Interpretations of Language: Words and Concepts," *British Philosophy in the Mid-Century*, ed. C. A. MACE. London: Allen & Unwin, 1957. Pp. 267–79.

HEMPEL, CARL G. *Fundamentals of Concept Formation in Empirical Science*. Chicago: University of Chicago Press, 1952.

HOSPERS, JOHN. *An Introduction to Philosophical Analysis*. New York: Prentice-Hall, 1953. Chap. V. 2d ed., 1967.

KLEMKE, E. D. "Universals and Particulars in a Phenomenalist Ontology," *Philosophy of Science*, XXVII (1960), 254–61.

KLEMKE, E. D. "The Laws of Logic," *Philosophy of Science*, XXXIII (1966), 271–77.

KÖRNER, S. "Some Types of Philosophical Thinking," *British Philosophy in the Mid-Century*, ed. C. A. MACE. London: Allen & Unwin, 1957. Pp. 115–31.

MACE, C. A. "Some Trends in the Philosophy of Mind," *British Philosophy in the Mid-Century*, ed. C. A. MACE. London: Allen & Unwin, 1957. Pp. 99–112.

MASTERMANN, MARGARET. "Metaphysics and Ideographic Language," *British Philosophy in the Mid-Century*, ed. C. A. MACE. London: Allen & Unwin, 1957. Pp. 293–357.

PASSMORE, JOHN. "Professor Ryle's Use of 'Use' and 'Usage'," *The Philosophical Review*, LXIII (1954), 58–64.

PAUL, G. A. "Is There a Problem about Sense-Data?", *PASS*, XV (1936), 88–101.

PRICE, H. H. *Perception*. London: Methuen, 1932. 2d ed., 1950.

QUINTON, M. "The Problem of Perception," *Mind*, LXIV (1955), 28–51.

RAMSEY, F. P. "Facts and Propositions," *PASS*, VII (1927), 153–70.

RUSSELL, BERTRAND. "Knowledge by Acquaintance and Knowledge by Description," *Mysticism and Logic*. New York: Doubleday-Anchor, 1957. Pp. 202–24.

———. *The Problems of Philosophy*. Oxford: Oxford University Press, 1912. 2d ed., 1946.

———. "On the Nature of Acquaintance," *Logic and Knowledge*, ed. R. Marsh. New York: Macmillan, 1956. Pp. 122–74.

———. "The Philosophy of Logical Atomism," *Logic and Knowledge*, ed. R. Marsh. New York: Macmillan, 1956. Pp. 122–74.

RYLE, G. "The Theory of Meaning," *British Philosophy in the Mid-Century*, ed. C. A. MACE. London: Allen & Unwin, 1957. Pp. 239–64.

Index

Index

External to our minds, 145
External world: knowledge of, 171–86;
proof of, 25, 65, 143–47, 191

Facts, 124–32

Hallucinations, argument from, 154
Hempel, Carl, 117n
Hospers, John, 104n, 142n
Hume, David, 118–19, 180–84

Idealism, 149; refutation of, 73, 111–14, 192
Illusion, argument from, 154–55
Inconsistency upon denial, criterion of, 22–24

James, William, 133n

Kant, Immanuel, 65, 143–44
Klemke, E. D., 12n
Knowing, ways of, 91–110
Knowledge: by acquaintance, 95–96;
actualized and non-actualized, 93; as
apprehension, 94–99; consciousness and,
111–20; dispositional, 92–93; immediate,
103n; indirect, 102–4; kinds of, 91–110,
189; of other selves, 172–78; three main
kinds of, 105; and true belief, 136–37
Knowledge proper, 99–102, 136–38, 179,
189
Knowledge that, 99–102; conditions for,
99–102, 104–10, 137

Langford, C. H., 83, 189
Lazerowitz, M., 38, 70n
Lewy, C., x
Locke, John, 119
Logic, 8
Logical constructions, 78–79

Malcolm, Norman, 31–34; criticism of, 35–38
Material objects: alternative views on
knowledge of, 184–85; defined, 184;
knowledge of, 177–84, 186
Meaning, 47–49, 188–89; as analysis, 62–
63; emotive, 53–54; and epistemology,
10–11; meanings of, 51–63; ordinary, 15,
65; as referent, 57–62; as sense of
ordinary expression, 55–56; and
significance, 53; as use, 48, 56–57; as
verbal definition, 57
Metaphysics: as general description of
universe, 7–8; importance to Moore of,
9–12

Mill, John Stuart, 168–69
Moore, G. E.: chief epistemological problems
of, x; importance of, ix; as ontologist,
193; summary of criticisms of, 187–91;
tribute to, 193

Necessity, 47–48

Observation, 173–78, 181–82
Ordinary language, 31–50, 188; common
sense and, 35–37, 41; identification
principle, 32; linguistic recommendation
principle, 34; Moore and, 31–35; Moore's
adding to, 44–45; Moore's appeal to, 40–
43; Moore's correction of, 45–46; Moore's
departure from, 44; refutational principle,
34; role of in Moore's philosophy, 39–44

Paul, G. A., 11, 154n
Perception: criticism of Moore on problem
of, 183–84; and the external world, 141–
48; problem of, 139–86, 190–91; problem
of, delineated, 141–42; solution to
problem of, 171–86
Perspectives, argument from, 155–56
Phenomenalism, 78–79
Philosophical method, 3
Philosophy, 3–12; divisions of, 7–8; source
of, 4–6
Philosophy of mind, 111–19, 190
Plato, 4
Proof, conditions of, 146
Propositions, 96–99; kinds of, 105; as names
of facts, 124–25; as objects of belief,
125–29

Quine, W. V., 86n

Reference theory of meaning: concept
theory, 61–62; object theory, 58–61
Russell, Bertrand, ix, 59n, 61n, 78, 95, 122,
125, 134, 135, 156n, 163, 168–69
Ryle, Gilbert, 122

Seeing, 152–54
Self-evidence, 24–26
Sense-data, 8–82, 149–70; causal theory of,
167–68; defined, 152–54; their *esse
percipi*, 158–61; existence of, 149–50, 190;
grounds for, 154–56; kinds of, 151–53;
as mental, 156–62; as neither mental nor
physical, 166; Mill-Russell theory of, 168–
70; ontological status of, 156–66, 191; as
parts of physical objects, 162–65; as
physical, 162–66; relation to physical